SOLDIERS, SPACE, AND STORIES OF LIFE

CHRIS GIBBONS

This book is dedicated to my brother, Jack, and my Dad.

"Those we love never truly leave us. There are things
that death cannot touch."
(Jack Thorne)

CONTENTS

STORIES OF LIFE

PREFACE

It was sometime in 2008, and I had been writing op-ed essays for the *Philadelphia Daily News* since 2004 when a co-worker unwittingly contributed to what would eventually become the title of this book. I handed him a copy of the *Daily News*, and said, "Check it out, I have another story in the paper today." "Let me guess," he said sarcastically, "It's about war, space, or a story from back-in-the-day."

Since that day, my essays have been published in the *Philadelphia Inquirer, Orlando Sentinel, Houston Chronicle, Washington Times, History Channel Magazine, America in WW 2 Magazine*, and *PhillyMan Magazine*, among others. But, whenever I think about that moment, I always laugh because my co-worker, of course, was right. Up to that point, and since that time as well, I suppose that my essays can be broadly categorized in such a way, and rather than object to it, I proudly accept it. I am, after all, a product of the baby-boomer generation - a true child of the 1960s and 1970s. Consequently, I've been heavily influenced by the historic events, social movements, and pop culture that have come to define those formative years of my youth, and I view my stories as a reflection of that era.

Some of the greatest war movies ever made premiered in the '60s, and I repeatedly watched them when they eventually made it to broadcast TV. Films such as *The Longest Day, The Great Escape, The Guns of Navarone, Where Eagles Dare*, and *The Dirty Dozen* were just a few of the many. These films helped promote my early interest in military history which was then further heightened upon hearing the harrowing stories of World War II and Korean War veterans who were neighbors, or friends of my father, or both. Unfortunately, the harsh realities of war cast an ominous shadow over my pre-teen years as horrific television images of the fighting in Vietnam, as well as the violent anti-war protests in America's streets, frequently invaded the normally safe confines of my family's living room. Additionally, I now suspect that my father, a Korean War veteran, quietly suffered during those years from the lingering effects of undiagnosed PTSD.

My enthusiasm for science fiction and space exploration resulted from the influence of my big brother, Jerry, and was further fueled by iconic television shows like *The Twilight Zone, The Outer Limits,* and *Star Trek,* which reached peak popularity among America's youth during the years when NASA and its heroic astronauts boldly rocketed towards the moon. The great science popularizer, Carl Sagan, was often a guest on *Johnny Carson's Tonight Show* and he fired my young imagination whenever he appeared. When Sagan, along with colleagues Bruce Murray and Lou Friedman, formed the Planetary Society in 1980, I immediately joined and have been a loyal member ever since. I still marvel at the sight of Saturn's rings, and Jupiter's moons when viewed through my backyard telescope.

Although many of the essays featured in the *Stories of Life* section of this book have the unique social and cultural aspects of the '60s and '70s serving as a backdrop, they touch upon themes that are common to every generation such as love, loss, longing, tragedy, triumph, discovery, and redemption.

While I've always known that my own interests and influences weren't unique among my fellow baby-boomers, I'm still instilled with a certain measure of comfort whenever I gaze upon the bookshelf of a friend or colleague from my age group and find the same books that sit on my shelf as well. The primary themes of this book seem to resonate with many of us. Indeed, one of the most famous members of my generation, Tom Hanks, often explores these subjects through his films. He co-produced two of the most popular mini-series in HBO history, *Band of Brothers* and *From the Earth to the Moon,* and starred in the blockbuster movies *Saving Private Ryan* and *Apollo 13.* I also wasn't surprised to learn that Hanks has watched *2001: A Space Odyssey* over 100 times. He also wrote and directed *That Thing You Do,* a wonderfully upbeat film that chronicles the meteoric rise and fall of a '60s one-hit-wonder pop band. Stephen King, another famous fellow 'boomer', wrote the short story that the film, *Stand By Me,* is based upon, and both are true masterpieces in depicting the coming-of-age theme that I tried to convey in many of my *Stories of Life* essays.

The 78 essays in this compilation were primarily published in the Op-Ed sections of the *Philadelphia Inquirer* or *Philadelphia Daily News*, but a handful were published in other outlets as well. I've listed where and when the edited versions of each essay were published. With one lone exception, that being my first published essay in 1997, they span the time period from 2004 to 2019. I've also included an afterword for each essay that provides interesting context, subsequent updates, or noteworthy e-mails I received in response to them.

I would like to thank a few of the Op-Ed page editors that I've worked with over the years: Michael Schaffer from the *Philadelphia Daily News*, Josh Gohlke from the *Philadelphia Inquirer*, and Kevin Ferris from the *Philadelphia Inquirer*. Without their support and encouragement, I don't believe I would have written on a regular basis. Their influence has been immeasurable.

I hope that you enjoy reading these essays as much as I enjoyed writing them.

Chris Gibbons
February 5, 2020
Philadelphia

SOLDIERS

THE GIANTS OF JUNE 6, 1944

(Edited version published in the June 4, 2004 *Philadelphia Daily News*)

American troops approaching Omaha Beach on D-Day (U.S. Army photo)

"They were chosen by fate and circumstance to represent us on the beaches that day." (Filmmaker and historian Charles Guggenheim)

On June 5, 1944, Dwight Eisenhower casually walked among the young paratroopers of the 101st Airborne Division who were preparing themselves for the D-Day invasion. He had just given the order for the invasion to commence early the next morning and the soldiers, with their blackened faces, rifles, and assorted equipment, momentarily stopped their preparations to talk to the General. The men were understandably apprehensive and Ike tried to calm their fears. He told them not to worry, and that he had confidence in them. "We ain't worried, General," a young sergeant said. "It's the Germans that ought to be worrying now."

Eisenhower watched all of the big C-47 transport planes carrying the paratroopers take off that night. He often affectionately referred to the soldiers as "my boys", and it was feared that the 101st would suffer 70 percent casualties. As the last plane left the runway, the General had tears in his eyes.

Although the Allies had meticulously planned every detail of the operation, the success of the invasion was by no means a given. Eisenhower and the other Allied generals knew that all of the planning in the world couldn't compensate for the courage and improvisation necessary for the invasion to succeed. Ultimately, it would all come down to the performance of the various combat units and their soldiers that would decide the outcome.

The individual acts of bravery on that day were astonishing. Despite witnessing several soldiers die in failed attempts to cut through barbed wire that had his platoon trapped on the beach, Sergeant Philip Streczyk of the 16th RCT ran through a barrage of German machine-gun fire to cut the wire, and then waved the rest of his troops through. Paratrooper Sgt. John Ray landed in the middle of a Ste.-Mere-Eglise town square full of alarmed German soldiers. Shot in the stomach and dying, Ray still managed to shoot a German soldier who was about to kill two other American paratroopers. Technician John Pinder, shot twice and terribly weakened by loss of blood, continually waded back into the surf to retrieve vital communication equipment. While struggling back out of the water, Pinder was shot for a third time and killed, but not before he had retrieved a workable radio.

Various allied combat units also performed brilliantly that day. The textbook capture of the critical Orne River Bridge by British paratroopers is still marveled at to this day by military strategists. The destruction of the German gun batteries at Brecourt Manor by the outnumbered 101st Division's Easy Company was immortalized in the HBO miniseries, *Band of Brothers*. And the sacrifice of that day was epitomized by the 29th Division at Omaha Beach. Of the 35 soldiers in the 29th from little

Bedford, VA, 19 died in the first 15 minutes and two more died later that day. Fittingly, Bedford is the site of the National D-Day Memorial.

These are just a few of the heroic individuals and military units that distinguished themselves that day. To list them all would surely require every page of this newspaper.

It's so easy to forget and take for granted what happened on the Normandy coast 60 years ago. Had the invasion failed, the resulting consequences to civilization would have been appalling. Accordingly, most historians regard D-Day as the most important day of the 20th century. However, its true meaning to each subsequent generation of Americans has been gradually diminished by the passage of time. Sadly, this 60th anniversary reveals the steadily thinning ranks of "Eisenhower's boys." So, if you happen to know a veteran of the D-Day invasion, take a moment while you have the opportunity to thank them for what they did. They represented us on the beaches that day, and all of us should feel privileged to have known them and lived among them. We are obligated to preserve and honor their legacy for all future generations to come.

AFTERWORD

The inspiration for this D-Day essay was Steven Spielberg's epic war film, Saving Private Ryan, *and I wrote it shortly after seeing the movie for a second time on HBO. It is still the most intense experience I've ever had while watching a movie in a theater. I was so moved by the film that shortly after seeing it for the first time, I wrote a letter to the* Philadelphia Daily News *that was published in the August 8, 1998 edition. Parts of the letter follow, and it still sums up my feelings quite well: "I was unprepared for the intense and realistic depiction of the Normandy invasion in* Saving Private Ryan. *Throughout the first 25 minutes of the movie, my fists were clenched so tightly that my palms had fingernail impressions that remained for days. How, I thought, could those American soldiers face such a murderous barrage of machine-gun and mortar fire and continue to assault that* beach? What was it that kept them moving forward? Fighting in a war thousands of miles from home, a generation of Americans was tasked with helping to liberate Nazi-occupied Europe. A madman, whose crimes against humanity were not yet fully known, had to be stopped. How well these men fought would determine our country's fate. I wondered if they realized that that they were not only fighting for those alive then, but also for those yet to be born?...I shudder to think of what might have been if Hitler had pushed the Allies back into the sea that day and the war had been delayed long enough for the Nazis to develop Atomic weapons before the United States did. Most of us would not be here today."

WHEN THE BULGE ALMOST BROKE

(Edited version published in the December 16, 2004
Philadelphia Daily News)

Massacre of American soldiers at Malmedy during the Battle of the Bulge

The light snow fell steadily in the Ardennes Forest of southern Belgium during the early morning hours of December 16, 1944. The American soldiers stationed in the area slept soundly that night as the prevailing opinion among the Allies was that the German army was in complete disarray and couldn't possibly regroup to mount an offensive of any significance. At 5:30am that morning, the stunned U.S. 1st Army division soon found out how badly they had miscalculated.

Eight German armored divisions and thirteen infantry divisions launched an all out attack. It was the beginning of what came to be known as The Battle of the Bulge, the largest land battle of World War II in which the United States participated. Hitler's plan was to trap the Allied troops in Holland and Belgium, and push to the key Belgian port city of Antwerp. He believed that the alliance between the U.S. and Britain was already fragile, and that this new offensive would further split the relationship, thus buying him more time to develop his secret weapons and rebuild his depleted and exhausted army. Hitler's plan was dependent upon speed and extended bad weather to keep the Allied air forces grounded. Hitler also believed he had history on his side as it was in the Ardennes that he launched his successful surprise attack against France only 4 years earlier.

The initial hours of the attack were wildly successful for the Germans. U.S. Army units were surrounded or destroyed by the fast moving Wermacht, and large numbers of G.I.'s were surrendering. Sergeant Ed Stewart of the 84th infantry recalled the initial chaos and fear among the Americans. "The screaming sound of 288s, which was a major artillery on the part of the Germans, is absolutely frightening, it's a nightmare", he said. It seemed that Hitler's impossible gamble just might succeed.

However, on December 17 the Germans made a fatal mistake. On a road leading to the Belgian town of Malmedy, SS troops committed one of the worst atrocities of the war. Some 86 American POW's were shot in a snow covered field. Those that tried to crawl away were shot as well. However, some did escape and as word spread of the massacre, the tide began to turn as determined and enraged American soldiers, some cut-off from their units and completely surrounded, began to take the initiative and refused to surrender.

82nd Airborne staff sergeant Ted Kerwood of New Jersey was one such soldier. His unit was quickly rushed in to the battle, and as they approached a bridge in the Belgian town of Bielsaim on Christmas Eve, they noticed a column of German tanks and infantry quickly closing to cross the bridge. A volunteer was needed to run down and set explosives to blow the bridge before the enemy crossed it. Ted said that he would do it. "We just had to go up there and take care of the situation", Ted told me in a recent interview. "You're not really scared until after it's over. You just have a job to do, and you do it." Kerwood was awarded the Silver Star for his actions that day. The fierce resistance of the U.S. 28th, 106th, and 101st divisions was also a key factor in delaying the German advance. But the most famous example of U.S. resolve occurred in the town of Bastogne, where the surrounded U.S. troops refused to yield to superior German forces. The stunned Germans were told to "go to hell" when they requested the Americans to surrender.

The tenacious defense across the battlefield by the American soldiers soon caused the German advance to slow, and ultimately signaled defeat for Hitler. As the German offensive ground to a halt, it was destroyed by superior Allied airpower when the weather cleared in late December.

This Christmas Eve, be thankful for the many blessings that we sometimes take for granted. Remember that 60 years ago on this date, in the freezing cold of the Ardennes Forest, a determined group of American soldiers helped to ensure the freedom we have today. They spent that Christmas Eve wondering whether it would be their last, and for many of them it was. During this holiday season, take a moment to remember the veterans of this battle, and those who gave their lives, and raise a glass in salute. Remember, that the likes of these men may never be seen again.

This article is dedicated to the memory of Battle of the Bulge veteran Lawrence W. Summers of Roxborough.

Grave of Lawrence Summers at Epinal American Cemetery

AFTERWORD

My interview of 82nd Airborne veteran Ted Kerwood for this essay was arranged by his nephew, Tom Kerwood, who has been one of my closest friends since childhood. It also served as a reminder of an idea for another story that I'd been thinking of writing for several years, and eventually culminated in my essay 6 months later titled, The Scars of War. *This essay was dedicated to the memory of Lawrence W. Summers of the Roxborough section of Philadelphia. He was my brother-in-law's uncle (Eddie Summers is married to my sister, Rose). Lawrence was a Sergeant in the 110th Infantry of Pennsylvania's 28th Division and was wounded during the Battle of the Bulge. Despite his wounds, he wanted to return to his battalion as quickly as possible so that he could be back with his men. Shortly thereafter, he was killed in action on February 7, 1945, and is buried in France at the Epinal American Cemetery.*

THE SCARS OF WAR

(Edited versions published in the July 13, 2005 *Philadelphia Daily News* and in the July, 2009 issue of *The History Channel Magazine*)

Jack Kerwood (photo courtesy of Tom Kerwood)

I can still remember the first time I saw the scar. It was on a warm summer day over 35 years ago in the working class Philadelphia neighborhood I grew up in, and my friend's father was lying on a float in his backyard pool while reading the paper and listening to the Phillies game. Running across the upper part of his thick chest and onto his beefy shoulder was a huge gash that, at first glance, didn't seem as if it could be real. It almost looked as if his flesh had been gouged out with an ice cream scoop. The scar was so deep, that there were puddles of pool-water inside of it. He noticed me staring at it and gave me a wink, which changed the astonished look on my face to an uneasy smile. As he resumed reading his paper, I wondered if he had any other scars that I couldn't see.

Jack Kerwood was a young Marine fighting in the Pacific during World War II, and he was part of the American assault on the Japanese Island of Okinawa that lasted from April through June of 1945. Ripped by shrapnel from a mortar, Kerwood almost had his arm amputated, but a young army surgeon heroically succeeded in saving it.

Okinawa was the largest amphibious invasion of the Pacific campaign, and it would also be the bloodiest. More people were killed during the battle of Okinawa than those that died in the atomic bombings of Hiroshima and Nagasaki. American casualties totaled more than 38,000 wounded and 12,000 killed or missing. Japanese casualties were more than 107,000 soldiers killed, and it's estimated that over 100,000 Okinawan civilians also died during the battle. Close quarters fighting with bayonets, hand grenades, and flame throwers was the order of the day. Unburied Japanese bodies littered the island and were left to decay in the monsoon rains. The stench was said to be unbearable. American soldiers watched in horror as Okinawan women hurled their children, and then themselves, off rocky cliffs rather than submit to the Americans. So horrific were the battle conditions at Okinawa, that psychiatric combat stress among American soldiers was an astonishing 48%. More than 26,000 U.S. troops were eventually removed from the battlefield for combat stress during the Okinawa campaign.

During World War II, the war in the Pacific took a back seat to Hitler and the campaign in Europe, as the Allies made the early decision to pursue victory over the Nazis first before focusing on defeating the Japanese empire. Even to this day, as we think of some of the brutal island hopping battles of the Pacific, many of us are unfamiliar with the names of those places. The battles of Tarawa, Tinian, Luzon, and Okinawa are not as widely known as the battles of Normandy, Holland, Sicily, and Bastogne.

This year marks the 60th anniversary of the end of World War II, and as we remember all of the veterans who fought in this great conflict, think of the veterans of the Pacific. They deserve to be remembered and honored in the same way as those who fought in Europe. In many instances, the battles fought in the Pacific were bloodier, and the conditions were more dismal.

To many members of my generation, these men were our fathers, or friends of our fathers, or our neighbors. We know their stories, and what they endured on those battlefields. They are our heroes, but now they are in their twilight of their lives and dying at an average rate of 2,000 per day. Time is running out for the younger generations to thank them for what they accomplished for all of us.

Unfortunately, Jack Kerwood is no longer with us to commemorate the 60th anniversary of the end of World War II. When he was laid to rest in December, 2001, a Marine honor guard was there, as well as a military bugler. As the final note of *Taps* echoed across the cemetery, I remembered that day when I first saw the scar, but I also thought of the psychological scars that Jack Kerwood and his fellow veterans of the Pacific must have stoically carried with them all of these years. It was at this moment that the tears began to well up in my eyes and stream down my cheeks as I realized that sometimes the scars we can't see leave the deepest wounds. I looked around at the faces of those in attendance, and all of them were crying too.

AFTERWORD

This essay marked a turning point for me in my writing. For the first time I not only focused on someone that I knew, but also decided to convey my personal feelings and emotions as well. I worried over my decision to do so, and actually thought that my submission was likely to be rejected by the Philadelphia Daily News *because of it. Instead, I received so much positive feedback via e-mails from readers following its publication, many of whom told me that they were in tears as they read it, that I tried to incorporate a more personal touch into most of my essays that followed. The gratitude that I received from the Kerwood family, especially from Jack Kerwood's son, Tom – one of my oldest and very best friends – placed this essay among the most rewarding I've published.*

REMEMBER THE FORGOTTEN

(Edited versions published in the November 11, 2005 *Philadelphia Daily News*, the April 18, 2018 *Washington Times*, and in the *Graybeards Magazine for Korean War Veterans*)

National Korean War Memorial in Washington, D.C. (Chris Gibbons photo)

And when we go to heaven, St Peter will surely yell,
"Here're the boys from Korea, they served their time in Hell."
(Excerpt from a poem written by a GI killed in Korea)

Those who have seen the memorial are struck by the stark beauty of its realism. It depicts a walking and weary platoon of 19 soldiers. These steel statues, with their helmets, guns, boots, and ponchos, are so accurately sculpted that you almost expect them to take a step forward. But it's their faces that haunt you. They wear the faces of war: looks of determination, fear, loneliness, and grim resolve that somehow the artist was able to capture. I've seen these faces before. My father is burdened with them on the rare occasions he talks of a certain place that his generation was asked to defend. That place was Korea, and the statues are part of the National Korean War Veterans Memorial.

The war is often referred to as "The Forgotten War", and it's easy to see why. While the conflict was raging from 1950 to 1953, it was not uncommon for newspapers to relegate stories from Korea to the back pages. With the horrific memories of WWII still fresh in their minds, Americans didn't want to deal with the harsh realities of this new conflict. The soldiers returning from Korea were greeted with little fanfare here in the U.S. When my father returned in 1952, the first thing my grandfather asked him was if he had a job lined up. My Dad told me "that's just the way it was back then", and like the other returning soldiers, he very quickly and quietly merged back into society. History books now barely mention it, and many young people know nothing about it.

With a determination and resolve characteristic of their generation, the veterans of the Korean War waged one of the fiercest fights in the annals of U.S. military history. In a conflict that witnessed American and Communist forces meeting each other on the battlefield for the first time, both armies hurled each other up and down the Korean peninsula. The battles were often as brutal as the harsh Korean winters. After enduring some initial defeats at the hands of the Communist armies, the U.S. and UN forces, under the brilliant command of General Matthew Ridgway, began to turn the tide of battle. American led UN soldiers repeatedly routed the massive "human wave" assaults of the Chinese, and after a prolonged stalemate, an armistice was eventually signed in 1953. The South Koreans remain free to this day. In addition, a message was sent to the Communist leadership in Moscow and Beijing: the U.S. will meet your aggression, with force and on the battlefield if necessary. Throughout the duration of the Cold War, Communist leaders surely remembered the bloody nose they received in Korea and set a much less aggressive agenda in the subsequent years that followed. Many historians now believe that the seeds of our eventual Cold War victory were sewn on the battlefields of Korea.

The brother of a GI killed during the war told me that he hates the term "The Forgotten War." He said, "My brother is not forgotten, and there's not a day that goes by that my family and I don't think about him." The time has come for all of us to remember the Korean War, and its importance in U.S. history. The United States emerged as the winner of the Cold War, but the first steps towards that victory were tread 55 years ago by American soldiers on the often frozen ground of the Korean peninsula.

2005 marks the 55th anniversary of the start of the Korean War, and on this Veterans Day, remember the men who fought there so long ago. If you ever get the opportunity, visit the Korean War Veterans Memorial in Washington, DC. And if you happen to see some older gentlemen there, with the same haunting faces as the statues, let them know that they're not forgotten.

AFTERWORD

The only time that my Dad would talk about his experiences during the Korean War was when I, or my brothers and sisters, would ask him about it. And when he did, his face would literally change. His eyes would glaze over, his lips would tighten and tremble, and he would vacantly stare ahead as he spoke. The best way to describe it was that his face suddenly had a "haunted" appearance to it. I remember that when I visited the Korean War Veterans Memorial in Washington, DC for the first time what immediately struck me were the faces of the statues. "That's my Dad's face", I whispered as the tears flowed down my cheeks.

THE LAST OF THE DOUGHBOYS

(Edited version published in the May 25, 2007 *Philadelphia Daily News*)

"To the world he was a soldier. To me, he was all the world."
Epitaph on the gravestone of a soldier killed in WW I

It must be a very strange and lonely feeling to realize that you are among the very last to still be alive. Being last has always held a somewhat negative connotation in our society: in last place, the last in line, the last to be picked, or the last to know. These men are the last of the doughboys, which some might contend is not such a bad thing. However, to have endured the deaths of so many of their comrades, both during and after the war, and to have witnessed the devastating wars that followed the "war to end all wars", must have slowly chipped away at their souls. In the prime of their youth they were among the 4.7 million Americans who served their country during World War I. Now, in the twilight of their lives, they are the

4 known surviving American veterans from one of the most devastating wars the world has ever seen.

The origin of the term "doughboys" remains sketchy. Some said it referred to the dough-like shape of their uniform buttons, others thought it was due to the dough-white trimmings on their uniforms. The dough-boys fought in one of the greatest conflicts of the 20th century, and its impact upon the world still reverberates to this day. The primary weapons of today's battlefields such as airplanes, tanks, submarines, and machine guns were either used for the first time or perfected for use during World War I. Weapons of mass destruction in the form of poison gas and chemicals were also used for the first time during this conflict. Unfortunately for the soldiers, these innovations resulted in appalling losses. The casualty numbers were staggering: 10 million killed, and 20 million wounded. Nearly 10% of the fighting soldiers in World War I were killed, as opposed to 4.5% in World War II.

When the U.S. entered the war in 1917, they brought with them a naive enthusiasm for combat. During the battle of Belleau Wood, Captain Lloyd Williams was urged to retreat by a French commander, and he replied, "Retreat? Hell, we just got here!" The Americans fought tenaciously, and the famous "Lost Battalion" of the 77th division, which refused to surrender to superior German forces, exemplified the U.S. fighting spirit. However, it wasn't long before the horrors of the war began to take their toll.

Although the U.S. entered the war near its conclusion, and only experienced 8 months of significant combat action, over 116,000 were killed and 200,000 wounded in that short period of time. My father still has disturbing childhood memories of disabled World War I vets begging for money on the streets of Philadelphia during the Depression. Tony Pierro, veteran of the Meuse-Argonne offensive, where U.S. fatalities averaged 1,000 per day, recently recalled the bitter memories he carries to this day. "Many of my buddies lost an arm or a leg. I want to forget all of those bad days." Moses Hardy, the last African American veteran, spent 39 days in combat. He told his son that so many of his buddies were killed that it affected him for many years after the war's end. John Babcock, an American who served in the Canadian army, recounted a chilling incident he witnessed during the war. A distraught young soldier grabbed everyone's attention by yelling "Boys....here goes!" He then put a gun to his head, and shot himself."

The entry of the U.S. helped to tip the balance in favor of the Allies. In 1918, in the 11th month, of the 11th day, at the 11th hour the guns finally fell silent. The veterans soon referred to it as the "war to end all wars." How tragically wrong they were.

We have a tendency now to view these surviving veterans as oddities or curiosities. We are amazed by the fact they are still alive, but fail to listen to what they have to say about war. As the last survivors of a war that clearly demonstrated the tragic human consequences that can result from our technological innovations, these men, and their stories, need to be heard. Perhaps the epitaph is right, and to the world they are just soldiers, only to be seen and not heard. But it doesn't have to be that way. On this Memorial Day, take a moment to salute the last of the doughboys, for their time on this Earth is nearly up, their words still echo with truth, and their like may never be seen again.

The remaining veterans (per the VA): John Babcock-106, Frank Buckles-106, Russell Coffey-108, Harry Landis-107. Moses Hardy and Tony Pierro recently passed away.

AFTERWORD

The veterans listed at the end of this essay were all of the doughboys who were still alive as of May 25, 2007. The last of them to die was Frank Buckles on February 27, 2011 at the age of 110. World War 1 has always held a special fascination for me that started when I was very young. At 12 years old, I worked on Saturdays at the Roxborough Gun Club as a 'trap-boy', putting the clay pigeons on a machine that would fling them out of the trap-bunker. There was an old man who also worked there that everyone called "Gunner". I never knew his real name, but I was told that he was a veteran of World War 1. I remember that Gunner was missing the tops of a few of his fingers and often wondered if that had happened in the war. In the years lead-ing up to the publication of this essay, I had immersed myself in learning as much as I could about the Great War by reading such brilliant books as Yanks *by John Eisenhower (Ike's son), and* Finding The Lost Battalion *by Robert Laplander. As the media started to focus on the war's last surviving American veterans, I wanted to honor these veterans by writing this essay. Little did I know that just 4 years after its publication the relation-ship between World War 1 and my alma mater, Roman Catholic High School, would not only lead to a series of new essays, also featured in this compilation, but also begin one of the most incredible journeys of discovery in my life.*

THE KID AND THE GENERAL

(Edited version published in the September 28, 2007
Philadelphia Daily News)

General Jonathan Wainwright (U.S. War Dept. photo)

The boys from Roman Catholic High School in Philadelphia stood along Broad Street, and some peered out from the school's 2nd and 3rd story windows on that crisp fall day in October, 1945. Thousands of cheering Philadelphians lined the parade route, and rumor had it that the general's car was going to stop at the corner of Broad and Vine streets. The boys were eager to get a close look at the general riding in the open-top car.

They remembered seeing him in the newsreel footage as he stood behind Douglas MacArthur to formally witness the Japanese sign the articles of surrender just a few months prior to that day. The boys strained their necks and stood on their toes as the general's car slowly approached. Some of the boys then shifted their attention to one of their classmates, the quiet kid with the embarrassed look on his face, for they knew that he was the reason why the general's car was stopping. A path was cleared among the boys, and a respectful silence fell over them. The kid's name was Joe Owens, and he stepped forward to meet the general.

The new Ken Burns World War II series, *The War*, is one of the most highly anticipated documentaries in the history of PBS. Advanced screenings have drawn critical praise, and the very first episode in the 7 part series has been cited for its powerful, brutal depiction of one infamous event: The Bataan Death March.

In April, 1942, General Jonathan Wainwright's beleaguered force of 70,000 Filipino and American soldiers was forced to surrender the Philippines to the invading Japanese army. The Japanese then force-marched the captured soldiers some 90 miles north from the southern tip of the Philippine peninsula of Bataan to POW Camp O'Donnell. The atrocities committed by the Japanese army during the march are almost unspeakable. The sick and the dying were left to rot on the roadside in the stifling heat of the Philippine jungle. The thirsty men weren't allowed to drink from the nearby streams, and those that tried were beheaded on the spot. Struggling men who couldn't keep up with the march were bayoneted by the sadistic Japanese guards. Bataan survivor Abbie Abraham witnessed a group of the diseased, starving men as they arrived at a small stream. "It was contaminated with filthy water from a bloated corpse filled with maggots. This filthy stream the POW's were allowed to drink from, as the Japanese guards laughed at them."

Wainwright himself was eventually captured and nearly died in a POW camp. He remained there until the end of the war when he was rescued by Allied forces. During his captivity, he felt that he had let his country down for surrendering Bataan and Corregidor. Upon his release, he was stunned to learn that the country regarded him as a hero, and he received the Congressional Medal of Honor in 1945.

It's estimated that approximately 5,000 – 10,000 prisoners died during the march, most of them Filipino. Of the nearly 10,000 Americans taken prisoner at Bataan, over 6,000 died in Japanese prison camps during their captivity. One of the men who died there was Joe Owens' father.

Each year, during the anniversaries of the atomic bombings of Hiroshima and Nagasaki, we hear the cries of anger over the cruelty of the Americans for dropping the bombs. But, those same voices are strangely silent when it comes to the Death March. Who speaks for Bataan, for the dead cannot and the survivors are few?

The open-top car carrying General Wainwright slowed to a stop. Apparently, the priests at Roman had gotten word to Wainwright about Joe's father, and he agreed to meet young Joe. In what must've been a surreal moment, the general who lost an army, and the kid who lost his Dad, shook hands in the shadow of Roman Catholic High School, which had lost nearly 110 alumni during WW II. It was said that Wainwright was haunted by guilt in the months following the war, and perhaps he hoped to find some solace in meeting the kid who now stood before him. We don't know what was said, or how Joe felt about meeting the man whose surrender at Bataan sealed his father's fate. He never spoke of the encounter with his friends or family for the remainder of his life.

AFTERWORD

Joe Owens was one of the greatest track athletes in the history of Philadelphia's Roman Catholic High School, and I never saw my Dad get as emotional regarding the death of a close friend as he did when Joe, his former classmate, died. His death hit my Dad hard, and when I saw how badly it was affecting him, I told him how sorry I was. He then proceeded to tell me the incredible story I recounted in this essay. The premiere of the Ken Burns WW II documentary presented a perfect opportunity for me to submit my story for publication. I can still recall the raw emotion in the voice of Joe's son, Kevin, as he thanked me for writing the story.

DEADLY BATTLE'S LAST VICTIM

(Edited version published in the October 17, 2008
Philadelphia Daily News)

U. S. OFFICIAL PHOTO

LIEUT.-COL. CHARLES W. WHITTLESEY
Commander of the "Lost Battalion"

Charles Whittlesey stood along the rails of the large steamship in the late autumn of 1921, and stared vacantly at the Atlantic Ocean below. Haunted by his experiences during World War I, Whittlesey was consumed by guilt, and his terrible memories of the great Meuse-Argonne offensive had left him with a broken spirit. He probably gazed down at the churning water with a macabre sense of relief as he realized that soon he would no longer have to endure the dreaded nightmares that slowly chipped away at his soul.

———

The autumn of 2008 marks the 90th anniversary of the start of the deadliest battle every fought by U.S. soldiers: the Meuse-Argonne offensive of World War I. More Americans were killed during this battle than in any other in U.S. history, as 26,277 Doughboys lost their lives and another 95,786 were wounded. Over 1.2 million American soldiers took part in the 47 day battle in 1918, and it eventually resulted in forcing an end to World War I.

Major Charles Whittlesey commanded 9 units of the U.S. 77th division. His battalion consisted of 554 men, most of whom were ethnic Irish, Italian, Jewish, and Polish street toughs from New York City, as well as Midwestern farm boys. Whittlesey himself was a Harvard Law School graduate. Because of his social status, one might assume that Whittlesey held himself above these men, but this wasn't the case. He had the utmost respect and concern for the men he commanded.

On the morning of October 2nd, the battalion advanced deeply into the Argonne forest of eastern France, but unbeknownst to them, the Allied divisions supporting their right and left flanks had stalled, and they were soon cut-off and surrounded. For the next 5 days the Germans relentlessly attacked the small American force and inflicted heavy casualties. The Americans fought back fiercely and refused to yield. Food, water, and ammunition began to run out as the number of dead and wounded piled up. At one point, the men were mistakenly shelled by their own artillery forces. Newspaper reporters picked up on the story, and dubbed them "The Lost Battalion."

On October 7th, a captured American soldier was released with a note for Whittlesey from the German commander. It read in part: "The suffering of your wounded men can be heard over here in the German lines, and we are appealing to your humane sentiments to stop. A white flag shown by one of your men will tell us that you agree with these conditions."

Whittlesey and his second in command, Captain George McMurtry, smiled when they read it because they viewed it as a sign of German desperation. Whittlesey ordered two white panels used to signal Allied planes to be removed lest they be mistaken for white flags. There would be no surrender. Word of the note spread among the men, and some of them yelled, "You Dutch bast****, come and get us!"

Once again German *Sturmtruppen (Storm Troopers)*, some equipped with flame-throwers, attacked the defiant Americans. The battalion was enraged as they viewed these weapons as immoral, and they tore into the attacking Germans, some with only their bare hands. The Germans retreated, but Whittlesey's men were barely hanging on. Finally, on October 8th, the battalion was rescued by advancing U.S. troops. The relieving soldiers watched in silence as the battered survivors emerged from the forest. "There was nothing to say," one of them said. "It made your heart lump up in your throat just to look at them." Of the 554 men who entered the Argonne, only 194 were rescued. The rest were either killed or missing in action. Whittlesey, McMurtry, and 3 others received the Medal of Honor.

The post-war years were difficult for Whittlesey as he was continually troubled by his memories and the decisions he made during the battle. He was a pallbearer in burial ceremonies of the Unknown Soldier at Arlington in 1921, and a friend said that the distraught Whittlesey "thought that the Unknown Soldier might have been one of his own men." He had recurring nightmares of the screaming wounded, and once had a disturbing dream in which a young soldier's "cold in death" face touched his own.

On November 26, 1921, Charles Whittlesey jumped to his death from the deck of the SS Toloa. His body was never recovered. Whittlesey's Will stipulated that the original surrender letter from the Germans be given to McMurtry.

The terrible memories would haunt Charles Whittlesey no more. Over 3 years after its conclusion, the great battle of the Meuse-Argonne had recorded its final casualty.

AFTERWORD

I never knew the story of Charles Whittlesey until I saw the excellent AMC movie, The Lost Battalion *starring Rick Schroder. Needless to say, I was deeply moved. Every year I give a presentation to the history students at Roman Catholic High School regarding my search for the alumni of our school who fought in World War 1. As part of the presentation, I play an intense 4-minute clip from the movie which graphically depicts the Battle of the Meuse-Argonne. The students' eyes are always riveted to the monitor as it plays. When the clip ends, I inform them that my research has revealed that most of the Roman alumni that I have found who gave their lives during WW I died during the Battle of the Meuse-Argonne, and that elements of Pennsylvania's famed 28th Division participated in the eventual rescue of the Lost Battalion. I tell them that "it is likely that Roman alumni, men who sat in this same classroom, were there that day." You can always hear a pin drop as that reality sinks in.*

GREG MAZZOTTA'S DREAM

(Edited version published in the April 6, 2009 *Philadelphia Daily News*)

Vietnam Memorial Wall in Wildwood, N.J. - dedicated in 2010

Greg Mazzotta had a dream, and he was determined to see it realized. He dreamed of a permanent Vietnam Memorial Wall in Wildwood, N.J. that would almost be an exact replica of the famous Vietnam Wall in Washington, D.C., but on a smaller scale. As President of the Vietnam Veterans of America – Chapter 955, Greg was instrumental in bringing a traveling exhibit of the Wall to Wildwood in 2008, but he wanted to bring something permanent to honor the Vietnam veterans, especially the 58,913 who gave their lives. Born and raised in Philadelphia, and a 25 year resident of Delaware County before moving to Wildwood, Greg knew the special ties that have always existed between the coastal towns of Southern New Jersey and the Philadelphia counties. He was convinced that Wildwood would be an ideal location for the new memorial, and would host thousands of visitors each summer.

"We are gonna work on a permanent Memorial Wall," Greg told his cousin and best friend, Vince DePrinzio. "This is our wall to honor and remember our brothers and sisters who fought in that war. We've gotta do this, especially to honor those that died."

Like so many of his fellow veterans, the war never really left Greg Mazzotta. It wasn't just the fact that Viet Cong shrapnel was still embedded in his body, it was also the persistent memories of his five buddies and that terrible day in 1966. Mazzotta was part of a small unit of 6 soldiers patrolling the jungles of South Vietnam who were suddenly ambushed by a fierce Viet Cong mortar attack. Greg was the only survivor, and received the Purple Heart. Those who knew the story, knew what was fueling Greg's passion and determination in having the Wall built. If anyone could push this project through to its completion, it was Greg.

With the help of Wildwood mayor Ernie Troiano, and City Commissioner Bill Davenport, Greg and Vince secured the land they needed for the Wall in Wildwood's Columbus Park. The property had previously been dedicated to the "Sons of Italy", who were honored to have the land used for such a special purpose.

Unfortunately, securing the land was just the beginning phase of the project, and Greg and Vince had their work cut out for them. Because of Wildwood's coastal climate, the 235 foot long Wall has to be made of graphite in order to withstand long term exposure to the elements. In addition, the frame has to be specially made as well. Consequently, the total cost of the project is estimated at $150,000, and the only way to fund it would be through donations. The long road ahead of them seemed daunting, but Greg was determined to see it through. Whenever he was having a bad day, and it seemed as if the project would never get off the ground, he would remember his five buddies and push himself to continue on. He had to do this, and he couldn't quit. "Greg was the driving force behind it all", Vince said. "He was determined."

On September 21, 2008, Greg Mazzotta suddenly died after suffering a massive heart attack. He would never get to see his dream realized, and many had doubts that the project would continue on without him. But people underestimated these veterans. As they've always done, the Vietnam Veterans rallied around their fallen comrade, and were more determined than ever to build their Wall. "Greg was a veteran's veteran," Vince told me, "and he was always there for the veterans. He would give you the shirt off of his back." The funeral home couldn't hold the huge crowd for Greg's viewing, and his funeral caravan stretched for 5 miles.

With a renewed determination, and Greg's spirit driving them on, Chapter 955 began to raise the money needed for the Wall. Starting in November, 2008 they solicited donations from individuals and companies to help turn Greg's dream into a reality. They had a wildly successful Beef-n-Beer fundraiser in February, and they've raised $19,000 so far, with additional commitments of $8,500.

"We know we have a long way to go, but we're confident we'll get there," Vince said.

The national motto of the Vietnam Veterans of America is *"Never again will one generation of veterans abandon another"*. Greg Mazzotta lived by this principle and refused to abandon the memory of his five buddies who perished that day in 1966. Now, his cousin Vince, and the other members of Chapter 955 will not abandon Greg or his dream.

AFTERWORD

I heard about Greg Mazzotta from my wife's sister, Barb. Greg is the father of one of Barb's neighbors, and when she told me about Greg's sudden passing and the project that he was involved in, I wanted to help spread the word by writing this essay. I've met so many wonderful Vietnam veterans from the Philadelphia area in my life, and when "Greg's dream" finally came to fruition in 2010, I couldn't have been happier for all of them.

INVISIBLE WOUNDS THAT KILL

**The Japanese didn't take the life of this soldier.
The horrible memories did.**

(Edited version published in the May 25, 2009 *Philadelphia Inquirer*)

Marvin Ravinsky (Photo courtesy of the Ravinsky family)

I stood there in the Har Nebo Cemetery on Oxford Avenue in Philadelphia, and looked out at the gravestones that surrounded me. The high autumn lawn of the cemetery undulated like an ocean in the wind, green grass waves breaking over tombstone shores. I was heading to the section for indigent Jews, searching for the gravesite of a World War II veteran. Although I never met him, I felt that I had to come and pay my respects. I found his grave, marked only by a 4 square inch plaque that bore his name, and knelt down next to it. I planted a small American flag and said a short prayer. The silence of the moment was only broken by the sound of the American flag as it whipped in the wind.

Marvin Ravinsky grew up in a tough Jewish section of North Philadelphia. He enlisted in the Army in 1943 and fought in some of the bloodiest battles of the Pacific Theater. He was at Okinawa, where psychiatric combat stress among American soldiers was an unbelievable 48%, as over 26,000 U.S. soldiers had to be removed from the battlefield because of "battle fatigue." During the fighting, Marvin and some other soldiers were trapped in a cave by the Japanese. They riddled the cave with bullets, killing everyone but Marvin. The Japanese entered the cave and began bayoneting the bodies. They were using the tactic to find and kill any survivors. Marvin played dead, and through his sheer will to live, didn't move or cry out when a Japanese bayonet pierced his thigh. Bleeding profusely, Marvin waited until they left the cave, and then crawled out from under the lifeless bodies of his friends.

Marvin returned home with a Purple Heart medal awarded for his injuries, but there was no recognition for the hidden wounds that eventually infected his mind. He fought a long, losing battle with the demons of Post Traumatic Stress Disorder (PTSD), as there was little government help given to the traumatized veterans of WW II. These men and their families were left to deal with the nightmares and debilitating effects of this affliction on their own. Unfortunately, Marvin slowly spiraled into the dark abyss of PTSD and eventually lost himself and his family. In his later years he was destitute and being taken advantage of by drug addicts in his neighborhood until rescued by social workers. He died of lung cancer on August 12, 2008.

I never knew Marvin Ravinsky. His cousin was going through his personal belongings and among his medals and other WW II memorabilia she found a copy of an article that I wrote in which I stressed the need to honor the WW II veterans who fought in the Pacific. Since I was a child, soldiers have always been my heroes, and to know that one of them kept my article among the things he cherished the most was a touching moment for me.

On this Memorial Day, honor all of our veterans, especially those who gave their lives. Remember that although some were killed on the field of battle, others, like Marvin Ravinsky, eventually succumbed to the hidden wounds of war, wounds that couldn't be seen, yet were fatal nonetheless. Marvin died a slow death that began the day he first witnessed the horrors of battle as a young soldier, and finally ended over 60 years later in the cold hospital bed of a lonely, disoriented, and forgotten old man. It doesn't seem fair. Heroes aren't supposed to die this way.

As I stood above his grave, I wished that there was something more that I could do to honor Marvin. I felt so helpless. How sad, I thought to myself, that we live in a world in which we praise people for acting in a movie, or putting a ball through a hoop, or singing songs on a stage. We misuse terms such as "great" and "courageous" when describing them, but conveniently forget about the people who fought for this country and who are much more deserving of these accolades. I can just hear the neighborhood junkies, "He was just some old, crazy Jew. Who cares?"

I turned to leave, but was compelled to carry out one final gesture that seemed somewhat clichéd, yet very appropriate. As I faced his grave one last time, I straightened my back and saluted. The wind howled in sorrow, and the green grass waves lapped at my feet as the American flag whipped above the grave of Marvin Ravinsky.

AFTERWORD

The article that they found when sorting through Marvin's belongings shortly after he died was my article about my neighbor, Pacific War veteran Jack Kerwood (The Scars of War). To say that I was deeply moved upon hearing this from Marvin's cousin would be an understatement, and I was once again reminded of the power of the written word. But, perhaps the greatest satis-faction that I received from writing this essay occurred some 5 months after it was published when I received an e-mail that read in part: "My mother just forwarded me the article that you wrote about Marvin Ravinsky. He was my Grandfather. I never knew him. I wanted to thank you for giving me a little bit of insight into Marvin and my family history. I am proud to know that my Grandfather was a hero...Life is short; so those of us who are still living should do our best to honor those who have passed on. We should especially remember our heroes. Thanks again."

RECALLING THE 'MOTHER OF NORMANDY'

A Frenchwoman dedicated herself to tending the graves of American troops

(Edited version published in the November 11, 2009
Philadelphia Inquirer)

Normandy-American Cemetery (Photo courtesy of Jack Dougherty)

"We have gone forth from our shores repeatedly over the last hundred years and…put wonderful young men and women at risk, many of whom have lost their lives, and we have asked for nothing except enough ground to bury them in." (Colin Powell)

The first letters from America started arriving at the home of Madame Simone Renaud shortly after the publication of the Life magazine article in August, 1944. The article included a photo of Renaud placing flowers at the grave of Brigadier General Theodore Roosevelt, Jr. It noted that she was the wife of the mayor of Ste. Mere-Eglise, the first town liberated by American soldiers on D-Day.

Most of the letters were heartbreaking. One from Pennsylvania read in part: *"Dear Madame….we have just received word today from the War Department that our son was buried in this cemetery, my wife has kept this issue of the magazine ever since…something seemed to tell her that this was where our boy was buried. If I am not asking too much… would it be possible for you to look up the grave that I am listing below and place flowers on same… She is heartbroken over the loss of this boy …."*

Renaud was soon inundated with letters asking her to take care of the grave of a loved one believed to be buried in Ste. Mere-Eglise. As she read the letters, Renaud's thoughts would often turn to the terrible memories of that night when the American paratroopers descended onto her town.

Seizing Ste. Mere-Eglise prior to the D-Day beach landings was crucial to the Allied offensive. A German counterattack would likely use the main road that ran directly through the town, and the Allies were determined to hold it. Mixed units of the American 82nd and 101st Airborne Divisions had hoped to use the elements of surprise and confusion to overwhelm the German garrison there, but stray incendiary bombs set many of the town's buildings ablaze. The German soldiers and the townspeople were fully alert and fighting the fires when the paratroopers suddenly began landing among them.

The Americans were shot as they landed. Some fell directly into the burning buildings, and their agonized screams could be heard above the loudly ringing church bells. Others got hung up on poles, buildings, and trees, but were shot before they could cut themselves down. Renaud's husband witnessed several Germans emptying their machine gun magazines on one paratrooper as he hung helplessly above them. It seemed that the assault on the town would end in failure and catastrophe.

But the young paratroopers fought back. They could see what was happening below and started firing their guns as they descended. Wounded paratroopers who were lying in the streets, some bleeding to death, shot the Germans as they tried to pick off their descending comrades. Renaud and her 3 frightened young sons huddled in their home as the fierce fight raged in the streets outside.

At 4:30am the town finally fell to the Americans. As the reinforcing soldiers arrived, they were stunned by the macabre scene before them. Dead paratroopers were lying on the streets and dangling from the trees, their blood staining the cobblestone streets. Lieutenant Gus Sanders said "the men just stood there staring." Lieutenant Colonel Edward Krause could only utter three words: "Oh, my God."

Madame Renaud personally answered each of the letters from the families of the fallen soldiers. With the help of the townspeople, she carefully tended to the 3 cemeteries where 15,000 American soldiers were buried. In 1948 the bodies were moved to the American cemetery overlooking Omaha Beach, but Renaud continued to visit the graves, place flowers, and send letters and photos to the families. Surviving veterans loved to visit her, and she often organized D-Day anniversary events up until her death in 1988.

Film producer Doug Stebleton's new documentary, *Mother of Normandy*, chronicles the life of this remarkable woman. "I could not believe her story hadn't been told on a grand scale", Stebleton told me. "Her motto was "never forget", and with this film we can remind people to never forget that these men gave their lives so other people can live in freedom." Stebleton hopes to have the documentary premiere on a major cable network in 2010.

France is sometimes criticized for minimizing the sacrifices made by American soldiers on their soil during WW II. But it's unfair to say this of all French citizens, especially those from Ste. Mere-Eglise. On this Veterans Day take a moment to remember Madame Simone Renaud, a woman who spent most of her life trying to ease the suffering of grieving American mothers by treating their fallen sons as if they were her own.

AFTERWORD

In the weeks leading up to Veterans Day, 2009, I had an idea for an essay that was inspired by the Colin Powell quote that precedes this essay (ie: "...and we have asked for nothing except enough ground to bury them in."). I had heard that what prompted Powell to say it, and what my essay would expand upon, was the apparent self-righteous, non-appreciative French society that routinely minimized the sacrifices made by American soldiers who helped liberate France during World War II. However, it was during my research that I stumbled upon the incredible story of Madame Simone Renaud. I also learned that Powell's remarks were not directed at France, and if there are French citizens who are not appreciative of the American sacrifices during that war, they are few and far between. Indeed, the town of Ste. Mere-Eglise is a living monument to the heroic American paratroopers of D-Day, with a museum, numerous historical markers featuring the 10st Airborne patch, and streets named after some of the American soldiers. An email that I received following this essay's publication confirmed my discoveries. The woman who sent me the email stated that she and her husband recently moved to Paris, and were looking to buy wine from a local chateau. She wrote: "It was Sunday morning, we knocked on the door and a very proper elderly French woman, clearly just back from Church and in her Sunday finest, answered the door. I explained that we were Americans living in Paris, were looking to purchase some wine and had been referred to her chateau by the proprietor of one her neighboring wineries. She scowled, but ushered us into her parlor and rang for some tea. After some awkwardness while I tried to make small talk, she raised her hand to interrupt me and said: "We do not entertain visitors here, but my dead husband, who fought in the Resistance, would never forgive me if I turned away two young Americans at my door." We concluded a brief visit, she was politely curious about what we were doing in Paris, I bought some wine and we left with a story I continue to tell whenever anyone criticizes the French (or at least the part about the French not liking Americans)."

RESPITE FROM WAR, SADLY BRIEF

The Christmas Truce of 1914 underscored the insanity of the fighting

(Edited version published in the December 25, 2009
Philadelphia Inquirer)

THE UNOFFICIAL CHRISTMAS TRUCE

BRITISH AND GERMANS EXCHANGE PRESENTS.

Writing on Boxing Day from the trenches to his wife in Lower Broughton, a Manchester soldier gives the following account of the exchange of Christmas greetings and hospitality between our troops and those of the enemy:—

The Germans had a lot of Christmas trees lit up with candles, and our men wrote on a board, "A Merry Christmas," and the Germans wrote on another "Extreme Thanks." Then they beckoned for one of our men to go for some cigars, and he met the Germans half way between the trenches. This was the Welsh Fusiliers. Then their officer brought a bottle of champagne, which was drunk between them. Then all the men came and shook hands. The Germans, having occupied a brewery, rolled two barrels of beer up to our men. There was a stoppage of war for twenty-four hours, but they are at it again this morning. The Germans

The Guardian newspaper, London - Jan. 1, 1915

The peace that night was said to have been somewhat eerie. "I remember the silence, the eerie sound of silence," recalled British WW I veteran

Alfred Anderson in a 2004 interview with *The Guardian.* "All I'd heard for two months in the trenches was the hissing, cracking and whining of bullets in flight, machine gun fire and distant German voices. But there was a dead silence that morning across the land as far as you could see."

It was Christmas Eve, 1914, and thousands of Allied and German soldiers were dug in their trenches as they opposed each other across the cold and muddy battlefields of Belgium. They were separated by a mass of barbed wire, dead trees, and scorched earth that came to be known as the "No Man's Land." The war was only entering its 5th month, but there had already been thousands of casualties, and the demoralized soldiers began to wonder if they'd ever see home again. That night, the silence gradually succumbed to a beautiful sound arising from the trenches. It was the German soldiers softly singing *Stille Nacht (Silent Night).* The British soldiers responded by singing *O Come All Ye Faithful.* The Germans knew the Latin version, and began to sing in unison with their foes. Throughout the cold, moonlit night, the voices of the singing soldiers drifted across the battlefield.

As dawn approached, the German soldiers held up signs in fractured English that read "You No Fight, We No Fight." Men on both sides cautiously climbed out of their trenches and onto the barren landscape that separated their lines. They met on "No Man's Land" and exchanged gifts of cigarettes, candy, whiskey, and uniform buttons. Christmas trees were hastily pieced together from the splintered pines. Incredibly, in at least one area, a soccer game was played. German private Carl Muhlegg carried a Christmas tree across the scarred land and presented it to a French captain. "Never was I as keenly aware of the insanity of war", Muhlegg wrote in his journal. The soldiers hopefully believed that maybe the killing was finally over.

Unfortunately, the impromptu peace would not last. Upon hearing the news of the unauthorized truce, angry generals on both sides ordered the men to resume fighting. "The silence ended in the early afternoon, and the killing started again", said Anderson. It would continue that way for another 4 bloody years. When the war finally concluded, nearly 10 million had been killed, and over 20 million wounded.

World War I is now just a dim memory, and there are only a handful of surviving veterans. It is estimated that there are fewer than 10 remaining around the world. Alfred Anderson, the last surviving Allied witness to the Christmas Truce, died in 2005 at the age of 109.

The veterans of World War I, certain that the brutality and devastation wrought by the Great War would induce nations to seek diplomacy rather than armed conflict to resolve disputes, referred to it as "the war to end all wars." One only has to pick up a current newspaper to realize that their hopes were nothing but naive dreams.

Sadly, the saga of the Christmas Truce of WW I still resonates today. Despite the fact that we shake our heads in disbelief over the insanity that followed that night, we still tacitly accept the grim prospect that somewhere in Afghanistan lonely and home-sick soldiers will once again softly sing *Silent Night* on a battlefield, as the specter of war continues to haunt humanity. Although I support our troops and believe our cause is just, I wish the WW I veterans had been right, and it had actually been the war to end all wars.

To all of our soldiers in harm's way: Merry Christmas and Happy Holidays! I know that the enemy who opposes you cares nothing for our traditions, and there will be no truce, nor singing in unison with them. But I hope that you will take some small comfort in knowing that when many of us sing *Silent Night* this holiday season, we will think of all of you, and pray that you have a safe and silent night this Christmas Eve.

AFTERWORD

In response to my essay, an Inquirer reader wrote a letter to the editor that read: "Chris Gibbons' piece "Respite from war, sad but brief" on Friday employs nostalgia to misleadingly contrast an incident in World War I with the current war on terror. Just because British and German soldiers sang Christmas carols together on a sacred holiday, and our present antagonists are non-Christian, scarcely means that the Taliban "care nothing for our traditions." A linchpin of President Obama's Afghanistan policy is to convert rank-and-file Taliban to noncombatants using the "traditional" inducements of secure livelihoods, freedom from war, and a philosophy of tolerance for the other."

I sent an e-mail to the reader in response that read in part: "Your letter in response to my article is amusing, to say the least. I guess I should have said that the enemies our soldiers face in Afghanistan (you failed to mention that our enemies are both the Taliban and Al-Qeda) care nothing for our "Christmas" traditions. I'm fairly certain that nearly all of the readers of the article knew that's what I was referring to... you were wrong to state that I concluded that they care nothing for our traditions only because they are non-Christian. No, the reason they care nothing for our Christmas traditions is because we are their enemy and the traditions I referred to are primarily Christian. If you believe that the Taliban and Al-Qeda combatants do, in fact, actually care about the U.S. soldier's Christmas traditions, then you are living in a dream-world. With that being said, you also tried to cleverly assert that the Taliban is merely interested in the same "traditional" inducements that are shared by all U.S. citizens (you stated: "secure livelihoods, freedom from war, and a philosophy of tolerance for the other.). Wow...that was an interesting comment, especially when you consider that you left out some of the other Taliban "traditions", such as: public stoning, public amputations for defying Sharia laws, banning TV and videos, and forcing women to adhere to Taliban dress code and way of life. Question for you - in light of these "other traditions" that you left out of your letter, where did you ever get the idea that the Taliban is interested in a "philosophy of tolerance for the other?" You strike me as the kind of person that will stand up and denounce injustice when you believe it is being imposed. That's a good thing, and you should be proud that you possess that noble characteristic. But, be careful who you side with. Remember, if the Taliban were running our country, and you maintained your trait of speaking out against injustice...you'd find yourself in the middle of a public amphitheater, surrounded by hundreds of

Taliban with arms raised and stones in their hands, poised, and ready to engage in one of their infamous "traditions."
I never received a response.

SOME WAR STORIES WON'T EVER BE TOLD

A veteran shared firewood, but few memories

(Edited version published in the March 12, 2010 *Philadelphia Inquirer*)

Murray used to leave small bundles of firewood in my yard. They were made up of fallen tree branches or old wood scraps he had gathered from his garage or attic. The bundles were always neatly tied with twine, and cut to a perfect size for my fireplace. His timing was uncanny because every time I ran out of firewood, a bundle would be waiting for me in the yard.

Murray DiGioia was in his mid-80's when I moved next door to him in Lafayette Hill, but he seemed 20 years younger. I told him about my passion for American history and he fascinated me with his vivid memories of seeing the returning WW I Doughboys parade up Broad Street in Philadelphia in 1919. He was just a young child at the time, but Murray recounted his excitement at seeing their distinctive wrapped leggings and boots through the legs of the taller onlookers. I thought it was remarkable that my neighbor was a living link to an era that I had only read and dreamed about, and I hung on his every word.

I can still remember the day that I was putting up my big American flag on the front of my house, and Murray came strolling over. "Hey, why are you putting up your flag today?" he asked me. "It's June 6th, Murray", I replied, "The anniversary of D-Day!" Murray's eyes widened and his jaw slacked. "That's right!" he exclaimed, and he scurried over to his house. Two flags proudly flapped in the breeze on our street that day.

I told Murray about some of the articles I'd written honoring WW II veterans, and gave him a copy of one of them. I knew that he was about 30 years old in 1945, and figured he was too old to have been a soldier, but I thought it was odd that he didn't share his thoughts about the article with me. Here was a man who captivated me with stories of seeing the WW I soldiers as a child, but he said nothing about my article, or what life was like for him during WW II. I assumed he just didn't like the article and left it at that.

As the years passed, Murray's wife's health deteriorated. One day an ambulance arrived outside of their house and they took her to the hospital. My wife and I worried about Murray, so I drove him to the hospital. It was raining and we drove in silence as Murray just stared out the passenger window. "That was a nice article you wrote that time, Chris", he suddenly said, his gaze never leaving the window. "I fought in the Pacific during the war and saw some terrible things, but I really don't like to talk about it." There was a long awkward pause, and then he started to weep. "What am I going to do without my wife if she dies?" he cried. I told him that everything would be OK, even though I really didn't know if it would. His soft sobs were barely heard over the sound of the swishing windshield wipers.

Murray's wife passed away just a few months after that day, and as so often happens with older couples, Murray soon passed away as well. I was saddened and stunned by the news because he seemed to be in great shape the last time I saw him, but I suppose it's not always easy to tell when someone is dying from a broken heart.

During the height of the last snowstorm, I remembered the time that Murray and his wife baked us a cake, thanking me and my sons for shoveling their driveway. As I sat by the fire, I noticed the bundle of wood next to my fireplace. It was the kind that you buy at the supermarket and comes in a plastic bag. It wasn't comprised of broken branches and old wood scraps, nor was it neatly bound with twine. It looked artificial and manufactured, like so many of the things in our society today. Some of the little human touches in life seem to be fading with the passing of the older generation. I looked out the window and watched the snow fall and cover up the broken branches lying in Murray's old yard.

The highly anticipated HBO WW II mini-series *The Pacific* premieres this Sunday night, and I know that I'll think about Murray as I watch. But I can't shake the feeling that he wouldn't want me to watch it because I'll finally see the terrible things he never wanted me to know.

AFTERWORD

Murray was a great neighbor, and I always think of him anytime I buy a bundle of wood. It still fascinates me that he was actually there as a child to witness the parade held in Philadelphia in 1919 for the returning 28th Division soldiers. His recollections of it were so vivid, that I had the impression that he was a time-traveler who'd just returned from an excursion to the past. I thought that HBO's The Pacific was very well done, but its depiction of the brutality of the fighting, and the hatred that the Japanese and American soldiers had for one another was not only revealing, but tough to watch as well. When the series concluded, I was certain of two things: Murray would not have watched it, and he wouldn't have wanted me to watch it as well.

60 YEARS AGO, A WORTHY STAND IN KOREA

(Edited version published in the June 20, 2010 *Philadelphia Inquirer*)

Korean War Memorial in Washington, D.C. (Chris Gibbons photo)

"If we stand up to them [the communists] ... they won't take any next steps. There's no telling what they'll do if we don't put up a fight now."
(President Harry Truman at the outbreak of the Korean War)

On June 25, 2008, the 58th anniversary of the start of the Korean War, my son Ryan and I wandered among the statues of the Korean War Memorial in Washington.

A local TV news crew had gathered around a man with his young toddler son. The man reverently placed a bouquet of flowers at the memorial and bowed his head in silence.

Later, I overheard him tell the reporter that he was of Korean descent and that "South Korea was saved by the American soldiers. I wanted to come today and pay my respects." As he spoke, I couldn't help but notice the statues behind him of a weary platoon of 19 soldiers walking in formation during the harsh Korean winter, their ponchos billowing up from the bitterly cold wind. The words of my father, a Korean War veteran, echoed in my mind: "It was so cold there … cold like you wouldn't believe." Despite the stifling heat and humidity that day, I shivered as I gazed at the statues while imagining the cold my Dad had to endure.

This Friday marks the 60th anniversary of the start of one of the fiercest conflicts in U.S. military history: The Korean War.

On June 25, 1950, communist-backed troops from North Korea invaded a hopelessly overmatched South Korea. American-led U.N. forces quickly came to the aid of South Korea, but the war unexpectedly escalated five months later when China, in support of North Korea, launched a massive attack on U.N. forces near the Yalu River.

Three years of brutal fighting followed as both armies hurled each other up and down the Korean peninsula. Over 54,000 U.S. soldiers died during the war, which technically has never officially ended but has been in a prolonged cease-fire since 1953.

North Korea often states that they are still at war, but the reality is that tenacious fighting by U.S. and U.N. soldiers successfully repelled the invading communist forces and pushed them back across the 38th parallel border. South Korea remains a free nation, one of the most prosperous in Asia, while North Korea is one of the most repressive.

The North often provokes South Korea, and recently torpedoed one of their naval vessels, killing 46 sailors. North Korea routinely faces economic and starvation crises, and there are frequent reports of human rights abuses — torture, slave labor, and public executions. It is frightening to think of what would have become of South Korea if the United States had not intervened in 1950.

During a modest ceremony that day at the memorial, South Korean Ambassador Tae-Sik Lee spoke of the admiration that his country has for the American soldiers who fought to preserve their freedom:

"In the brutal heat of summer, and the bitter grip of winter, over every kind of tough terrain — it was through countless acts of courage, sacrifice, and faith — that South Korea's freedom was preserved. To the veterans here today, you are our heroes and we remember you. And we hope that you believe that Korea was a country worth saving — a people worth protecting — and a war worth fighting."

As I walked along the memorial's path, I thought about our country's history. We haven't always done things right, but we've tried to do the right thing. We've stumbled at times in our history, but there have also been countless moments when we've exhibited great courage and compassion as well. The Korean War was one of those moments.

A handwritten note attached to one of the floral bouquets simply read "Thank you." A tear ran down my cheek as I thought about my Dad and all of the brave Korean War veterans, especially those who gave their lives.

In the striking irony of that moment, the warm sun shone upon the Korean man's little boy as he skipped within the shadows of the statues dressed in their winter ponchos and prepared to battle not only the bitter cold of Korea, but a bitter enemy as well. His laughter hung in the warm summer air, and as I looked at him I could think of only one thing: Harry Truman was right. Korea was a place where we had to take a stand, and the right thing to do was to put up a fight.

AFTERWORD

This essay was a direct message to my Dad. I would often ask him if he realized that the incredible success and economic growth of South Korea since the 1953 Armistice would not have been possible if he and his fellow soldiers had not come to their aid. He would always respond with a very lackluster, "I guess so", which bothered me. I had the feeling that, because of the death and destruction that he had witnessed during the war, he was conflicted as to whether or not it was worth it in the end. When I saw the little boy that day at the memorial, I realized that there was another way that I could help my Dad understand that what he and his fellow veterans did was not only noble, but worth the fight that they put up. Did this essay change my Dad's feelings? I don't know, but on the day that it was published, my Dad called me and said, "That was a great article." He had never done that before.

NO BETTER PLACE TO DIE: LOST AMONG THE MANY LEGENDS OF D-DAY – THE BATTLE FOR THE BRIDGE AT LA FIERE

(Edited version published in the November 11, 2011 *Philadelphia Inquirer*. This version was updated in 2018)

The small bridge spanning the Merderet River at La Fiere in France

The little bridge sits in a quiet, bucolic area of Southern France, about 2 miles west of the town of Ste. Mere-Eglise. It spans the scenic Merderet River, and thousands of tourists flock to the area every year because of its rich history and beautiful scenery. Right next to the bridge is the charming *a la Bataille de La Fiere Bed and Breakfast,* which was built in 1180 and originally used as a grain mill by Viking settlers. For those looking for a quiet vacation in a beautiful, historic setting, this area is the perfect destination. But when the tourists are told the story of what happened on this little bridge nearly 70 years ago, and how significant that event was in WW II history, many are stunned. Those from the U.S. will often beam with pride or are moved to tears.

Although it is described by renowned military historian S.L.A. Marshall as "the bloodiest small unit struggle in the history of American arms", the heroic saga of the battle for the bridge at La Fiere from June 6 to June 9 in 1944 has now become lost among the numerous legendary stories of D-Day. But it was at this bridge that a small group of lightly armed U.S. 82nd Airborne paratroopers fought in one of the most epic battles in U.S. military history, and in doing so, likely saved the lives of thousands of U.S. soldiers who landed at Utah beach on D-Day. The bridge was one of only two in the Utah beach landing area that would enable German armor to cross the river. If the Germans could get their tanks and infantry to the beach, they could wipe out the U.S. forces on Utah beach. The 82nd was given the difficult task of seizing and holding the bridge.

Led by Lieutenant John Dolan, the paratroopers assaulted and eventually took control of the bridge in the late morning hours of D-Day. They set mines and pulled a disabled truck onto the bridge to help block the inevitable German counterattacks. The fields surrounding the causeway (raised road) that led to the bridge had been flooded by the Germans prior to the invasion, and the men could see the parachutes and backpacks of dozens of drowned paratroopers floating in the water. The sight likely served as a reminder to them of what was at stake, stiffening their resolve.

The Germans still controlled the high ground of the western causeway leading to the bridge, and late in the afternoon of June 6, they sent three tanks, followed by infantry, rumbling across in their first attempt to seize it. Private Lenold Peterson stood with his bazooka, bravely exposing himself to the enemy machine gun fire. He took out the two lead tanks, and forced the third to retreat back with the German infantry.

The following morning, the Germans launched an even heavier assault against the paratroopers. The brutal, close-quarters combat that followed reduced Dolan's force to only 14 men, but the paratroopers held. The fighting was so bloody, that the Germans asked for a truce so that they could retrieve their wounded. When Dolan's men asked if they should fall back, he told them that they were staying. "I don't know a better place to die", he said, and his words lifted the morale of the decimated platoon.

On June 8, Dolan's men were finally reinforced by the 507th Paratroop Infantry Regiment. U.S. tanks from the 4th Infantry Division had also arrived but couldn't cross the bridge until the Germans had been cleared from the western end. The paratroopers attacked across the bridge and down the causeway in a suicidal frontal assault. The first wave of men was cut down, and those following behind dropped to the ground, paralyzed with fear. Lieutenant Bruce Hooker, shot in both legs, turned to his men as he lay on the ground and tried to urge them on. "Come on…get up!", he shouted. As the dead and wounded piled up, the chaos on the bridge mounted.

Just when the battle seemed lost, a group of some 90 men led by Captain R.D. Rae charged across the bridge. Again, many were cut down, but this time, many more kept moving forward. They ran down the causeway and started taking out the enemy positions. The tank commanders then seized the opportunity and streamed across the bridge, destroying the remaining German opposition. The Americans had finally secured the bridge, but at a terrible cost: 60 paratroopers were dead and 529 wounded.

Tom Hanks announced in February, 2018 that he has signed on to act in, and serve as Executive Producer for, the highly anticipated war drama, *No Better Place to Die*. Written and directed by actor and former Marine, Dale Dye, the film will finally reveal to the general public the gallant story of the U.S. paratroopers at the La Fiere Bridge.

Take a moment this Veterans Day to remember the American paratroopers who courageously decided during a pivotal battle in WW II that there was no better place to die than the bridge at La Fiere.

AFTERWORD

Shortly after this essay was published in 2011, I was surprised to receive an e-mail from Vivian and Rodolphe Roger who own the *La Fiere Bed and Breakfast in Normandy, France. Their website states that their B&B faces the La Fiere Bridge and is a "converted WW II barn where the battle of Normandy began on June 6, 1944!" They wrote that my article "was a tribute to the men who fought the battle that took place here 67 years ago. I think we all look forward to the film in process* No Better Place to Die*...thanks to Chris Gibbons for writing and publishing this article. Our guests read this article at breakfast here this morning. I think that you will be hearing from them." They were right. I did hear from them, as well as from actor/director Dale Dye, who thanked me for writing it. Following the announcement in 2018 of Tom Hanks joining as an Executive Producer for the film, I sent Dale an updated version of this essay and he posted it on his* No Better Place to Die *Facebook page.*

A SOLDIER CONSIDERS HIS FORTUNE

(Edited versions published in the December 7, 2011 *Philadelphia Inquirer* and *America in World War II* magazine)

Dave Coonahan (Photo courtesy of the Coonahan family)

It was Sunday, December 7, 1941, just a few minutes before 8am, and a large formation of planes was traveling west in the clear, blue Hawaiian sky, towards the U.S. Naval Base at Pearl Harbor. Initially, Army Tech Sergeant Dave Coonahan of Philadelphia didn't think there was anything unusual about the planes. He was riding in a truck with some fellow soldiers headed for Sunday Mass, and planes were always taking off or landing at Kaneohe Naval Air Station, so Dave assumed it was just normal flight traffic. But as the drone of the planes grew louder, Dave thought the situation was somewhat odd. He looked up and was puzzled not only by the large numbers of planes, but their strange shapes as well. Suddenly, a voice came over the truck radio: "This is not a drill…this is not a drill!" Then one of the men shouted, "They're Japanese Zeros!"

The droning engines of the Zeros changed to a terrifying whine as they quickly dove down into attack formation. The truck stopped and the men scrambled out, but they were totally unprepared for what was happening. "We had our guns and rifles", Dave said, "But no ammunition." Although the men were a relatively safe distance away from Kaneohe when the attack started, they could see and hear the devastation that the Zeros were inflicting on the air station.

"An older sergeant finally retrieved some ammunition, but by the time he brought it back, the Japanese had already destroyed over 32 planes at Kaneohe," Dave recalled. "Some of our planes got off the ground and got a few of the Zero's, but they gave it to us pretty good that day."

After neutralizing Kaneohe, the Japanese then focused their assault on their main objective – destroying the U.S. naval fleet at Pearl Harbor. When the infamous sneak attack was over, the U.S. fleet was in ruins with over 2,400 Americans killed and nearly 1,300 wounded. 20 Americans were killed at Kaneohe - 2 civilians and 18 sailors.

That night, Dave's battalion was ordered back to the beach at Kaneohe to defend against a Japanese amphibious assault. Although the attack never came, the battalion remained on the island for months. "If they decided to attack after our preparations, we were ready," Dave said.

Dave grew up in North Philadelphia and graduated from Northeast Catholic High School before he was drafted into the Army. Prior to the attack on Pearl Harbor, Dave's 34th Combat Engineer Battalion helped with the construction of the Army fortifications on Oahu, and built the soldier's barracks near Kaneohe. The men were initially quite pleased with their assignment in Hawaiian "paradise", as they called it, and Dave thought the "luck of the Irish must be with me." But his luck wouldn't last as the dark clouds of war soon dimmed the army life he once knew.

Incredibly, Pearl Harbor wasn't the worst of what Dave would experience. He fought throughout the Pacific for 47 months without receiving one furlough. His unit participated in the invasion of Saipan in June 1944, and he was part of the initial invasion of Okinawa in 1945. During my interview with him, Dave choked-up a few times as the bitter memories of Okinawa came flooding back. "It was awful there," Dave said. "My worst memories of the war were at Okinawa." When the Japanese finally surrendered in 1945, Dave's unit was preparing to invade the Japanese islands of Kyushu and Honshu. "Thank God that never happened. It would have been a nightmare," he told me.

When Dave finally returned to Philadelphia, the city buses were running hopelessly late, and he had to pick up his heavy barracks bag and walk home. I asked Dave if he thought the "luck of the Irish" had deserted him again that day, but he laughed and said, "Oh no, it was with me. I was home."

Dave and his late wife, Mary, raised 4 children, and he worked for the Prudential Insurance Company for 33 years. He's now 92 years old, and still resides in the same Oreland, Pa house where he raised his children.

On that fateful morning in December 1941, Dave never did make it to church. But when I asked him if he had anything special planned to mark the 70th anniversary of the attack, I wasn't surprised by his response: "I'll just go to church and pray for those who died that day."

AFTERWORD

Dave Coonhan's daughter, Kate, set up my interview with him at her home, and, like so many of the war veterans that I've interviewed over the years, Dave was humble, unassuming, and proud of his wartime service. I was unaware until the interview that Dave also fought in the Battle of Okinawa following the attack on Pearl Harbor. He kept his emotions in check when he spoke of Pearl Harbor, but the memories of Okinawa must have been his most haunting as Dave became visibly emotional when discussing them. The fact that he spent 47 straight days on the battle-lines is almost unimaginable. Dave was also a member of Sandy Run Country Club in Flourtown, Pa. for 69 years, and I was informed by a fellow member that shortly after my essay was published, it was framed and hung on a wall for all the members to see, as most knew nothing of Dave's service during WW II. He died in January, 2016, and I sincerely hope that Dave's story still hangs on that wall at Sandy Run.

A SALUTE TO RIDGWAY'S LEADERSHIP

(Edited version published in the August 11, 2013 *Philadelphia Inquirer*)

Lt. General Matthew B. Ridgway talks to Major James H. Lee in Korea,
March, 1951 - (Associated Press)

In March 1951, my father and his small platoon of American soldiers marched along the muddy street of the South Korean capital in a two-column formation that lined both sides of the road. After weeks of bitter fighting, the Americans had finally recaptured Seoul, and although the platoon was dog-tired, there was a renewed confidence in the soldiers' stride.

Just a few months before, in the closing weeks of 1950, Dad's unit, the Second Combat Engineer Group, had been badly mauled and forced to retreat during the Chinese army's surprise assault across the Yalu River. But the U.S. soldiers were now thriving under a new leader whose bold initiatives and concern for their well-being not only boosted their morale but likely saved many of their lives. This commanding general let his troops know that while they may have been forgotten by the American public back home, he still cared about them and had confidence in them.

"Brass coming!" a soldier suddenly shouted from the back of the lines. The platoon turned toward the sound of a jeep's groaning engine as the vehicle slowly moved between their lines. One of the officers in the jeep stood up. At first, the men didn't recognize him, but then they noticed the small stars on his cap and the trademark grenade hanging from his chest. Their initial confusion was understandable, for although Matthew Ridgway was their commanding general, he was wearing the same common soldier's uniform that they wore.

———

When Matthew Bunker Ridgway assumed command of the Eighth Army after the accidental death of Gen. Walton Walker in December 1950, the U.S. military in Korea was reeling from one of the worst crises in its history. Douglas MacArthur, the U.N. forces commander whom Ridgway would eventually replace, had downplayed U.S. intelligence reports that Chinese troops were massing along the Korean border in October 1950.

When Chinese soldiers finally stormed across the Yalu in November, the U.S. military was in disarray. The Eighth Army's retreat was the longest in U.S. Army history, and 15,000 Marines from the First Marine Division, as well as more than 3,000 soldiers from the Seventh Infantry Division, were surrounded at the frozen Chosin Reservoir. Korea's subzero temperatures and blizzard-like conditions added to the soldiers' misery, and the memories of that cruel winter still haunt my father and the other Korean War veterans. The steadily mounting U.S. casualties were in the thousands, and on Dec. 15, President Harry S. Truman declared a national emergency.

CHRIS GIBBONS

The situation was so grave that Truman told a stunned press corps that he was prepared to use atomic weapons if necessary.

Under Ridgway's leadership, the tide began to turn. His initial message to the demoralized troops not only revealed his character but also won their admiration: We are in this together. We will no longer retreat. We will begin to fight back.

Ridgway analyzed the strengths and weaknesses of the Chinese and North Korean armies and devised strategies that capitalized on superior U.S. artillery and airpower, strengthened his defensive positions, and employed high concentrations of flares to illuminate the battlefield at night. He would not tolerate officers who distanced themselves from the front lines, and he had a deep concern for the common foot soldier. Ridgway once said, "All lives on a battlefield are equal, and a dead rifleman is as great a loss in the eyes of God as a dead general."

His carefully planned and executed offensives in the winter/spring of 1951, code-named Operations Killer and Ripper, drove the communist armies back across the 38th Parallel and enabled U.N. forces to recapture Seoul for the final time. Ridgway then formed impregnable defensive lines that inflicted heavy casualties on the enemy during its massive counterassaults. His "give no more ground" mandate helped force a negotiated end to the war, culminating with the armistice of July 27, 1953.

After the war, Ridgway was praised by his superiors. Gen. Omar Bradley, the first Joint Chiefs chairman, said Ridgway's accomplishment during the Korean War was "the greatest feat of personal leadership in the history of the Army." And when Ridgway died July 26, 1993, at the age of 98, Joint Chiefs Chairman Colin Powell spoke at his graveside: "No soldier ever performed his duty better than this man. . . . Every American soldier owes a debt to this great man."

Perhaps the most enduring tribute to Ridgway and the Korean War veterans was given by British military historian Max Hastings in his seminal book, *The Korean War*: "The men who turned the tide on the battlefield in Korea in the first weeks of 1951 may have also saved the world from the nightmare of a new Hiroshima in Asia."

My father vividly remembers that day in March 1951 when Ridgway stood in his jeep as it slowly moved between the two columns of soldiers in his platoon. When I asked what happened as the jeep passed by, the emotions induced by the memory made it difficult for Dad to speak. He simply responded with a "salute" gesture.

"That must've been a proud moment when you saluted Ridgway," I said. But my father quickly corrected me, and with what I'd learned of Matthew Ridgway, I wasn't surprised. "No, it was the other way around," Dad said, as his eyes filled and his raspy voice quivered. "It was Ridgway who saluted all of us that day."

Pvt. John "Jack" Gibbons - Korea, 1951

AFTERWORD

In May of 1985 I was watching a news broadcast with my Dad of a wreath laying ceremony at the Bitburg Military Cemetery in Germany to commemorate the 40 year anniversary of the end of World War II in Europe. U. S. President Ronald Reagan attended, as well as West German Chancellor Helmut Kohl. The TV broadcast showed Reagan walking with a short, balding old man during the brief ceremony. "There's old Ridgway", my Dad said. I remember thinking to myself, "So that's General Ridgway...the guy from my Dad's story." My Dad had been telling me the story recounted in this essay for quite a few years, and I never understood who Ridgway really was, or why it meant so much to my Dad until many years later. My later research into the career of General Matthew Ridgway not only revealed a leader who achieved "the greatest feat of personal leadership in the history of the Army", but also revealed a man who cared deeply for the soldiers under his command – "my boys" as he affectionately called them. Ridgway's quote that "all lives on a battlefield are equal, and a dead rifleman is as great a loss in the eyes of God as a dead general", not only exemplifies his true character, but why my Dad respected him so much. Following this essay's publication, I received an e-mail from an Inquirer reader who helped Ridgway with his finances over 30 years ago. He wrote: "I found (Ridgway) to be just as you described. When we first started to chat on the phone, I was naively unaware of him and his background. It wasn't until my boss, a veteran, pointed me in the right direction. General Ridgway was very easy to talk with – and, I found him to be very humble – I guess maybe the opposite of his friend, Douglas MacArthur. He shared lots of stories, such as running a department at West Point, going to the Tunney/ Dempsey fight with MacArthur, running the Presidio, and being one of the first to officially cross the Golden Gate Bridge. Thanks for sharing your Dad's story."

GOODWILL IN WARTIME

(Edited version published in the December 25, 2013
Philadelphia Inquirer)

"A Higher Call" painting by John D. Shaw. Courtesy ValorStudios.com

It was December 20, 1943, just five days before Christmas, and the 21 year-old pilot of American B-17F bomber *Ye Olde Pub*, First Lieutenant Charles "Charlie" Brown, was desperately trying to keep his heavily damaged plane aloft in the skies over Germany.

As recently chronicled in the 2012 award winning book, *A Higher Call* by Adam Makos (with Larry Alexander), the *Pub* had just completed its bombing run of a Focke-Wulf airplane manufacturing plant in the German city of Bremen, but it was attacked by a swarm of Messerschmitt fighter planes, as well as ground based anti-aircraft guns. The crew fought back as best they could, and even shot down one of the German fighters, but they clearly absorbed the worst of the fight. The bomber's nose, wings, and fuselage were riddled with gaping holes, and it was leaking oil and hydraulic fluid. Half of its rudder was missing, and one of its engines was out. When Brown asked for a damage report, one of the crew replied, "We're chewed to pieces."

Nearly half the members of the *Pub's* crew were wounded, their blood splattered throughout the interior of the bomber. The ball turret gunner, Hugh "Ecky" Eckenrode, was dead, his body slumped over the machine gun. His dripping blood formed icicles in the freezing air that now rushed in through the shattered turret's Plexiglas.

At one point, Brown told his crew that he was going to try to fly the damaged bomber back to England, but he gave them the option to bail out while they were still flying over land. They all decided to stay with their commander. Brown knew that their chances of making it back were slim, but he still had hope.

As the bomber limped towards the North Sea, a dark shape just off the right wing of the B-17 caught Brown's attention. He looked through the cockpit window and was terrified by what he saw. It was a German Messerschmitt Bf-109 fighter plane, piloted by Luftwaffe ace Franz Stigler. The fighter plane was so close that Brown could clearly see Stigler's face. The co-pilot of the B-17, Spencer "Pinky" Luke, said, "My God, this is a nightmare." Brown responded, "He's going to destroy us."

When Stigler initially encountered the B-17, he was prepared to fire. He was not only just one more air victory from qualifying for the prestigious Knight's Cross, but Stigler also sought vengeance for his older brother August, who had been killed earlier in the war.

But as he closed on the stricken bomber and surveyed the damage, he couldn't believe that it was still flying. Stigler could clearly see the dead tail gunner and his blood stained jacket. The holes in the fuselage were so large that he could even see the *Pub's* crew caring for the wounded.

Stigler, a Catholic who once studied to be a priest, placed his hand on his jacket pocket and felt the rosary beads that were inside. His thoughts turned to his brother, and he also remembered the words of his former commander, legendary German Luftwaffe fighter ace Gustav Rodel, who once told him: "You follow the rules of war for you — not your enemy. You fight by rules to keep your humanity." Stigler decided that he could not shoot and "would not have this on my conscience for the rest of my life."

Stigler pulled up alongside the bomber and tried to get Brown's attention. He was waving his hands and mouthing the word "Sweden" in an attempt to get the American pilot to land his severely damaged aircraft there, as Sweden was a neutral country and only 30 minutes away. But Brown and Luke couldn't understand what Stigler was doing. They still thought that he was going to attack, and were determined to go down fighting. Brown ordered one his gunners to prepare to fire.

Finally realizing that the Americans would never understand, Stigler saluted Brown and said "Good luck, you're in God's hands." Brown was puzzled, and the image of Stigler saluting him before he peeled away stayed with him for the rest of his life.

Fortunately, the crew of *Ye Olde Pub* made it back to England that day and survived the remainder of the war. Brown eventually married, raised two daughters, and worked for the State Department for many years before retiring to Florida. But that day in 1943 always haunted him. In the 1980's, Brown started to have nightmares about the incident, and decided to try and find the German pilot. He diligently searched military records, attended pilot reunions, and placed an ad in a newsletter for former German WW II pilots with the story of what happened.

Stigler, who moved to Canada in 1953, saw the ad and sent Brown a letter in 1990, letting him know that he was the German pilot who spared his crew. As Brown read the letter, tears streamed down his cheeks. When the two finally met in a Florida hotel lobby, they embraced and wept.

Franz and Charlie became great friends, went on fishing trips together, attended military reunions together, and spoke at schools and other events. Charlie even organized a reunion of the crew of *Ye Olde Pub* that was featured in a *CBS This Morning* segment in which a video was played for Franz showing pictures of the children and grandchildren of the crew. The message to Franz was obvious, and he broke down in tears. "The war cost him everything," Makos said. "Charlie Brown was the only good thing that came out of World War II for Franz. It was the one thing he could be proud of."

Franz Sigler died in March 2008, and Charlie died just 8 months later. Franz once gave Charlie a book with a note he had written on the inside cover, and his words not only reveal his love for Charlie, but also serve as a reminder to all of us of the true meaning of Christmas:

> *In 1940, I lost my only brother as a night fighter. On the 20th of December, 4 days before Christmas, I had the chance to save a B-17 from her destruction, a plane so badly damaged it was a wonder that she was still flying. The pilot, Charlie Brown, is for me, as precious as my brother was. Thanks Charlie.*
>
> *Your Brother,*
> *Franz*

AFTERWORD

A friend of mine, Pat Mundy, gave me the book, A Higher Call, and said "You must read this book. It's an amazing story and right up your alley." Pat was right. It truly is a fantastic book that chronicles one of the most incredible stories I've ever come across. An e-mail I received from an Inquirer reader eloquently captured my feelings about the bond shared by Charlie and Franz, as well as my hopes for all of humanity: "Your essay reminds us of our immense capability for love and compassion, but also of our immense capability for savagery, a duality recognized by Abraham Lincoln in his first inaugural address: 'We are not enemies, but friends. We must not be enemies. Though passion may have strained, it must not break our bonds of affection. The mystic chords of memory will swell when again touched, as surely they will be, by the better angels of our nature.' Here's hoping the 'better angels of our nature' prevail for all in the coming year. Merry Christmas."

In April, 2020, I sent an e-mail to Adam Makos, the author of
A Higher Call, asking if he could provide a photo to accompany
my story for this book. His brother, Bryan, replied and granted
me permission to use an image of the painting of the incident
by John D. Shaw.

THE HIDDEN TRUTHS WITHIN A PICTURE

(Edited versions published in the November 23, 2014 *Philadelphia Inquirer,* the December 1, 2014 *Desert Sun,* the December 1, 2014 *Savannah Morning News,* the December 1, 2014 *Knoxville New Sentinel,* the December 1, 2014 *Stars and Stripes,* and the December 7, 2014 *Arkansas Democrat Gazette)*

AP Photo/Eddie Adams

My father's booming voice filled the living room. "That wasn't right," he yelled at the TV. "You can't do that to people!"

It was the early 1980's, and Dad and I were watching a news program that showed an infamous incident from the Vietnam War.

The video is chilling. A Viet Cong prisoner stands along a roadside, his hands tied behind his back. A South Vietnamese officer positions himself next to the prisoner, raises his pistol, and fires a point-blank shot to the man's head. His lifeless body crumples to the ground.

Dad cursed again. "That wasn't right," he shouted. I was somewhat stunned by his angry reaction. If I hadn't known better, I would have thought that he knew the man who was shot. I looked at Dad's hands, and noticed that they were slightly trembling.

———

2014 marks the 45th anniversary of the awarding of a Pulitzer Prize for a photo taken of one of the most infamous incidents of the Vietnam War as South Vietnamese general Nguyen Ngoc Loan executed Viet Cong officer Nguyen Van Lem. AP photographer Eddie Adams and an NBC cameraman filmed the execution, and Adams' still picture of the incident soon appeared on the front pages of newspapers and evening news telecasts across the U.S. The picture outraged the American public, and it seemed to galvanize the growing anti-war sentiment. The picture soon became a symbol of the apparent brutality of the U.S. supported South Vietnamese regime. In 1969, Adams' photo won the Pulitzer Prize for Spot News Photography.

But the picture didn't tell the whole story, and Adams later came to regret the damage that it did to Loan. The Viet Cong prisoner who he shot was reportedly part of a "death-squad" that targeted the families of South Vietnamese policemen. According to witnesses, the prisoner was captured near a ditch where 34 bound and shot bodies of policemen and their families were found. Adams later said, "I killed the general with my camera. Still photographs are the most powerful weapon in the world. People believe them, but photographs do lie, even without manipulation. They are only half-truths. What the photograph didn't say was, "What would you do if you were the general at that time?" Adams later apologized to Loan and his family.

General Loan eventually escaped Vietnam, and opened a pizza restaurant in a Virginia suburb. Unfortunately, he couldn't escape his past. Word got out to an angry public of who he was. Someone once wrote an ominous message on the restaurant's walls, "We Know Who You Are F***er." Loan eventually had to close the restaurant because of the negative publicity. He died of cancer in 1998, leaving a wife and five children. Adams sent a note to the family that read: "I'm sorry. There are tears in my eyes."

As for my Dad's reaction that day, I assumed that, like so many Americans at that time, the execution in Saigon was the final straw. The Vietnam War had once sharply divided the nation, but by the late 1960's even its staunchest supporters had seen enough. I concluded that my Dad finally realized this as well, and seeing the video again that day must've brought back those bitter feelings of anger and betrayal. I quickly forgot about the incident, and never asked my father about it.

It wasn't until many years later that I finally came to understand the hidden truths behind the picture, not only the story of general Loan, but my Dad's story as well. We had a quiet moment alone in 2008 on the 55th anniversary of the end of the Korean War, and I asked him if he could tell me of his worst experience during the war. He said it would be too difficult for him to tell me the worst, but there was one incident that still haunted him. Shortly after his company had set up a defensive perimeter around their base in South Korea, two frightened and dirty Chinese prisoners were brought before a company sergeant. This sergeant was a WW II veteran who my father and the other young soldiers in his company admired and looked up to. "We were very young, and often scared," my Dad told me. "But he helped us get through some of the toughest times during the war."

The sergeant needed to understand how these two Chinese soldiers had gotten through so he could fix the weakness in their perimeter. If they escaped and revealed the weakness to the enemy, the lives of his men could be at risk. "Ask them how they got through!", he barked to the interpreter. The prisoners replied that they didn't "get through", but were separated from their outfit, and simply hid in covered fox-holes when the Americans moved into the area. The American soldiers unknowingly piled the dirt and barbed wire right on top of them, and the prisoners simply climbed out later and surrendered. "I don't believe them. Ask them again!" shouted the sergeant, as he raised his rifle and pointed it at the head of one of the prisoners. My father believed the prisoners and was shaken by the horrible scenario that was now being played out in front of him and his fellow soldiers. Again, the frightened prisoners told the same story.

The sharp sounds of gunshots echoed across the Korean sky, as two lifeless bodies crumpled to the ground.

"It wasn't right", my Dad said softly as he remembered the incident and vacantly stared ahead. I looked down and noticed that his hands were slightly trembling.

———

I originally wrote this story in 2008. I sent a copy to my Dad prior to publication to ensure that my facts were correct. After reading it, he immediately called me and told me that he didn't want it published because one of the soldiers who witnessed the incident with him was severely traumatized by it. "He was never the same again, he had a lot of issues from it," my Dad said. He told me that even after they returned home, his friend continued to struggle and the remainder of his life was difficult. My Dad was concerned that seeing the story in the newspaper might adversely affect his friend's already fragile psyche.

My Dad passed away earlier this year, and a few months before he died I asked him if I could ever publish the story. He didn't mention his friend this time, possibly because the man had passed away. My Dad simply responded, "When I'm long gone." It was then that I knew that the picture and its hidden truths would now haunt me as well, as I realized that there were actually two young soldiers who witnessed the execution that day who were never the same again.

AFTERWORD

Former National Security Advisor and retired lieutenant general, H.R. McMaster, grew up in the same Philadelphia neighborhood (Roxborough) that I did. My brother, Pat, married his cousin Maureen. McMaster was all too familiar with the complexities of war and combat as he was awarded the Silver Star for his actions during the Gulf War at the Battle of 73 Easting. He read this essay after publication and wrote in an e-mail to Pat: "Just read it. It is great. And I appreciate it even more that it was your Dad…knowing that you behaved humanely in war is one of the keys to preventing PTSD."

A Knoxville News Sentinel *reader also sent me an e-mail: "I chanced across your very thoughtful and heartfelt article that included an anecdote regarding your father's Korean War experience. Like your father, I am a combat vet (Vietnam). I, too, saw terrible things I didn't understand. Later, as a more experienced soldier, I realized there was a "good" practical reason for what was done. You shouldn't be too judgmental regarding that nameless WW2 sergeant mentioned in your piece. As repugnant as it may have seemed at the time to your father, that sergeant's actions may be the reason your father survived to sire you."*

THE SOULS OF DACHAU

(Edited version published in the April 26, 2015 *Philadelphia Inquirer*. This version updated for the 2020 75th anniversary)

Ernie Gross (left) and Don Greenbaum in 2014 (Photo courtesy of the Holocaust Awareness Museum and Education Center in Phila.)

"All the Dachaus must remain standing. The Dachaus, the Belsens, the Buchenwalds, the Auschwitzes - all of them. They must remain standing because they are a monument to a moment in time when some men decided to turn the Earth into a graveyard. Into it they shoveled all of their reason, their logic, their knowledge, but worse

of all, their conscience. And the moment we forget this, the moment we cease to be haunted by its remembrance, then we become the gravediggers." (Rod Serling's ending narration for Twilight Zone *episode* Deaths Head Revisited*)*

On the day the Americans came, it was a Sunday, and unseasonably cold for late April. So cold, in fact, that just a few days later a light snow would fall. Current Philadelphia resident, Ernie Gross, was only 15 years old and had just been imprisoned at Dachau that morning. Weak and resigned to his fate, Gross told me that he was simply "standing in line outside of the crematory waiting to die."

As detailed in *Dachau Liberated: The Official Report of the U.S. 7th Army,* a few of the inmates from the east side of the compound suddenly noticed a lone American soldier at the edge of a field outside the camp, and he was running towards the gate. Then, more U.S. 42nd Division soldiers appeared behind him. Unaware of what was happening outside the gate, Gross was puzzled when "all of a sudden, the Nazi guard next to us threw down his weapon and started to run."

Excited shouts in disbelieving tones echoed within the walls of the compound in multiple languages: "Americans! Americans!" A prisoner rushed toward the gate, but was shot by the Nazi tower-guard. Undeterred, more prisoners ran towards the gate. The American soldiers opened fire on the guard tower, and the SS guards surrendered. One of the guards still held a pistol behind his back, and was shot by an American soldier.

"The Americans were not simply advancing; they were running, flying, breaking all the rules of military conduct", wrote Dachau prisoner and Turkish journalist Nerin E. Gun. The 7th Army soldiers, primarily from the 45th "Thunderbird" Division and 42nd "Rainbow" Division, had been told by newspaper reporters about the camp, and rushed to liberate it. But nothing could have prepared them for what they would find at Dachau.

Philadelphian Don Greenbaum of the 283rd Field Artillery Battalion attached to the 45th Division remembers that as his unit approached the camp they were stunned to find numerous abandoned train rail-cars which contained thousands of decaying corpses. He told me that as the soldiers entered the compound, they were "sickened by the sight of thousands of emaciated prisoners who looked like walking skeletons." As chronicled in *The Liberator* by Alex Kershaw, soldiers from the 45th Division moved through the camp and found metal poles where naked prisoners had been tied while guard dogs tore into them, a building where prisoners were subjected to sadistic medical experiments, and stacks of decomposing bodies left to rot because the SS had run out of coal for the crematory.

Lt. Col. Felix Sparks of the 45th wrote in a personal account that "a number of Company I men, all battle hardened veterans, became extremely distraught. Some cried, while others raged." Kershaw's book described SS guards and prison "informers" being torn apart by the vengeful prisoners with their bare hands. Enraged U.S. troops started to execute the Nazi guards until Sparks forcefully stopped them. Private John Lee of the 45th said, "I don't think there was a guy who didn't cry openly that night."

Those interred at Dachau between 1933 and 1945 were considered "enemies of the Reich" for one reason or another. Ernie Gross said that he was there simply because he was a Jew. Prisoners were from over 20 different countries and numerous religious denominations: Catholics, Jews, Protestants, Greek Orthodox, and Muslims among others. Thousands died there, but the exact number will probably never be known. General Dwight Eisenhower was concerned that someday there would be those who doubted what happened at the concentration camps. He ordered detailed films and photos taken of the camps and requested that representatives from the major newspapers visit the camps so that there would be "no room for cynical doubt." American soldiers ordered the German citizens from the towns surrounding the labor camps to view the bodies. After visiting the Ohrdruf labor camp, the town's mayor and his wife returned home and then killed themselves.

Unfortunately, as we mark the 75th anniversary of the liberation of many of the death camps, Eisenhower's fears have come to fruition. Despite the film records, soldiers' accounts, survivors' recollections, testimony of former SS guards, and physical evidence gathered, there are millions around the world who believe the Holocaust never happened, or has been greatly exaggerated. In 2005, former Iranian President Mahmoud

Ahmadinejad said that it was a fabricated legend, and the Palestinian terror group, Hamas, has referred to it as "an invented story." Here in the U.S., a 2010 Harvard study found that 31 Facebook groups had "Holocaust Denial" as their central purpose. Recent polls in 2018 and 2019 reveal that 10% of Britons, and 4% of Americans believe the Holocaust never happened. "I cannot understand them," Gross said of the deniers, and Greenbaum added: "I was there. I saw it for myself."

Amazingly, after all that he's been through, Ernie Gross still has faith in humanity. He and Greenbaum will often speak together at various organizations as arranged by the Philadelphia Holocaust Awareness Museum and Education Center, and in 2015, they traveled together to Germany for the 70th anniversary liberation ceremonies at Dachau. Gross hoped that his presence there might "change the way people think. Every time you hate somebody, it's not good. It's better to help somebody than hate."

If you ever happen to hear the doubters spewing their Holocaust-denial drivel, remember the stories of the Allied soldiers who witnessed it, the testimony of the survivors and the Nazi guards who experienced it, but more importantly, remember the dead who cannot speak. Then hand the deniers a shovel. And if you fail to challenge them, or if you ever begin to doubt the truth of the Holocaust, grab a shovel for yourself as well. Then, after you've buried your conscience, pray to whatever God you worship that you're never confronted by the souls of Dachau.

U.S. soldiers order German citizens to view the corpses at Ohrdruf
(U.S. Army photo)

AFTERWORD

Lt. Col. Felix Sparks was the subject of Alex Kershaw's riveting book The Liberator, *but prior to reading the book, I had already seen Sparks interviewed in a documentary about the liberation of the concentration camps. His extremely emotional interview in the documentary was not only compelling, but difficult to watch. It wasn't until I watched that documentary that I realized the psychological damage and permanent scars suffered by the soldiers who liberated these camps. This was further reinforced by a few of the e-mails I received from Inquirer readers in response to my essay. Among them was the following: "Thank you for remembering, and writing of this place. My Great Uncle... was with the forces that liberated that camp. For better or worse, I was given pictures of what he saw. He only spoke of this in his older years, lest we may have not known. We have shared his history with the Delaware County Veterans Museum, but I have the originals, and would be glad to share the heroism that took place during this event. My Uncle was a kind man at heart, but I know that he was forever scarred by his witness."*

THE FORGOTTEN HERO OF THE FORGOTTEN WAR

(Edited version published in the December, 2015 edition of
PhillyMan Magazine)

Roman Catholic High School's Edward Seeburger –
Class of 1940 (Photo courtesy of R.C.H.S.)

Although it was 20 years ago, Paul Sweeney still remembers that momentous evening well. On July 28, 1995, the Marine Barracks outdoor facility in Washington D.C. was filled to capacity as the attendees patiently waited for the awards ceremony to begin. Dignitaries in the audience included former Marine aviator, astronaut, and United States senator, John Glenn, Jr. A Marine announcer asked for everyone's attention. The guests quieted.

"Lieutenant Edward Seeburger, center walk", the announcer said. The Marine Corps band's drums beat a military cadence and bugles echoed across the barracks. All eyes then shifted to a gray-haired man in his early 70's, sharply dressed in a navy-blue suit, as he stood and proudly walked towards the center stage with a noticeable limp, the result of an old war injury. Tears filled the eyes of his family members as they watched Seeburger approach the stage where Marine Commandant Charles C. Krulak waited to present the graduate of Philadelphia's Roman Catholic High School with the prestigious Navy Cross – only one grade below the Congressional Medal of Honor. "It was quite a moment to see", Seeburger's son-in-law Paul Sweeney told me recently, but when you consider what Edward Seeburger did during the Korean War's Battle of the Chosin Reservoir, it is hard to believe that this award was overlooked and nearly forgotten.

On December 2, 1950, First Lieutenant Edward Seeburger, a veteran of WW II, was leading the remains of his Dog Company Unit as they desperately fought their way south to reach the U.S. held Korean town of Hagaru. Of the 220 Marines originally in his Company, only about 20 were still fit to fight as the rest were either dead or wounded. Out of seven officers, only Seeburger remained. The men were not only fighting the enemy soldiers, but the weather as well. The snow impeded their progress in temperatures that plummeted to minus 20.

Seeburger was near the lone tank at the front of the convoy when it was suddenly attacked by well positioned Chinese troops with small arms, automatic weapons, rockets, and mortars. "One minute there was no action, and then there was artillery and mortar fire," Seeburger said in a 1995 Philadelphia Inquirer article. "We couldn't move. Everybody stopped."

The Marines took cover, but the American tank gunners could not see where the enemy fire was coming from. The convoy was being decimated. Seeburger knew that he had to do something or he, and his men, would die on the frozen Korean hills. He climbed on top of the lead tank so that he could locate the enemy positions, exposing himself to the enemy fire. "Somebody had to give them some direction," he said in the article. "We were being hit from both sides and the front. I told them to open up with their weaponry to help our men out."

Seeburger's direction was working as the tank's guns began to neutralize the enemy positions. Suddenly a bullet tore into his right knee, knocking him to the ground. The soldiers advised him to go back with the other wounded, but Seeburger refused. The official Navy Cross citation reveals what happened next: "With well-entrenched machine guns defending a roadblock to the front, and with his ranks depleted by eight further casualties, and he himself painfully wounded and unable to walk, he staunchly refused evacuation, and directed his men in an enfilade movement which wiped out the obstruction and enabled the entire column to move forward. By his great personal valor and dauntless perseverance in the face of almost certain death, First Lieutenant Seeburger saved the lives of many Marines..."

For his actions, Seeburger was immediately recommended for the Navy Cross by his Major, James Lawrence. However, unknown to Lawrence, the paperwork was destroyed when a regimental building burned down. Lawrence long assumed Seeburger received the award but was stunned to learn over 40 years later that Seeburger never received it. Lawrence then spoke to Navy officials and his recommendation was approved.

Edward "Bud" Seeburger from the R.C.H.S. Class of 1940 proudly received the Navy Cross that night in 1995, and it also coincided with the formal dedication that day of the new Korean War Veterans Memorial in Washington D.C. How fitting it was that on the day that the "Forgotten War" was finally recognized, one of its forgotten heroes was finally honored as well. Sweeney told me that Seeburger never really talked about that night in Korea until he received the award. "It couldn't have been in a better setting," Seeburger said in a 1995 *Philadelphia Daily News* article. "It was quite an honor. My daughter and grandkids are able to see me get this award whereas, 45 years ago, they would not have been around for this...it's amazing to me."

Seeburger worked as a park police officer, and then later as an engraver for 32 years at Becks Engraving Co. After retiring, he and his wife moved to Ocean City, N.J., and he worked part-time for the Claridge Casino in Atlantic City. He died in 2007 at the age of 85.

Philadelphia's Roman Catholic High School, founded in 1890, is still thriving today. In one of the classrooms at the historic school are various plaques honoring alumni who distinguished themselves in battle, and one of those plaques bears the remarkable story of Edward Seeburger. They serve as a reminder to the students of the proud legacy of their school, which is the only Philadelphia Archdiocesan high school, and one of the few in the country, whose alumni have served in the Spanish-American War, WW I, WW II, Korea, Vietnam, the Persian Gulf, Iraq, and Afghanistan. Over 150 alumni have given their lives in these conflicts. On March 8th of 2015, several of these veteran alumni were honored during Roman's 125 Year Anniversary celebratory banquet where the school formally recognized Roman's "125 Persons of Distinction". The Seeburger family was there to accept the award on behalf of their father. Roman's Alumni Association felt that it was important to remember and recognize men like Edward Seeburger, whose actions and achievements are so remarkable that they reveal, not only to fellow alumni, but to the rest of our country as well, those quality characteristics that Roman has always strived to instill in its students.

Edward Seeburger receives the Navy Cross
(Photo courtesy of the Seeburger family)

AFTERWORD

One of the unexpected outcomes of my research into Roman Catholic High School's alumni who fought in World War I has been the discovery of other unrelated stories while sorting through the school's archives. In 2014 I came upon a 2001 booklet put together by noted Roman alumnus, Jim McSherry '40, and Roman's Cahill Club, that was dedicated to the Class of 2001 - the first graduating class of the new Millennium. The booklet provided interesting historical facts about Roman alumni with a "Did You Know" section that detailed the incredible story of Edward Seeburger. Upon reading it, I immediately nominated Seeburger for Roman's "125 Persons of Distinction" award that coincided with the school's 125 year anniversary in 2015. I was so happy that his family was there at the banquet in 2015 to accept the award on behalf of their father. They provided me with the picture of Seeburger wearing the Navy Cross on the night it was presented to him in 1995.

DURING THE KOREAN WAR,
A CHRISTMAS MIRACLE

(Edited version published in the December 22, 2015
Philadelphia Inquirer)

*Demolition charges destroy Hungnam port facilities and remaining U.N.
supplies at the conclusion of evacuation operations,
24 December 1950 (U.S. Navy photo)*

"The greatest rescue operation by a single ship in the history of mankind."
(U.S. Maritime Administration)

On Dec. 22, 1950, Capt. Leonard LaRue, of Philadelphia, peered through his binoculars from the deck of his merchant cargo vessel, SS Meredith Victory, as it approached the besieged North Korean port of Hungnam.

LaRue could see thousands of shivering refugees lining the harbor in a desperate attempt to escape the marauding Communist Chinese and North Korean soldiers who surrounded, and were quickly closing in on, the city.

"It was a scene of 'Dante's Inferno,'" LaRue would later recall. In the book, *Ship of Miracles*, by Bill Gilbert, LaRue remembered that "Korean refugees thronged the docks. With them was everything they could wheel, carry, or drag. Beside them, like frightened chicks, were their children." Rumors were swirling that the Communists were executing fleeing refugees for "collaborating" with the American soldiers.

U.S. Navy gunships fired at the enemy on the city's outskirts, shuddering the harbor with each salvo. Smoke billowed into the overcast skies as elements of the 3rd Infantry Division fought to save the now encircled Hungnam. Outnumbered but undaunted, the brave Americans were desperately trying to buy time for the evacuation of the frightened refugees.

Just a few days prior, LaRue, a Merchant Marine captain who had been employed by the Navy to carry supplies for U.S. servicemen during the initial months of the Korean War, met on board his ship with U.S. Army officers who revealed their plans for a "Dunkirk-like" rescue of the refugees. Staff officer J. Robert Lunney recounted the scene in *Ship of Miracles*. "We can't order you to take them," one of the colonels said, "but we ask if you would volunteer." Lunney remembers that LaRue didn't hesitate: "He neither turned to his left or right, nor conferred with anyone. He responded that he would take his ship in and take off as many refugees as he could."

Code named "Christmas Cargo" by the military, and now commonly referred to as the "Christmas Miracle," the incredible evacuation at Hungnam by military transports and merchant ships resulted in the rescue of nearly 200,000 troops and civilian refugees. But it's the forgotten story of the S.S. Meredith Victory that truly defines the miracle.

As chronicled in *Ship of Miracles*, the Meredith was designed to haul cargo and only had accommodations for 12 passengers and a 47-person crew. On the afternoon of Dec. 22, in gale force winds and swirling snow, the crew began to load the refugees into the cargo holds using makeshift booms and gangplanks.

First mate Dino Savastio recalled that "the temperature was well below freezing, but the holds were not heated or lighted. There were no sanitary facilities for them ... children carried children, mothers breast-fed their babies with another child strapped to their backs, old men carried children. ... I saw terror in their faces."

It took nearly 24 hours, but the crew somehow managed to fit 14,000 refugees within the ship's five cargo holds. The Meredith finally departed Hungnam on Dec. 23. After a harrowing two days in mine-infested waters patrolled by enemy submarines, the ship safely arrived at Koje Do Island on Christmas Day. Not only did all of the refugees survive, but five babies were born during the journey.

LaRue and his crew would receive citations from the U.S. and South Korean governments. In 1954, LaRue joined the Benedictine monastery at St. Paul's Abbey in Newton, N.J. He was known as "Brother Marinus," and lived there until his death in 2001. When asked about the Christmas Miracle many years later, LaRue said, "I was always somewhat religious, even in my youth in Philadelphia. ... I think often of that voyage ... and as I think, the clear, unmistakable message comes to me that on that Christmastide, in the bleak and bitter waters off the shores of Korea, God's own hand was at the helm of my ship."

On the 65th anniversary of that miracle, the United States again faces a refugee crisis wrought by war. The situations are very different, but the courageous actions our country has taken on behalf of refugees in the past has set a high bar. Like it or not, the world looks to the United States to lead in a crisis.

As I look back on what the brave men of the Meredith Victory accomplished in 1950, I sadly recognize just how much our country has changed. While many will read this story and marvel at how the lives of 14,000 refugees were miraculously saved, others will conclude that the real miracle was that LaRue and his crew volunteered to do it at all.

AFTERWORD

After reading Ship of Miracles *I was not only amazed at Leonard LaRue's courage, but his unassuming demeanor as well. An e-mail I received from an* Inquirer *reader confirmed LaRue's character. It stated: "I read your story today in the* Inquirer *today and it brought back a lot of great memories. I knew Brother Marinus in the 1960's when I was a seminarian at Saint Paul's. He ran the Abbey gift Shop there and I believe he ran it for the whole time he was a monk. We had a certain bond as both being Philadelphians and he would tell stories of his family's variety store on Cottman Avenue (LaRue's) that his sister ran and his growing up there in Burholme. One day he pulled out a scrapbook with news stories about that Christmas voyage. He told it as a matter of fact; no boasting or bragging. He acted as if anybody else would do the same thing if they were in his shoes. At first I could not believe that this mild man was the same Captain Larue. But the more I looked and listened to him I could see that he may have been the only sailor able to pull this rescue off. I last saw Brother Marinus in 1972 when I made a visit to Saint Paul's. Times changed but he was still the tall, thin, ramrod straight monk in the black habit tending to the gift shop. Quiet and unassuming, he always wished everyone well and said he would keep you in his prayers."*

SURVIVING WAR AND THE BITTER COLD

(Edited version published in the November 26, 2017
Philadelphia Inquirer)

Marine Cpl. Ed Aversa (Photo courtesy of Ed Aversa, Sr.)

It was late November 1950, and the biting wind and snow relentlessly swirled around the 1st Division Marines at the Chosin Reservoir in North Korea as they desperately fought their way south towards the American held town of Hagaru. Marine Corporal Ed Aversa from the Roxborough section of Philadelphia, began to wonder if he'd make it out of Chosin alive. In the midst of an unprecedented Siberian cold front that gripped the Korean peninsula, as temperatures plummeted to minus 30 degrees, the Chinese had launched a massive, surprise assault against the U.N. forces in North Korea. One of their main objectives was to encircle, and then annihilate, the Marines at Chosin. Although Ed, still spry and feisty at 87 years old, thought that he might die at Chosin, he wasn't going down without a fight. He smiled at me as he echoed the famous words of his heroic Division Commander, Oliver Smith: "We weren't retreating, we were just fighting in a different direction."

But when I pressed him for more details of the battle, his smile quickly faded, and his eyes glazed over as a haunting memory of what he witnessed during the worst of the fighting seeped back into mind. "When we first arrived at Chosin", Ed recalled, "a truck backed up to the cargo plane we just got off of. It was loaded with dead Marines…naked….not a stitch of clothing on them. Frozen bodies in all different positions. They were so unprepared for the winter, for what happened, that they stripped them of their clothes so they could re-use them. One of our officers said 'Gentlemen, we are here for one reason now – to survive.'"

In the chaotic days following the Chinese attack, with the army of U.N. forces commander Douglas MacArthur in full-scale retreat, the senior military leaders in Washington ineptly struggled to deal with the crisis. David Halberstam's brilliant book on the Korean War, *The Coldest Winter*, revealed that as MacArthur began to unravel, incoherently mumbling to his aides while refusing to heed the advice from Washington, the Joint Chiefs meekly sat "around waiting for someone else to do something". But with American soldiers dying by the hundreds each day, there was one senior officer who was outraged by Washington's impotence and "vacuum of leadership": General Matthew B. Ridgway. Halberstam's book details a meeting that took place with the Joint Chiefs on December 3rd that very likely led to the eventual decision to replace MacArthur with Ridgway. It was "another long meeting where, in Ridgway's mind, they were unable to issue an order…Finally, Ridgway asked for permission to speak and then – he wondered later whether he had been too blunt – said that they had all spent too much damn time on debate and it was time to take some action. They owed it to the men in the field, he said, 'and to the God to whom we must answer for those men's lives to stop talking and to act'. When he finished, no one spoke." When the meeting concluded, Ridgway asked Air Force Chief of Staff, Hoyt Vandenberg, "Why don't the Chiefs send orders to MacArthur and tell him what to do? Vandenberg shook his head. "What good would that do? He wouldn't obey the orders. What can we do?" Ridgway then exploded. "You can relieve any commander who won't obey orders, can't you?!"

The drama unfolding in Washington paled in comparison to the fierce fight being waged by the Marines at Chosin. Fortunately for them, a brilliant tactical decision made in the weeks prior to the Chinese surprise attack by 1st Marine Division commander, Oliver P. Smith, not only enabled the Marines to escape encirclement, but to also inflict heavy casualties on the marauding enemy soldiers. "Oliver Smith was a smart man, and a good general", Ed said. In early November, Smith expressed concern with his orders to continue heading north towards the Chinese border because he believed that his Marines were walking into a carefully planned and deadly trap. His request to slow their advance was denied by MacArthur, but, unbeknownst to his superiors, Smith cleverly left supplies and established airfields along their route so that they could fight their way out if his instincts were right.

Ed recalled one particular night of intense combat during their withdrawal from Chosin. "An officer said, "anything moving – hit it. They (the Chinese troops) were 20 yards in front of us, and we didn't know they were there. Then, all of a sudden, they started with the noise – bugles, whistles – anything to try and rattle us. They didn't know that every Marine was wide awake waiting for them. When daylight came, their dead were everywhere...only 15 yards away...frozen." As the fighting withdrawal continued, what initially appeared to be a disaster for the Marines, is now regarded as one of their greatest military moments. "When we got to Hagaru, (Marine 1st Regiment commander) Chesty Puller was standing there with his pipe in his mouth", Ed recalled, "He said 'A lot of boys went up that hill, but a lot of men coming down now'." When the battle finally concluded in mid-December, the Chinese had succeeded in driving the Marines out of Chosin, but at a terrible cost. Although the Marines were outnumbered 8-1, and sustained over 11,000 casualties, U.N. estimates show that Chinese casualties were a staggering 40,000 to 80,000. Following the battle, Chinese General Song Shi-Lun offered his resignation. Unfortunately for Shi-Lun, Ed and his fellow Marines didn't go down without a fight.

Today, Ed is extremely proud to count himself among the "Chosin Few", those Marines who stunningly turned certain annihilation into one the most remarkable feats of courage and survival in the annals of military history. He told me that when he looks at how far South Korea has come since the war, he almost can't believe it's the same country he left in 1951. "When I first arrived, I thought, what is this place, and what the hell are we doing here? But I look at the country now, and I'm proud of what we did. And the Korean people and the Korean government have not forgotten us."

In my short time with Ed, I learned that he does not seek recognition, and prefers to keep his emotions in check. Perhaps his most endearing quality is his sense of humor. Following my interview, I put on my coat and said, "It's supposed to get cold tonight." Ed shot me a sarcastic look and replied, "When someone says it's getting cold, I just give 'em a look and say, 'Really?'"

AFTERWORD

Ed Aversa's son was one of my childhood friends, and a few times we were teammates on the same little league baseball and basketball teams in our old Roxborough neighborhood. Like so many of my friends from those days, our fathers were veterans of the Korean War, but I didn't know that Ed's father fought at Chosin until many years later when I ran into Ed Jr. at a friend's Communion party. When I finally sat down to interview his father, I hung on his every word as Ed Sr. vividly described his harrowing battlefield stories of Chosin. Invariably, whenever I interview veterans about their war experiences there will come a moment when they are visibly overcome with emotion. At one point during the interview I asked Ed to tell me the worst thing that he had seen at Chosin, and, anticipating what I had experienced before with veterans, I let him know that if it was too difficult to talk about, we could move on in the interview. Ed looked at me, then looked down at the scrapbook in front of him, and began to slowly turn the pages. He kept his head down as he turned the pages, acting as if he didn't hear the question. A very awkward minute passed as we both sat there in complete silence. Suddenly, he looked up at me and described the scene with the truck loaded with the dead, frozen bodies of his fellow Marines. Ed had taken that minute to gather himself and was determined to keep his emotions in check. He later told me that he had only recently been diagnosed with PTSD, 65 years after the Battle of the Chosin Reservoir.

A PHILADELPHIA LIEUTENANT AND THE TRAGEDY OF THE USS JUNEAU

(Edited version published on the May 28, 2018 *WHYY.org* website)

Lieutenant Charles Wang surrounded by Roman Catholic High School
alumni sailors during his visit to the school in early 1945
(Photo courtesy of Roman Catholic High School)

"They remotely maneuvered the underwater vehicle until the letters
emblazoned on the stern began to come clear. 'That's going to be the J,
there's the U,N,E, here's the A – that's it. That is the Juneau,' said Robert

Kraft, the director of underwater operations..."
(New York Times, *March 22, 2018)*

As I recently read through the various news articles that detailed the discovery of the USS Juneau by the South Pacific research exploration vessel, Petrel, on March 17, 2018, I immediately thought of the conversation I had with my Dad several years ago. Former Roman Alumni President Paul Pincituro had initially informed me that a Roman alumnus was the only officer to survive the sinking of the Juneau. I asked my Dad about it, also a Roman alum, and he said that the officer was from his old St. Columba parish in the North Philadelphia neighborhood known as "Swampoodle". I compiled a research file on the ship's sinking because I thought that it would make for a good story someday. Following the news of the discovery of the Juneau, I sorted through my notes in the file, and could almost hear my Dad's voice, and "straight-to-the-point" delivery style as I read them: "They called him "Chick" Wang. Lived on Lehigh Ave. Graduated from Roman in '34. Quarterback. Class President. Naval Officer. Became a doctor." I remembered initially thinking at the time that he never mentioned the Juneau, and that if I researched the story I may be able to reveal some things about the tragedy that my Dad did not know. Suddenly, the memories from that conversation, as well as my earlier research into the story of the USS Juneau, came flooding back.

━━━━━━━

As chronicled in Dan Kurzman's riveting book, *Left to Die: The Tragedy of the USS Juneau,* on the morning of November 13, 1942, Lieutenant Charles Wang, torpedo officer, had just finished inspecting the damage sustained by the USS Juneau during the previous night's battle. Although the Juneau had taken some hits, she could still fight, and her crew had performed admirably. Wang was resting at his station, eating a sandwich, when "a panicky voice cried into the earphones, "Fish! Torpedo heading toward us!" Seconds later, at 11:01 AM, Friday the thirteenth, it smashed into a magazine, and the Juneau blew up."

Wang was thrown onto the deck by the explosion. As he laid on his back, he opened his eyes and saw the radar antenna "spiraling straight down toward him." It smashed into Wang's right leg, badly breaking it in two places, his bones protruding through the skin. Wang managed to make it into the churning water and clung to the floating nets from the ship. Many of the survivors, most of whom were badly wounded, held on to the nets as well. Others found rafts, or simply floated in the water wearing their life preservers. These survivors eventually consolidated into a large floating group, desperately hoping for a rescue that would not come. As night fell, the wounded began to die, and the despairing cries of George Sullivan could be heard in the darkness as he searched for his four brothers. "Al, where are you?" he repeatedly cried out as tears streamed down his face. "Red, Matt, Frank, answer me! Where are you? It's your brother George."

The following morning, the sharks began to circle. Screams pierced the air as the sharks tore into the sailors still clinging to the nets. As the days went by, the initial group of about 150, now slowly dwindled down to a handful. The badly injured Wang was in a state of delirium from the pain. Two sailors volunteered to try to take Wang on one of the rafts to the island of San Cristobal some 55 miles away as the large flotilla of survivors was making "little headway because of the waves and the drag of the nets." If they made it, they would try to send a rescue ship for the survivors. Lieutenant John Blodgett agreed, and the men set off for the island.

The next several days would test the limits of human endurance. The blistering sun burned the skin off of their backs, and the extreme hunger and thirst drove some to madness. Some drank seawater, and dove underwater to imaginary "havens" where the sharks finished them off. A despondent and unstable George Sullivan told the group that he was going "to get some buttermilk and something to eat." He swam away before anyone could grab him, and the men soon heard his pitiful cries of "Help me!" as the sharks tore into him. Only seven men from this larger flotilla of survivors would be rescued. On November 19th, a PBY seaplane picked up five of the men, and the USS Ballard retrieved the remaining two the following day.

Wang and the other two sailors, in a remarkable feat of seamanship, eventually reached San Cristobal on November 19th where they were rescued by natives. The unbearable pain that Wang endured while still helping to navigate the raft to safety endeared him to the two sailors who were with him. "The courage that man showed during those days was something to behold," one of them said.

A total of 687 men from the USS Juneau lost their lives, including the five Sullivan brothers. Only 10 men survived the sinking. Lieutenant Charles Wang was the only officer to survive.

In 1947, Charles Wang married his wife, Marie, at St. Stephen's Catholic Church in Philadelphia. The parents of the Sullivan brothers were special guests. The Wang's raised three daughters, Celeste, Deborah, and Patricia, and Charles went on to a successful medical career as a pathologist. After enduring years of excruciating pain, he finally had his damaged leg amputated in 1980. Wang died in 1985 at the age of 70. He was chosen as one of Roman Catholic High School's "125 Men of Distinction" during the school's 125th anniversary in 2015.

———

I asked my Dad if he ever met Charles Wang. He said, "Once. I was just a kid. He came back to Roman during the war. He said that if any of us ever went to war, to try not to be afraid, do what you're told, and listen to your officers." My Dad's eyes then welled up, and his raspy voice cracked as he vacantly stared at a distant memory that only he could see. "He was on crutches...his leg was bad. He told us what happened."

It was at that moment that I realized that there was nothing I would discover in my research of Charles Wang and the brave crew of the USS Juneau that my Dad didn't already know.

Sullivans Attend Marriage of Last Juneau Officer

Mr. and Mrs. Thomas F. Sullivan, 98 Adams street, have returned from Philadelphia, Pa., where they attended the marriage of Charles Wang and Miss Marie Patricia Schaeflein in St. Stephen's Catholic church Monday.

Mr. Wang, formerly a lieutenant in the navy, is the only surviving officer of the USS Juneau with which the Sullivans' five sons were lost early in World war II. Mr. Wang, who was wounded in the catastrophe, has now almost completely recovered.

The wedding was followed by a reception at Hotel Mayfair. Mr and Mrs. Sullivan were special guests at the nuptials.

Waterloo Daily Courier 4-11-47

*Charles Wang is guest speaker at Roman's Alumni
Memorial Mass and Breakfast - Dec. 1944*

AFTERWORD

*Several years ago, following a Roman Catholic High School
Board of Trustees meeting, I was approached by former Roman
Alumni President, Paul "Pinch" Pincituro '69, and he said, "I have
an idea for a possible story for you. A guy by the name of Wang
was a Roman alum, and he was the only officer that survived the
sinking of the ship that the Sullivan brothers were on in World
War 2." Pinch then handed me a note with the information that
he had. I then asked my Dad about it, and, fortunately, he was
very familiar with Charles Wang. My Dad's memory was always
razor-sharp, and he not only provided some of the missing background information, but his personal recollections as well. I
wrote down a lot of what my Dad told me, and also read Dan
Kurzman's book with the intention of someday writing a story*

about it, but then completely forgot about it. Fast-forward to March, 2018, and as I was sitting on a beach in Jamaica scrolling through the top news stories, a story about the discovery of the wreck of the USS Juneau popped up. I thought that this recent discovery represented an opportune time to search for my old notes and write the story. On the day that it was published on WHYY's website, the first person that I e-mailed with the link to my essay was Paul Pincituro. I wrote: "Thanks for telling me about him, Pinch...you were the one who first told me about Wang and prompted me to ask my Dad." He responded: "Excellent job, thank you". In a sad twist of fate, four days later, Pinch died suddenly. I'll miss him and his frequent encouraging words regarding my essays featuring Roman alumni.

DUNNIE'S RED WAGON

(Edited version published in the November 11, 2019 *Orlando Sentinel*)

Dunnie's grave at the Normandy-American cemetery (Photo courtesy of Jack Dougherty)

During the early morning hours of Tuesday, June 6, 1944, Philadelphia Mayor, Bernard Samuel, was awakened by his secretary with urgent news: the long awaited invasion of France by the Allied forces had finally begun.

The *Philadelphia Inquirer* reported that that the mayor, "accompanied by his secretary and a few policemen, went to Independence Hall shortly before 7(am) o'clock. With a wooden mallet he tapped the Liberty Bell 12 times…The tapping of the Bell was carried throughout the Nation over an NBC hookup, and to other parts of the world by short wave." The Mayor then asked all to pray for a "victorious outcome", and to "remember the fathers and mothers of those who are fighting on the battlefields of France."

Word of the invasion spread across the neighborhoods of Philadelphia, and for many families it was the start of a period of great fear and anxiety. Like so many streets in Philadelphia, Stillman Street in Fairmount was lined with numerous row-homes that proudly displayed flags with blue stars in their windows, indicating a family member in the service. At the Keenan home, there were 2 blue stars on their flag. "They were for my two older brothers, Joe and Dunnie," Ed Keenan recalled. "I was only 8 years old at the time, but I remember the flags vividly – our's and our neighbors. My brothers, like a lot of the guys in our neighborhood, were alumni of Roman Catholic High School. Joe enlisted during his junior year and was serving in the Pacific. Dunnie enlisted after graduating in 1943, but the last that we heard following his recent Christmas visit home was that he was somewhere in England. On the day of the invasion, and the days that followed, we just kept thinking, 'Where's Dunnie? I hope that he's OK.'"

Unknown to the Keenan's was that Charles "Dunnie" Keenan's 330th Infantry Regiment of the 83rd Infantry Division was not part of the initial invasion force on June 6th, but was with the second wave of forces that landed at Omaha Beach in Normandy on June 23, 1944. The 83rd sustained heavy losses during the bitter "hedgerow" battles that followed the invasion as Allied forces tried to push inland. On July 4th, Dunnie's regiment began a series of attacks just southeast of the key French town of Carentan. Colonel R.T. Foster, Commander of the 330th Infantry Regiment, wrote that "we attacked every day for twenty-three straight days, from dawn til dark. We repulsed the enemies' counter-attacks and we moved forward. We became exhausted, physically and mentally. It showed in our dirty and drawn faces. We lost our closest friends."

Dunnie's regiment was met with near-fanatical resistance, as opposing the 330th were some of Hitler's best troops: the 37th and 38th SS Panzergrenadier Regiments. On July 5th a captured SS soldier from the 37th informed American interrogators that the Germans were ordered to hold the line "to the last drop of blood."

Back home in Philadelphia, young Eddie Keenan and his buddies, Billy Lamb, Billy McGahey, and Charlie Czarnecki, wanted to do something to help the war effort. They had heard the radio promotions urging Americans to collect scrap-metal so that it could be recycled for use by the military. "We wanted to try and help the war effort", Ed recalled. "Some of our older brothers were fighting, and we wanted to do something too. So we decided to go door-to-door in our neighborhood with my old wagon to collect scrap-metal pieces. But, my wagon was a hand-me-down, and we felt that for an effort like this, we needed to spruce it up a bit. So we got some bright red paint and started to paint it."

On the day that the boys were putting the finishing touches on the wagon, they were startled by a woman's voice. It was Billy McGahey's mother, and she had an odd look on her face. "Eddie," she said. "You have to go home. Something is wrong with your Mom." Eddie ran home and found his mother and sister sobbing. Time seemed to slow down. Words and phrases became jumbled, heard only in fragments. Something about a "telegram from Washington"…"deepest regret"…"Charles Keenan had been killed in action on July 8th". Dunnie was gone, and a gold star would replace a blue.

As the house began to fill with grieving relatives, a despondent Eddie returned to his friends and told them what happened. One of the boys had an idea, and after all of them heard it, they agreed it was a great way to honor Dunnie.

A few hours later, Eddie returned to his home, now filled with relatives and neighbors. He found his grief-stricken father, tugged on his shirt, and said, "Come to the window, Dad. Look outside!" His father walked to the window, pulled back the curtain, and there was the red wagon. Emblazoned upon it, in bright white paint, were the words: "PFC Charles T. Keenan."

His father quickly closed the curtain. With sad, red-rimmed eyes, he looked down at Eddie. "Oh Eddie", he said. "Please take that off. It's too soon." A confused and dejected Eddie painted over his brother's name. "I was just a little boy," Ed told me. "I didn't understand then why my father wanted it removed."

The innocence of childhood is often lost to the cruel indifference of tragedy, and life would never be the same again for Ed and his family. "The red wagon fell by the wayside", Ed said. "The joy of what we had done was diminished after Dunnie died."

On June 20th, to commemorate the 75th anniversary of D-Day, and the death of his brother, Dunnie, Ed Keenan returned to a place he has been once before. It is a place of honor, that's filled with the names of the fallen. And when Ed arrived there with his son, he sought one name in particular: Charles T. Keenan PFC. There, it is not emblazoned in white paint on a child's red wagon, but it's permanently carved upon a stone cross. And as Ed looked out among the 9,387 gravestones of the Normandy-American cemetery in France, he remembered the wisdom of his father, a World War 1 veteran who understood that there would be a proper place and time for Dunnie's name - it would be at Normandy, forever beside the names of his fellow heroes.

Charles "Dunnie" Keenan - 1943 (Photo courtesy of Ed Keenan)

AFTERWORD

When Ed Keenan returned from his visit to Normandy in the summer of 2019, he presented me with a gift: a vial containing sand from Omaha beach (see photo above). Although it's marked as being from "Gold" beach, the gift shop assured Ed it was from "Omaha" – they simply ran out of vials marked as such. Regardless of which beach it's actually from, each time that I look at the vial, I can't help but think of how many gave their lives just to gain a small foothold on that sand.

THE ROMAN CATHOLIC HIGH SCHOOL ALUMNI OF WORLD WAR I

R.C.H.S. WW I alumni logo
Designed by Gene Burns '81

In the autumn of 2011, I started a quest that has not only resulted in the publication of the essays found within this section, but also some of the most gratifying experiences of my life. It began as what I naively assumed would be a relatively straightforward search for the names of the alumni of Philadelphia's Roman Catholic High who gave their lives in World War I. And although finding the names of these "lost boys" of Roman has become a very difficult task, with numerous instances of frustration wrought by lost or missing records, chasing numerous false alarms, and finding the time to devote to this search, it has also resulted in incredibly rewarding moments of discovery. I quickly came to the realization that my search for names had also become an unexpected and remarkable revelation of stories, not only of those alumni who gave their lives in the Great War, but also those who survived as well. The discovery of their stories, and not just their names, would be among the most compelling and captivating of my search.

IN SEARCH OF ROMAN'S 'LOST BOYS' OF WORLD WAR I

(Edited version published in the May 27, 2012 *Philadelphia Inquirer*)

*1st floor hallway at Philadelphia's Roman Catholic
High School (Chris Gibbons photo)*

*"I resolved to find what remained of Company D for (my grandfather),
and for (his fellow soldiers), and for myself, as well, and complete a story
begun on a hot July day so long ago, when young men raced across open*

fields toward machine guns and disappeared into history." – (From The Remains of Company D: A Story of the Great War *by James Carl Nelson)*

As I recently walked down the first-floor hallway of my old high school, located at Broad and Vine, my footsteps sharply echoed off the walls, a stark reminder that it was late afternoon and that I was alone in the normally bustling, but now deserted, corridors.

Before that day, I had been poring over old yearbook photos, and I immediately noticed that the interior, with its beautiful early 20th-century architecture, looked strikingly similar to the way it had looked in 1917. Sunbeams escaped through open classroom doors, and their ribbons of light streamed across the hallway. Dust motes hung motionless within their illumination, but then suddenly swirled into motion. Just an errant draft? Or do the spirits of the boys I had been searching for still walk these halls?

I stopped at the end of the hall and looked up at the plaques that display the names of Roman Catholic High School alumni who had lost their lives in World War II, Korea, Vietnam, and the Persian Gulf wars. As I stared at the long list of names, well over a hundred of them, I knew that the young men who had been eluding me would not be found there. However, I hoped that my visit would serve as motivation to not give up on what had now become a very difficult task.

I touched the raised metal letters of the names on the plaques and could only shake my head in frustration. "Who were the boys from World War I?" I softly whispered. I futilely hoped that the ghosts of the past would somehow miraculously answer my question, but as the dust motes swirled back into motion, the deserted hallway remained silent.

Roman was founded by the son of an Irish immigrant, Thomas Cahill, in 1890, and was the first free Catholic high school in the country. By the time the United States had entered World War I in 1917, the school was already more than a quarter-century old. Yet many alumni, myself included, had long assumed that there was no commemorative plaque for World War I because no Roman alumni had died in that war. However, as my interest and knowledge of the Great War deepened over the years, I began to doubt this assumption. After I read James Carl Nelson's brilliant book *The Remains of Company D*, I resolved to finally learn the truth regarding World War I and the lost boys from Roman.

I began my search by talking to my father (Class of 1948) and other older alumni, hoping that they might remember a World War I commemorative plaque from their time as students. None did. My hopes were briefly raised when I learned that a group of students attempted to find an answer in 2008, but the project was never completed.

I contacted Roman's resident historian, Ed Keenan (Class of 1954), and we soon found ourselves behind a chain-link fence in the dusty basement of Roman's Alumni Annex building, sorting through some of the school's voluminous records and documents. Ed and I looked over old trophies, certificates, flags, banners, and plaques that had been collected over the years, but came up empty. However, during a review of the 1919 yearbook, our first clue finally emerged. A passage in the Alumni section read: "Some fourteen of our Alumni have made the supreme sacrifice and laid down their lives on the fields of France for their country."

We now knew the number, but still no names.

It was during a second review of the 1918 yearbook that the names of the first two alums who gave their lives were finally revealed. A short passage stated that on Nov. 28, 1917, Roman alumni formally presented to the school a "sad Memorial Flag ... the first of its kind in Philadelphia, [with] two gold stars on a purple background ... [to] commemorate the deaths of E.J. Kelly ... and W. Kimmel."

As I read the passage, I was momentarily shaken. Purple and gold holds special meaning for Roman grads. In addition to being our school's colors, they are also the title of our alma mater, which opens with the line: "When day mounts the East, what flag does he hold? He flings out his banner of Purple and Gold." That line kept repeating in my mind as I envisioned this solemn memorial flag and stared at the names.

Last month, I presented my findings to Roman's board of trustees. Their enthusiastic response was overwhelming, as numerous board members volunteered to help find the remaining 12 names. Many of us now believe that there once was a commemorative plaque, but it was probably lost during the school's numerous renovations or possibly destroyed in a 1959 fire.

A new plaque to commemorate the 14 is now being designed, with a formal unveiling planned during the school's annual Veterans Day ceremonies.

Thomas Cahill never had any children of his own, so Roman alums often refer to themselves as "sons of Cahill," and we are now more determined than ever to find our lost brothers from World War I. These boys have somehow disappeared into history, but we will find them, and they'll soon take their rightful place of honor on the wall of the legendary school at Broad and Vine.

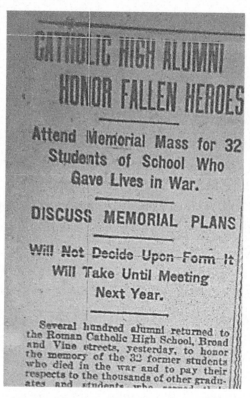

AFTERWORD

Two years following the publication of this essay, I discovered that it was not 14 alumni who had given their lives, but it was actually 32, as revealed in the newspaper image of the 12-29-19 Philadelphia Record. A task that I knew would be difficult, became that much harder. But, perhaps the most puzzling mystery of the search thus far has been trying to find the reason why Roman never dedicated a Memorial plaque to honor its fallen alumni of World War I. It has perplexed all of us involved in the search, especially upon discovering that in December 1918, Roman's Alumni Association announced plans to erect a bronze plaque to honor those who served and died during the war. The following year, the Alumni again publicly stated that it still planned to move forward with a Memorial (see 12-29-19 Philadelphia Record image), but it is unknown as to what became of those plans. Was there once a Memorial or a plaque to honor the Roman alumni of World War 1? If so, what happened to it? In addition to trying to find the names of the fallen, we hope to answer these questions as well.

BEAT THE DRUMS SLOWLY

(Edited version published in the May 26, 2013 *Philadelphia Inquirer*)

The grave of Louis R. McGinnis - RCHS Class of 1913

"Then beat the drums slowly, play the fifes lowly,
Sound the death march as you carry me along,
And fire your muskets right over my coffin,
For I'm a young soldier cut down in his prime"
(The Soldier Cut Down in His Prime - *old Irish ballad*)

I huddled in the cold rain with my sons, Jack and Ryan, in Yeadon's Holy Cross Cemetery and unfolded the paper that listed the burial registry information of the soldier that I was looking for. It was Easter Sunday, and many of the graves had fresh potted flowers beside them which brought a welcome respite of color among the drab gray sky and headstones. The tapping of the raindrops on the paper steadily increased, which hastened our search. "It states that he's in this section here, Section 19-Lot 48-Range 9, but I don't see any markers", I said to my boys as I surveyed the numerous headstones in front of us. "We'll have to split up, each take a row, and hope that we find him."

We searched for nearly 10 minutes before I finally saw the headstone that bears his name. "I found it!", I yelled. "He's over here." As my sons hurried over, I noticed that there were no flowers at his gravesite, and my initial feeling of satisfaction was quickly overwhelmed by an unexpected sense of sadness. Although he died in 1918, I felt that this was the grave of someone I knew.

My ongoing two-year search for the Roman Catholic High School Alumni who died in World War I led us to the cemetery that day to find the grave of Louis Robert McGinnis from the Class of 1913. Roman's records revealed that 14 alumni died during WW I, but only listed two of their names. A third name was found when a relative of that alum contacted me directly. But McGinnis was the first alum that I found through a meticulous and time-consuming process of comparing names from old Roman yearbooks to a list of Philadelphians who died during WW I.

McGinnis was born August 24, 1895, and his nickname was "Zeke". He was one of six sons of Andrew and Anastasia McGinnis, and, like me, his paternal grandparents were Irish immigrants. He lived on 58th street in Southwest Philadelphia, and prior to that, on Snyder Ave. in South Philly. At Roman, McGinnis was a popular kid, and the 1913 yearbook eerily stated that "McGinnis will never be forgotten by the members of the Class of 1913. Not only was he popular among the fellows of his own class, but with the whole student body of R.C.H.S." It also stated that "Lou" was on the track team, won a big race at Fairmount Park as a junior, and was a hit in the school play.

Following Roman, he went on to the University of Pennsylvania. In 1917, he joined the U.S. Army's new Aviation Section, a forerunner to the Air Force, and achieved the rank of 2nd lieutenant before he died on August 16, 1918, just eight days shy of his 23rd birthday. The circumstances surrounding his death are unknown. Perhaps he was a fighter pilot and was shot down, or maybe his death was more mundane – during a training exercise or from the deadly 1918 flu pandemic that killed thousands of U.S. soldiers. I'm hopeful that I'll eventually find the answers.

After we found his grave, Ryan ran back to the car and retrieved the small American flag and Roman Catholic High School Alumni plaque that we had brought with us. We fixed them in the ground and observed a moment of silence. I then realized that my search for the lost boys from Roman who died in World War I had reached a level of difficulty that I never anticipated. I had naively assumed it was simply a search for 11 missing names, but my research had revealed much more, and now Louis McGinnis was no longer just a name to me. He seemed more like an old friend or classmate, and it made for a poignant moment as three Cahillites from Roman stood at the grave of another who graduated 100 years prior. "He died a long way from home," I said aloud as we watched the rain pelt his headstone.

We headed back to the car, and while I was proud of my sons for helping me, I certainly wasn't surprised. Jack's a recent Roman graduate, and Ryan is a junior there now. Our school's motto is "Brothers for Life", so they were as determined as I was to find his grave.

A graveyard is a changeless place, seemingly immune to the passage of time, and as we drove along the cemetery's narrow path towards the exit, I wondered what it was like on that day in 1918 when Zeke was laid to rest. Was it a gray, rainy day like today? Were the mourners in attendance able to provide some measure of comfort to his grief-stricken family? Were his former classmates from Roman there? And did his military honor guard beat the drums slowly, play the fifes lowly, and sound the death march as they carried our brother to his grave?

Lieutenant Louis McGinnis - 1918
(Photo courtesy of the McGinnis family))

PHILADELPHIA AIRMAN DIES

Lieut. McGinnis, Instructor, Fails to Survive Operation

Second Lieutenant Louis McGinnis, of the Army Aviation Corps, died last Friday following an operation in the hospital at Camp Carlstrom, an aviation field near Arcadia, Fla., where he was an instructor. The body was brought back to Philadelphia, arriving at his home, 5337 Chester avenue, last night.

His funeral will be held tomorrow. Solemn requiem mass will be sung at the Church of the Blessed Sacrament, Fifty-sixth street and Chester avenue, and interment will be in Holy Cross Cemetery, with full military honors.

Lieutenant McGinnis was commissioned in May last and sent at once to Camp Carlstrom. He was the son of Andrew P. McGinnis, of the legal department of E. W. Clark & Co., bankers and brokers, Chestnut street near Fourth.

A brother, Walter, is in the navy and another brother, Joseph, is in the aviation corps.

Lieutenant McGinnis was a graduate of the Roman Catholic High School, class of 1913, and was employed in the Bureau of Health and taking a night course at the University of Pennsylvania when he enlisted in the air service.

AFTERWORD

The McGinnis family contacted me after reading my essay in the Philadelphia Inquirer. *They informed me that Louis became ill during pilot training. The illness led to a severe infection. Despite an operation at the Army hospital to save his life, Louis succumbed to the infection. His family sent me this picture of him in uniform, and I later found a newspaper clipping from the August 20, 1918* Philadelphia Public Ledger.

PHILADELPHIAN GAVE HIS LIFE AS NATION FOUND ITS SOUL

(Published in the May 25, 2014 *Philadelphia Inquirer*)

Edward J. Kelley - RCHS Class of 1908

It is Sept. 26, 1916. Six French soldiers, three on each side, carry the plain pine coffin from the little Catholic church in the French town of Rampont. It is unusually warm for late September, and the familiar booming sounds of the German and French artillery can be heard in the distance as the mourners slowly file out of the church.

The coffin holds the body of a young Philadelphian, Edward J. Kelley, and following behind the French soldiers are more than 35 solemn Americans dressed in the simple khaki uniforms of Kelley's unit, the all-volunteer American Ambulance Corps. During the funeral Mass, the best singers among the French soldiers had given a moving rendition of *La Mort d'Homme*, and their beautiful voices seemed to magically drift within the warm air and stay with the congregation as they slowly walk toward the graveyard some 300 yards away.

English poet John Masefield called these brave American volunteers "the very pick and flower of American youth." The military escort at Kelley's funeral was a sign of how highly regarded they were by the French army. A large French flag was draped over his coffin, and a folded U.S. flag rested on a pillow carried by one of Kelley's fellow Americans. Pinned to the U.S. flag was the prestigious French Croix de Guerre (Cross of War) medal with a gold star, the next to highest honor for service to France.

At the gravesite, the French division commander read the citation for bravery, and then gave a speech honoring Kelley and the other American volunteers. "It was a speech that one could never forget," W. Yorke Stevenson wrote for the *Philadelphia Public Ledger*. "I wish I had it word for word." It was so moving that many in attendance fought back tears. Some openly wept.

I learned of the amazing story of Edward J. Kelley during my search for the alumni of Roman Catholic High School who gave their lives in World War I. Kelley, Class of 1908, was one of the first names discovered, but Roman's records, as well as the initial newspaper reports of his death, mistakenly spelled his name "Kelly," which hampered my search for information surrounding his death.

But the primary reason that Kelley's story had eluded me was the date of his death: Sept. 23, 1916 — nearly seven months before the United States entered the war. But then I read a passage in the book, *Philadelphia in the World War: 1914-1919*, by the Philadelphia War History Committee (1922). I learned that while the United States officially remained neutral in the early years of World War I, there was a small group of young men in the American Field Service who volunteered to help the French fight

Germany. These Americans "offered their services to France for the trans-portation of wounded at the fighting front... This little group of American volunteers at no time amounted to more than 2,000 men, but, at the time of France's greatest need, they were a tangible expression of American sympathy."

The book listed Kelley as one of the first of these volunteers to lose his life. A more thorough investigation of Roman's student records, as well as a search of the archives of the *Philadelphia Public Ledger*, not only confirmed that he was the same alum, but also revealed the sad details of his death.

Kelley had been in his sector for only a few days during Verdun, the longest battle of the First World War. He was helping transport wounded French soldiers from the front when a shell exploded in front of the ambu-lance in which he was a passenger. Shell fragments killed Kelley instantly, and severely wounded the driver, another young American volunteer.

Kelley's funeral three days later touched the hearts of all who attended. In a letter to the Kelley family, the head of the Ambulance Corps, A. Piatt Andrew, wrote: "The scene was one which no one there could ever forget; they could only wish that you and those who were closest to Edward Kelley might have been there and might have felt the beauty and the sincerity of the tribute being paid to him." Before his coffin was lowered into the ground, Kelley's comrades from the Ambulance Corps placed a gold cross upon his chest and, into his breast pocket, a photograph of a young Philadelphia woman they had found among his letters from home. It was a photo of Kelley's girlfriend. Despite repeated inquiries, she remained anonymous. The reporter for the *Public Ledger* wrote, "Somewhere in Philadelphia a young woman is grieving for the hero, but his sister refused to reveal her name."

As I've done for the past two years, I reported on the results of my search for the Roman alumni who gave their lives in the First World War to my alma mater's A.P. history students, two of whom have been assisting in this effort. Thus far, we have named seven alums, out of what we initially thought was a group of 14, based on an old yearbook passage. But news-paper articles indicate that the number is at least 32, and possibly more, who died in the war that began 100 years ago. There is still more work to do. But what we already have learned about the valor of these young men from Roman captivated the school's current students, and they applauded at the end of the presentation.

In the early years of the 20th century, a relatively young and tentative United States was still unsure of its place in a world then engulfed in conflict. But before we could find our place, the country needed to save something, something we were in danger of losing as a result of our isolationist, almost selfish tendencies. I reminded the boys at Roman to take pride in their historic school, for a young man who once attended class in the same rooms where they now sit was among a small group of American volunteers who helped the United States save this most crucial attribute, which would be desperately needed in the chaotic decades that followed. Former President Theodore Roosevelt revealed what that attribute was when he praised the likes of Edward J. Kelley and his comrades in the American Field Service: "The most important thing that a nation can possibly save is its soul, and these young men have been helping this nation to save its soul."

AFTERWORD

The Kelley family contacted me after reading my essay in the Inquirer. They sent me the 3 previous photos - A French soldier during Kelley's funeral, a letter signed by all of the French soldiers in attendance at Kelley's funeral, and Kelley's great-great nephew at his gravesite at the Meuse Argonne Cemetery in France. (All photos courtesy of the Kelley family).

THE ROMAN CATHOLIC HIGH SCHOOL ALUM WHO BEAT THE CHAMP

(Edited version published in the September 25, 2014
Philadelphia Inquirer)

Tommy Loughran, 1929 (Chicago Daily News)

Atlantic City - September 11, 1926. The kid from Philadelphia looked across the ring at the much feared and seemingly indestructible heavyweight champion, Jack Dempsey, and for the first time in his boxing career he was visibly nervous. Although it was only a sparring session to help Dempsey prepare for his upcoming title defense vs. Gene Tunney in Philadelphia, Tommy Loughran knew of Dempsey's fearsome reputation for routinely knocking out his sparring partners. "In the corner, (my trainer) looked at me and said, `What the hell's the matter with you, Tommy?", Loughran recounted in a 1979 *Sports Illustrated* article by Sam Moses. "I can't understand you. You never get excited about fights.' "I said, `Joe, this isn't just a fight.' "`Don't worry, Tommy,' he said, `you'll knock his block off.' "I said, `Joe. I sure wish I had your confidence.'

My continuing search for the alumni of Roman Catholic High School who fought in World War I not only revealed the incredible story of Thomas "Tommy" Loughran from the Class of 1920, but it also enlightened me to a remarkable time in Philadelphia's history when our city was buzzing with excitement.

By September 1926, Philadelphia's Sesquicentennial International Exposition, celebrating our country's 150th anniversary, had hosted millions of visitors, and preparations for one of the biggest sporting events in our nation's history were in high gear. On September 23, 1926, Jack Dempsey and Gene Tunney would meet for the heavyweight championship in front of a record crowd of 130,000 in Philadelphia's new Sesquicentennial Stadium, later known as JFK Stadium. The result of that fight signaled the beginning of the end for a legendary, larger-than-life sports personality, but it was a little known sparring session just a few weeks before that foretold the fight's outcome, and led to the rise of one of the greatest fighters in Philadelphia's rich boxing history.

The son of Irish immigrants, Loughran was born and raised in South Philadelphia as a member of Saint Monica's parish. At the beginning of his sophomore year at Roman in 1917, Loughran, just 14 years old, was eager to fight for his country in World War I, and enlisted in the Army without revealing his age. When the Army finally realized Loughran's age, they released him from the armed services. Rather than return to school, he found work with a neighborhood blacksmith and also began to hone his boxing skills in the gym. Loughran built an impressive record through the mid-1920's, and was known for his great footwork, speed, and accurate counter-punching. His style was similar to Tunney's, and Dempsey personally requested Loughran to spar with him in preparation for the big title fight.

———

In the first round of the sparring session, Loughran's footwork and quickness enabled him to avoid Dempsey's relentless onslaught and his confidence grew. "He couldn't hit me to save his life, see, and it made him furious", Loughran recalled in the SI article. "Ooh, was he mad. I'd stay against the ropes and say, `Let's see if you can hit me, Jack.' I'd go this way, then I'd go that way; next time he came at me I'd step back, he'd step forward. I'd step back another way. He didn't know what to do."

Emboldened by his first round performance, Loughran became more aggressive in the second round and began to land his combinations. "I let him have it on the nose", Loughran said. "Blood squirted in all directions. He stepped back and cussed me out loud, and when he did, I grabbed him and turned him around and put him up against the ropes. Gees, I poured it on him, I gave him such a beating. I hit him in the belly, hit him with uppercuts, hit him with a hook, caught him with another. I had his eyes puffy, his nose was bleeding, he was spitting out blood. I had him cut under the chin, and I think his ear was bleeding. I don't know whatever held him up. He always came tearing back in, no matter how hard I hit him."

Dempsey's corner stopped the sparring session before their fighter could absorb more punishment. The sportswriters and spectators were stunned. Two weeks later, Gene Tunney used that same combination of footwork, speed, and accurate counter-punching to defeat Jack Dempsey and become the new heavyweight champion. Paul Gallico, the renowned *N.Y Daily News* sportswriter, chronicled after the title fight that Loughran "wrote Dempsey's finish in letters large enough for all of us to see, except that we, too, were blinded by our own ballyhoo and the great Dempsey legend that we had helped to create."

Loughran would go on to win the light heavyweight championship the following year, and successfully defend it 6 times before vacating it to fight as a heavyweight. He eventually fought for the heavyweight title and lost by decision to Primo Carnera, but his boxing career was truly extraordinary. Loughran had 169 total bouts and fought many middleweight, light heavyweight, and heavyweight champions in his career, including Harry Greb, Jack Sharkey, and Gene Tunney. As a light heavyweight, Loughran defeated two future world heavyweight champions: Max Baer and James J. Braddock. He was *The Ring Magazine's* Fighter of the Year in 1929 and 1931, and he was elected to the *Ring Magazine* Hall of Fame in 1956.

Tommy Loughran died in 1982, and there is a Historic Marker at 17th and Ritner in South Philly in his honor. He was posthumously inducted into the International Boxing Hall of Fame in 1991, and he is often ranked among the Top 5 Light Heavyweights of All Time by boxing historians.

The stories that I have uncovered in my search for the alumni of Roman Catholic High School who fought in World War I not only inspire me and my fellow alums, but they also seem to resonate with many Philadelphians. In 1979, Tommy Loughran reflected on that long forgotten sparring session against the great Jack Dempsey, and his words from the *SI* article not only revealed the key to his eventual success, but they also serve as a reminder to all of us as to how to we should confront life's seemingly insurmountable obstacles: "Those two rounds with Dempsey gave me confidence in myself. I learned an important lesson that day: never to be defeated by fear."

AFTERWORD

Many years ago, my father had told me that Tommy Loughran, the former great light-heavyweight champion from Philadelphia, was a Roman alum. I decided to do a little bit of research into Loughran's life with the hopes of possibly writing an essay about him. In doing so, I was somewhat startled to discover his connection to Roman's alumni of World War I. An article in the Jan. 19, 1937 Philadelphia Inquirer stated "...Tom decided to get a job after the school term closed at Catholic High. They needed an elevator boy at the Millionaire's Club, 12th and Walnut sts...The World War broke out and Tommy had the urge because so many members of the club joined the service. The youngster failed to return home...Mrs. Loughran (his mother) investigated and discovered that Tommy was in Washington D.C., all set to sail the High Seas...Tommy finally came home, a much disappointed youngster."

Loughran was proud of his association with Roman, and stayed active in the school's various alumni activities over the years. He was the guest speaker on multiple occasions at their annual alumni gatherings, and actually fought a bout in Roman's legendary 3rd floor gymnasium in 1922 (see the accompanying Philadelphia Public Ledger article image from 10-19-22). He even enlisted in the Marines when WW II broke out. However, the most surprising thing that I discovered during my research of Loughran was the heavy press coverage around the country surrounding his sparring session with Dempsey, as nearly every major U.S. newspaper covered the story. It was a testament not only to the public's fascination with the legendary Jack Dempsey, but to the incredible popularity of boxing in the early half of the 20th century as well. Loughran's nephew, Tom Dooley, commented on my story and wrote to me: "I enjoyed the story. It would have been better if you included Jack Dempsey's comment when Loughran started walking back to the showers, Dempsey yelled, 'Get back here! I want to break your nose!' Loughran replied, 'You have to hit me first.' The two men were the best of friends until they died many years later."

REVELATIONS IN QUEST FOR ROMAN ALUM IN WORLD WAR I

(Edited version published in the September 11, 2015
Philadelphia Inquirer)

Philadelphia Evening Public Ledger - 3-18-19

As I recently walked down the narrow, row-house lined South Philadelphia street searching for Robert Rongione's address, I was momentarily struck by just how far I'd come in my four-year search for the Roman Catholic High School alumni who died in World War I, and how the meandering path resulting from it had led me to this moment. What started out as a basic search for names, has developed into a revelation of their stories - not only of those who died, but those who survived as well.

After searching through various public records and archives, I had finally found a living relative of Vincent Diodati, a Roman graduate from the Class of 1906. Rongione is his nephew, and I was heading to his home to present him with the "Roman Catholic High School 125 Persons of Distinction Award", which was posthumously awarded to his uncle by Roman's Alumni Association to commemorate the school's 125 year anniversary. Rongione had told me over the phone that the details of what his uncle experienced during the Great War were sketchy, so I also brought a copy of the March 18, 1919 issue of the *Philadelphia Public Ledger* newspaper which prominently featured a story about his uncle.

After I found the address and rang the doorbell, I was warmly greeted by Rongione's brother, James and Robert's friend, Phyllis. They graciously invited me in to sit and chat, and we talked for an hour. They were very appreciative that Roman had recognized their uncle, and were not only interested in what I'd learned about Vincent, but what I'd also discovered about the other Roman alumni who fought in World War I.

As chronicled in the *Public Ledger*, Vincent Diodati graduated from Jefferson Medical College in 1911 and practiced medicine for 7 years at 1222 South 12th Street in Philadelphia. On April 6, 1917, the United States declared war on Germany, and Diodati enlisted that very day. Before any American troops were sent overseas, Diodati was commissioned an officer and immediately assigned to British forces who were in desperate need of battlefield surgeons. He was the first American to be placed in command of the 35th Royal Army Medical Corps, and during his entire time in France he was constantly under fire. In the battles that Diodati's unit was involved in ("...bloody places they were," he remarked in the *Ledger*), he was wounded three times and gassed twice. Despite being badly gassed at Annequin and hemorrhaging, Diodati refused to go to the hospital as he wanted to continue to tend to the wounded Allied soldiers. Out of his original outfit of 220 men, Diodati was one of only 14 survivors. For his gallantry in battle, Diodati was awarded the coveted British Military Cross and it was personally bestowed upon him by King George of England in the spring of 1919.

I then told the Rongiones some of the other amazing stories that I'd discovered thus far during my search. The story of Edward Kelley from the Class of 1908 who was killed during the Battle of Verdun, and posthumously awarded the Croix de Guerre medal for bravery by the French

Army. The extraordinary story of William Armstrong from the Class of 1912, a fighter pilot whose dogfight in 1918 over the skies of France against 4 German planes was headline news in the Public Ledger. The sad story of Walter Spearing from the Class of 1908, who was killed in action while serving with the 5th Marine Regiment during the Battle of Belleau Wood. Spearing was held in such high regard by his fellow soldiers, that one of them wrote a touching letter to his mother that was published on the front page of the *Public Ledger* in 1918.

Some of the Roman alumni who served during World War I went on to achieve local and national prominence. Among them, John F. McCloskey from the Class of 1896 was a veteran of the Spanish-American War, as well as WW I, and co-founded Chestnut Hill Hospital, Vincent Carroll from the Class of 1909 went on to become the first President Judge of Philadelphia's Court of Common Pleas, and James McGranery from the Class of 1913, served as an Army Balloon Observation Pilot and went on to become U.S. Attorney General under President Harry Truman in 1952.

The Rongiones were pleasantly surprised to learn that Tommy Loughran, the former great light heavyweight champion from nearby St. Monica's parish, left Roman as a 14 year old sophomore to fight in World War I. I also told them of a remarkable recent discovery that links the past with the present: Gabe Wilson from the Class of 1907 served as a lieutenant in the Army during the war, and his great-grandson, Joseph Wilson, graduated in June with Roman's Class of 2015.

When I visited the Rongiones that day, I arrived thinking that I would simply present them with the award, and reveal a story about their uncle that they might not have known. I also held out the slim hope that they would be able to provide me with something that would help in my search - perhaps a list of names from the Memorial Mass held at Roman after the war. Thus far we have learned that 32 Roman alumni died in World War I, and we have found the names of 12. Unfortunately, the Rongiones did not have any additional information that could lead to the discovery of more names, but they did tell me a story about Vincent Diodati that is the saddest and most poignant I've heard thus far in my search. It revealed the depth of the burdens that Diodati must've carried with him throughout his life, but, ironically, the story took place before World War I.

In the years prior to the war, Diodati and his wife, Margaret, had a child. When the little girl was just a toddler, she somehow pulled a boiling pot of water from atop the kitchen stove down upon herself and died. They never had any more children, and became distant from the rest of the family. Perhaps it was this terrible tragedy that drove Diodati to heroically save as many lives as he could during the war.

My search for names continues to be a revelation of stories.

AFTERWORD

Pictures: James Rongione (left) and Robert Rongione display the "125 Men of Distinction Award" from Roman Catholic High School to commemorate Roman's 125 Year Anniversary in 2015. The men accepted the award on behalf of their Uncle – Vincent Diodati, Class of 1906. Also shown - Diodati's British Military Cross, courtesy of his great-niece, Kathy Liston.

LOVE AND LOSS ON THE HOME FRONT

(Edited version published in the May 9, 2016 *Philadelphia Inquirer*)

THE EVENING TELEGRAPH

PHILADELPHIA, SATURDAY, AUGUST 17, 1918

TO A MARTYR'S MOTHER

The following letter from a marine overseas to the mother of another marine, killed in action,—a Philadelphian—was sent by the mother to Representative J. Hampton Moore to "demonstrate the spirit of the boys in the district you represent." The mother asked that Representative Moore call the attention of his colleagues in Congress to it. It is here reproduced in full because of its unusual appeal. The mother is Mrs. C. M. Spearing, of 1552 North Fifty-fourth street. The son, Walter Joseph Spearing, was a member of the Fifth Regiment, U. S. Marine Corps.

At the Front, June 26, 1918.

Dear Mrs. Spearing:

There is grief in my heart and in the hearts of all my comrades for the great sorrow that this war has brought to you and to us. We all unite to express our heartfelt sympathy and condolence to the Mother and family of one who has fallen in a cause as imperishable as will be the names of those who have fallen to defend it.

Should there be anything my comrades and I can do to mitigate your grief and to allay your sorrow—some little keepsake of Walt as a marine, perhaps; but name it, dear lady, and it shall traverse the ocean to you.

Because you do not know me, please do not think it presumptuous for me to write. You are Walter's Mother—I was his inseparable friend and comrade; that makes us two kindred souls in common grief for our nearest and dearest. Then too, this letter fulfills a duty that I am bound by oath and will to perform. Many months ago, Walt and I promised each other, that should the "God of Battles" call to one, the other would console the sorrowing Mother. Now Walt has gone West to Home and to you forever, but Walt, his voice, his wonderful

MEXICO ALTERS OIL TAX; AVERTS CRISIS WITH U. S.

Carranza Modifies Decree Imposing Excessive Levy on American-Owned Properties

By the Associated Press

Washington, Aug. 17.

The threatened crisis in the relations of Mexico with the Entente Allies and the United States apparently has been averted by a modification of the new Mexican oil tax decree by President Carranza.

It was learned today that on August 12, Carranza, in effect, canceled provisions of the decree of July 31, under which undeveloped oil lands might be seized by the Mexican Government upon failure of their owners to make declarations and submit to what they regarded as excessive taxation.

LOSSES OF 110TH PROBABLY HEAVY, MARCH ASSERTS

FOE'S OUTER DEFENSES AT ROYE TAKEN

French Plunge to Gates of City in New Advance

DRIVE ENEMY BACK OF ROAD TO LASSIGNY

Germans Prepare to Evacuate Salient and Construct New Hindenburg Line

HAIG GAINS IN FLANDERS

British Troops Press Further Eastward in Somme Battle

Philadelphia Evening Public Ledger - 8-17-18

"It is an image that has haunted me all my life," Patch said some 90 years later, "seared into my mind". Patch was haunted, in particular, by (a) dreadfully wounded soldier who had begged to be finished off. The young man had cried out "Mother!" as he died."
(From Peter Parker's, *The Last Veteran*)

On June 26, 1918, shortly after World War I's Battle of Belleau Wood, Private Sol Segal of the 5th Marine Regiment gathered his thoughts as he sat beneath the swaying pine trees of Belleau, France and next to the grave of Roman Catholic High School alum, Walter J. Spearing. Many months before, Segal and Spearing had promised each other that if one of them fell in battle, the survivor would "console the sorrowing Mother." On captured German paper, Segal then began to write the letter (excerpt below) that, in his words, "fulfill a duty that I am bound by oath and will to perform."

"Dear Mrs. Spearing:

There is grief in my heart and in the hearts of all of my comrades for the great sorrow that this war has brought to you and to us. We all unite to express our heartfelt sympathy and condolences to the mother and family of one who has fallen in a cause as imperishable as will be the names of those who gave fallen to defend it….You are Walter's Mother – I was his inseparable friend and comrade: that makes us two kindred souls in common grief for our nearest and dearest…Beneath the green in Belleau Woods, forever connected with the "Honor of the Marines", lies Walt with two comrades, dead on the "Field of Honor". Above their graves the stately pines sway in their grandeur, an imperishable monument…Dear lady, the very thought of you in grief tears my heart….in the name of the Twenty-third Company, in the name of the Marines, I salute you and all my comrades salute you."

The pledge between Segal and Spearing, as well as the letter sent to Spearing's mother, Ellen, are certainly not unique in the long, tragic annals of warfare. However, they do serve as touching reminders of the loving bond that exists between a mother and her son, and the anguish that mothers have always endured in times of war. But it was during World War I, as well as in the years that followed, that American mothers organized for the first time in a large scale, coordinated effort.

In September of 1917, nearly 6 months after the United States entered World War I, the American War Mothers organization first formed in Indiana, and quickly spread across the country. These mothers, who had children then serving in the military, displayed a flag in their home windows with a blue star denoting the service of a child. If a son was killed in action, a gold star was sewn over the blue. These women became known as the "Gold Star Mothers", a phrase coined by President Woodrow Wilson. The American War Mothers was also very active in helping men and women in military service, as well as promoting government calls for food conservation at home. Many of these women also helped the war effort by joining the labor force and working in factories due to the shortage of men.

Following the war, the American War Mothers organization had grown to 23,000 members and assisted families who wished to have their son's bodies brought back for burial in the U.S. Also, in the early 1930's, the organization assisted the U.S. government with the "Gold Star Mothers Pilgrimages", in which the government paid the travel expenses of mothers and widows who wished to visit the European grave sites of their sons and husbands who had died during the Great War.

Shortly after receiving the letter from Sol Segal in the summer of 1918, Ellen Spearing sent a copy to J. Hampton Moore, a Pennsylvania Republican then serving in the U.S. House of Representatives, and who eventually became the mayor of Philadelphia. She sent it to Moore "to demonstrate the spirit of the boys in the district you represent", and wanted him to share it with his colleagues in Congress. The letter was then published on the front page of the August 17, 1918 *Philadelphia Evening Public Ledger*.

In 1921, Ellen and Cornelius Spearing had the body of their son exhumed from the Belleau Wood battlefield grave, shipped to the U.S., and reburied in St. Denis cemetery in Havertown. My ongoing search for the Roman Catholic High School alumni who died in World War I led me to St. Denis. Like Sol Segal had done nearly 100 years ago, I sat next to the grave of Walter Spearing and gathered my thoughts. However, there were no "stately pines sway(ing) in their grandeur" above his grave at St. Denis - just a simple grass field neatly lined with rows of tombstones and bounded by a chain-link fence. As I placed Roman Catholic High School and American flags next to Spearing's gravestone, I was surprised to see that his mother's name was not chiseled into the granite. I reconfirmed with St. Denis that Ellen is, in fact, buried there. Perhaps when she died in Philadelphia in 1943, her family did not have enough money to engrave the headstone, or Ellen may have specifically requested that her name not be added before she passed. I cannot say. But I do know that her name's absence is symbolic of the often forgotten, selfless devotion of war-mothers, not only those in World War I, but in all the wars. I could only shake my head in frustration as I stared at the gravestone. It's almost as if Ellen Spearing, the mother who ensured that her son's sacrifice would not be forgotten, had never existed.

The search for Roman's "lost boys" of World War I continues, but it has now taken on a new meaning for me. It will carry on, and many more stories are likely to emerge from it, however, my admiration and motivation will no longer be limited to the soldiers. I'm confident that we will eventually find all of their names, and we'll do it not only for them, but for their families as well – especially their mothers. And on this Mother's Day, let's not only remember Ellen Spearing, but all of the devoted, selfless, and forgotten mothers of war.

Spearing's grave at St. Denis Cemetery

AFTERWORD

After reading my essay in the Inquirer, *Father Kevin Gallagher, pastor of St. Denis parish, sent me an e-mail. He wrote: "Your recent commentary in the* Inquirer *was very well written and most inspiring. I would like you to know that I was so inspired by its content, that we have decided to have the name engraved on the stone ourselves in the very near future. Having lost my own mother, who is also buried in this very cemetery, I feel that a Mother's name missing from that memorial is something that needs to be changed. I am happy to pay for this myself. Please know of my gratitude for you taking the time to write this commentary."*

A PHILADELPHIA CHAPLAIN'S HEROIC WORLD WAR I ACTS

(Edited version published in the January 1, 2017 *Philadelphia Inquirer*)

Rev. Joseph L. N. Wolfe, 1918
(Photo courtesy of C.H.R.C. of the Philadelphia Archdiocese)

In autumn 1918, during World War I's great Meuse-Argonne offensive in France, a badly wounded young American soldier lay on his back, clutching the hand of a chaplain, Lt. Joseph Wolfe, as the priest administered last rites.

Although the battle raged around them, an eerie calm enveloped the fallen soldier as he looked up into Wolfe's eyes — knowing that they were likely the last he'd gaze into upon this Earth. The chaplain held his emotions in check, finished his prayer, and made the sign of the cross above the young soldier's body.

Wolfe's grim tasks were just beginning. Dead and wounded soldiers littered the floor of the Argonne forest. Cries for help pierced the air amid the hissing bullets, rattling machine gun fire, and exploding mortar shells. Wolfe crawled over and knelt next to another wounded American soldier, trying to help him in any way he could.

Other 28th Division soldiers, who had taken cover, were stunned by what they saw. "Calmly and without fear [Wolfe] administered to the boys who were hurt and those who were in danger," wrote fellow soldier John J. Mangan in a letter to the *Philadelphia Public Ledger* in November, 1918. "This is but one instance of the work of this noble priest that the boys who were out there were able to see." A wounded soldier told Mangan that Wolfe "spent three days on the line without a bite to eat ... out there in the thickest of the shelling, not knowing the minute when it would come his turn."

My continuing search for the Roman Catholic High School alumni who gave their lives in World War I led me to the heroic story of Rev. Joseph L.N. Wolfe. I had come across numerous newspaper articles lauding Wolfe's acts of bravery during the Great War and unexpectedly discovered that he graduated from the historic school in 1899.

Born in Philadelphia in 1881, and raised in the city's old Logan Square section, Wolfe pursued theological studies at St. Charles Borromeo Seminary following Roman, and was ordained a priest in 1906. He was serving as assistant pastor at St. Patrick's Church in Rittenhouse Square when the United States entered World War I in 1917. Wolfe enlisted at the age of 35 and was assigned as a chaplain in the 110th Infantry Regiment in the 55th Infantry Brigade of Pennsylvania's 28th Division.

Wolfe saw some of the bloodiest fighting of the war as his division fought in nearly every major U.S. Army engagement: Champagne, Marne,

Marne-Aisne, Aisne-Oise, Meuse-Argonne, and Metz. His letters home, frequently published in the *Catholic Standard and Times*, not only revealed the horrors of war, but also the incredible bravery of American soldiers.

"During these days of terrible fighting there were many acts of heroism performed," Wolf wrote. "Litter bearers bravely running out on the battle-field to carry in the wounded, ambulance drivers disregarding their own safety, boldly driving their machines over roads exposed to enemy view and often under shell fire. ... Then there were the runners, often mere boys, stationed every few hundred yards to relay messages back and forth. And they ran and delivered their messages, taking amazing risks, sometimes giving up their lives in the effort."

But it was Wolfe's own heroic exploits that won him the admiration of the 28th Division soldiers. The *Public Ledger* referred to him as the "Father Duffy of the 28th" in deference to the nationally known Father Francis Duffy of New York's famed Irish-American 69th Infantry Regiment. Soldiers returning to Philadelphia continually praised Wolfe for his courage under fire.

"That man is right up in the front lines all the time, encouraging and administering to the boys," said Capt. James McMonigle in the *Ledger*. "I've seen him stay out for days at a time under fire, administering the rites of his Church to the boys and burying the dead. I've laid with him in a ditch at times for hours. If a man deserves a monument, and a big one, for bravery, it is our chaplain." For his gallantry in battle, Wolfe was awarded the Citation Star, WWI's equivalent to the Silver Star, by General of the Armies John J. Pershing.

Upon returning home to Philadelphia in May 1919, Wolfe consoled many grieving parents who wanted to learn of their son's final moments. Over the years, he delivered sermons at numerous memorial services throughout the city, and remained active in veterans' affairs. In 1926 Wolfe was selected as the national chaplain of the American Legion on the first ballot.

Wolfe also served as pastor in the West Philadelphia parishes of Saint Barbara's and Saint Gregory's. He died in 1949 at age 67 and is buried at Holy Cross cemetery in Yeadon.

As we approach the 100th anniversary of America's entry into World War I, Wolfe's words in 1919 during a war memorial service at St. John's Church in Philadelphia's Manayunk section still resonate today. He stated that America betrays her war dead and abandons her principles if "she harkens to the clamor of selfish men for material gain … and fails to bring liberty and justice to all without exception, fails to insist that the rights of small nations be respected or that the principle of self-determination be applied to all."

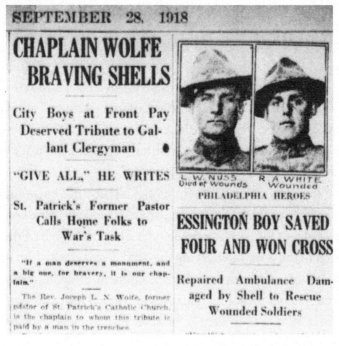

Philadelphia Evening Public Ledger - 9-28-18

AFTERWORD

Unfortunately, the warning from Rev. Joseph Wolfe in 1919, that 'America betrays her war dead and abandons her principles if "she harkens to the clamor of selfish men for material gain …"', has fallen upon deaf ears. In the last 4 years alone, the following members of the U.S. House of Representatives have either been convicted of financial crimes or plead guilty: Corrine Brown (D-FL) was convicted in 2017 on 18 felony counts of wire and tax fraud, conspiracy, lying to federal investigators, and other corruption charges, Chaka Fattah (D-PA) was convicted in 2016 on 23 counts of racketeering, fraud, and other corruption charges, Dennis Hastert (R-IL) Speaker of the United States House of Representatives pleaded guilty in 2016 for illegally structuring bank transactions related to payment of $3.5 million to quash allegations of sexual misconduct with a student when he was a high school teacher and coach decades ago, and Michael Grimm (R-NY) pleaded guilty in 2016 of felony tax evasion. These are but a few examples of financial crimes among our elected government officials, Republican and Democrat, since 2016. To list them all since the end of the Great War would likely require an additional 15-20 pages. It seems that some of our elected officials have, in fact, abandoned America's principals, and betrayed our war dead.

THE DOUGHBOYS OF ST. COLUMBA'S

(Edited version published in the April 6, 2017 *Philadelphia Inquirer*)

The World War I Memorial Plaque at St. Columba (Chris Gibbons photo)

It was Thanksgiving Day, November 27, 1919, and the Solemn Military Memorial Mass for the doughboys of Philadelphia's St. Columba parish had just concluded. The attendees, led by an armed guard and color bearers, two from the Army and two from the Navy, filed out of the beautiful church and gathered in the school yard at 24th and Lehigh.

The December 6, 1919 *Catholic Standard and Times* noted that during the Mass, seats were reserved in the middle aisle for the members of the families of the twenty seven boys of the parish who gave their lives during the Great War, and now these same family members were accorded the area closest to the cloaked structure now positioned at the front of the school yard. The late-autumn chill and overcast, sullen grey sky not only reflected the somber mood of the crowd, but many of the faithful likely believed that on this day, even God was sad. A ten year old boy stood next to the structure. A respectful silence fell among the crowd, and some wiped away tears, as the sorrowful eyes of the parishioners fell upon the boy. They knew why he had been chosen to unveil the large memorial tablet in honor of the St. Columba's doughboys who fought in World War I.

———

St. Columba's parish was founded in 1895, and the beautiful Gothic church at 24th and Lehigh was constructed in 1904. The parish was primarily comprised of Irish immigrants from the surrounding neighborhood known as "Swampoodle." I visited the church, now known as St. Martin de Porres, in March of 2014, and as I glanced up at its facade the Irish heritage of the masons and original parishioners was readily evident within the Gothic architecture of the building itself. High above the main entrance was a huge Celtic Cross, and just under it was a statue of St. Columba, the Irish missionary and Patron Saint of Derry. Statues of St. Brigid and St. Patrick also adorned the front exterior, and as I glanced up at them, I thought I heard my grandfather's voice, with his thick Irish brogue, whispering in the wind: "Ya see...the saints are lookin' down upon ya, lad." Although I knew it was just the wind and my imagination, I smiled anyway and softly answered, "I hope so, Grandpop."

My search for the Roman Catholic High School alumni who gave their lives in World War I had stalled, and it led me to St. Columba's that day. My father, an alumnus of both St. Columba's parochial school and Roman, suggested that I head down to the old church for some new leads. "There's a big monument in the vestibule", he told me. "It has the names of all of the guys from the parish who fought in World War I, and it also lists the ones who were killed. St. Columba's was a big feeder parish to Roman back then. Some of them might have gone to Roman."

I entered the church and was immediately struck by its beauty. Ornate stone, tiles, and brick trimmed in gold and green lined the walls and ceilings, with elaborate carvings, statues, and stained glass throughout the interior. I entered the vestibule and there, on the far wall, was the largest World War I Memorial tablet I had come across thus far. The December 6, 1919 *Catholic Standard and Times* described it as "a beautiful massive bronze tablet, 4 feet high and 6 feet wide, said to be the most elaborate of any erected in the city, and which is the gift of the parishioners." Carved upon the tablet are the names of the 486 members of the parish who served in the armed forces during the Great War. A special section contains the names of the 27 boys who gave their lives. My father turned out to be right, as subsequent research revealed that one of the boys killed, Frank T. Schommer, was a Roman alum. However, there were two names among the 27 that immediately caught my attention: Charles J. Fischer and John J. Fischer. I couldn't help but wonder if they were related.

⸻

Ten year old Joseph Fischer stood at the front of St. Columba's school yard that Thanksgiving Day in 1919, and unveiled the Memorial Tablet that held the names of the doughboys of St. Columba's, including his brothers, Charles and John. A street parade of the parish soldiers who returned home under the command of Lieutenant Joseph Yates followed the unveiling ceremony, and the women of the parish held a banquet that evening for the doughboys. But for the parish families of the boys who never returned, the moment was bittersweet. The parents of St. Columba's Daniel Lee wrote a poem about their son that was published in the Philadelphia Inquirer just one month before the unveiling of the Memorial tablet that conveys the deep sense of loss and anguish these families must have endured:

> *"A precious son from me was taken,*
> *A voice we loved is still,*
> *A wound within my heart is sealed,*
> *Which never can be healed,*

To France he went a volunteer,
His love, his life was given,
His body was not returned to me,
But his soul was sent to heaven."

Private Daniel E. Lee, of Philadelphia's 315th Infantry Regiment, is buried at the St. Mihiel American Cemetery in France.

Facade of St. Columba Church, now St. Martin de Porres (Chris Gibbons photo)

AFTERWORD

After I obtained the names from the plaque of the 27 parishioners from St. Columba who gave their lives in World War I, I was actually quite surprised to find that only one, Frank T. Schommer, was a Roman alumnus. I expected that there would be several.

The parish has been sending students to Roman since its founding in 1895, and, now known as St. Martin de Porres, that tradition continues to this day. In 2018, after I had concluded my annual presentation to the students that details my search for Roman's WWI alumni, one of the students introduced himself to me and told me that he was from St. Martin de Porres, and he never really took notice of the plaque until my presentation. Indeed, it came as no surprise to the Alumni Association that the parish that had the most members on Roman's 2015 list of "125 Persons of Distinction" was St. Columba.

PASSING THE TORCH OF HEROISM

(Edited version published in the May 28, 2017 *Philadelphia Inquirer*)

Civil War Veterans line the parade route in Philadelphia – May, 1919
(Photo courtesy of Peter Williams: Philadelphia – the World War I Years)

It was Monday, May 29, 1911, and the students of Roman Catholic High School in Philadelphia were gathered in the 3rd floor auditorium to honor "Our Soldier Dead" in commemoration of Memorial Day. The school newspaper, *The Purple and Gold,* noted that three Union Army veterans, Captain McGuigan, Private McCue, and Comrade Early, addressed the students on the origins of Memorial Day with Comrade

Early stating that it "was instituted to commemorate and honor those heroes who died to save the Union."

The veterans then vividly recalled for the students the Battle of Gettysburg, and Early described the now famous incident during the battle in which Irish Brigade Chaplain, Father William Corby, stood on a large boulder among the soldiers. "He gathered the troops around him and addressed them as follows: 'Boys, you are going into a battle, and God only knows how many will return from it. Now, kneel down and I will give you absolution, and always remember, even when in the thickest of the fight, that the Catholic Church does not recognize a man who turns his back on the American flag.' That same rock on which he stood has been preserved, and on it now stands a bronze statue of Father Corby."

———

Within the archives of Roman Catholic High School are many remarkable documents, such as the 1878 Will of Thomas Cahill which allocated the bulk of his estate for the establishment the first free Catholic High school in the country, the personal Civil War maps and records of original school trustee, Colonel Francis J. Crilly, and a 1940 letter from President Franklin D. Roosevelt congratulating the Alumni Association on the school's 50th anniversary. However, the article from the school newspaper in which three Civil War veterans vividly described the Battle of Gettysburg is certainly one of the most fascinating I'd come across. The men were described as "three well known veterans of the G.A.R." (Grand Army of the Republic), indicating that Philadelphians of that era were likely well aware of the crucial role our city played in the Union victory, particularly the heroic exploits of a local Army regiment that was part of The Philadelphia Brigade.

The Brigade was comprised of the 69th, 71st, 72nd and 106th Pennsylvania Infantry regiments. Although most of the Brigade were Philadelphians of Irish descent, the 69th was often referred to as the Brigade's "Irish Regiment" as it was the only Pennsylvania regiment to carry a green Irish flag into battle. Unfortunately, this was during a time of great discrimination of the Irish in Philadelphia. Patrick Young, in his essay, *The Irish Regiment That Ended Pickett's Charge*, described the harsh scene at a Philadelphia train station as the regiment prepared to board for Washington: "...a mob formed around the "Paddies in uniform." One member of the regiment recalled that: "Hisses, derisive cries, and shouts of contempt were bestowed on us and on more than one occasion...bricks and stones fell thick and fast...as [we] marched through...the city of brotherly love."

At Gettysburg, the commander of the 69th was Colonel Dennis O'Kane, an Irish immigrant who had settled in Philadelphia. Ironically, O'Kane was court-martialed a few months prior to the battle for beating his commanding officer, Joshua Owen, after Owen directed lewd comments towards O'Kane's wife. But at the trial, General Winfield Scott Hancock ruled in O'Kane's favor, and because the 69th had fought courageously at the battles of Antietam and Fredericksburg, the regiment was assigned the difficult task of defending a critical position at Gettysburg along Cemetery Ridge that became known as the "Bloody Angle."

As chronicled in *Dennis O'Kane and the 69th Volunteers*, by Walter Fox, on July 3rd, 1863, the third and final day of the battle, with the Confederate regiments closing on the 69th, O'Kane climbed upon a stone wall and faced his troops. "Men, the enemy is coming," he said, "but hold your fire until you see the whites of their eyes. I know that you are as brave as any troops that you will face, but today you are fighting on the soil of your own state, so I expect you to do your duty to the utmost."

The fighting that day was among the bloodiest in U.S. history. Although decimated by the Union artillery during their assault, the Confederate soldiers still breached the Union lines. The fighting was hand-to-hand, with bayonets, rifle-butts, and fists. But the Irishmen of the 69th stood their ground, beating the Confederates back until they retreated. During the battle, O'Kane was shot in the head, and succumbed to his injuries the following day. He is buried at Old Cathedral Cemetery in West Philadelphia. A monument to the 69th now stands at Gettysburg at the very spot where O'Kane was mortally wounded.

———

After the three Civil War veterans concluded their addresses to the Roman students that day in 1911, the Memorial Day Hymn was sung by all. In keeping with a tradition that continues to this day, the students then closed the assembly with the singing of the school's Alma Mater, the *Purple and Gold*. Filled with a renewed patriotic spirit, the boys proudly sang the school song in unison, their voices drifting out the open windows of the 3rd floor auditorium, and down onto Broad Street below. However, what the boys could not have known then was that eight years from that day, many of them would be marching up that same street as returning soldiers in a homecoming parade, after fighting in a conflict whose horrors far surpassed those of Gettysburg. Nor could they have known that at least six of the boys who sang with them that day – Raymond Hummel, Louis McGinnis, Richard Currie, John Boyle, Francis Schommer, and Walter Wiegand – would give their lives in that war.

PURPLE AND GOLD 9

Through an error on the part of the printer, the names of Rt. Rev. E. Prendergast and Rt. Rev. P. R. McDevitt were omitted from the list of donors. The complete list is as follows: Rt. Rev. E. Prendergast, Rev. H. T. Henry, Rev. H. C. Schuyler, Rt. Rev. P. R. McDevitt, Rt. Rev. W. Turner, Rt. Rev. N. F. Fisher. The Faculty and the Cahill Club.

SENIOR CLASS MEETING.

On Monday, May 22d, the regular monthly meeting of the Class of Nineteen Hundred and Eleven was held in Room 35. This will probably be the last meeting of the class as a body of undergraduates.

Final arrangements for the Class Record were made. The proceeds of the Class Play, it was decided, were to be apportioned between the Athletic Association and the PURPLE AND GOLD, for the purpose of clearing up their debts.

The committee to arrange for the Class Banquet was appointed as follows: Mitchell (chairman), Toohey and Harmon. A committee on class reunions was also appointed.

Upon the motion of Mr. Pope, a dramatic association was formed, with the following officers: Business manager, stage manager and property man. So far the class has been requested to give aid to three parishes by dramatic efforts, and to these calls it has willingly responded.

DECORATION DAY EXERCISES.

On Monday, May 29th, the students assembled in the auditorium to honor "Our Soldier Dead" and were treated to interesting and informing addresses by three well known members of the G. A. R., Comrade Early, Captain McGuigan and Private McCue.

Comrade Early first gave a brief exposition of the founding of Memorial Day. "It was instituted," he said, "to commemorate and honor those heroes who died to save the Union." He then gave a short account of the Civil War, dwelling mainly on the battles fought in Pennsylvania. Very vividly he brought to our minds the scene of the battle of Gettysburg, and his description of the battle was thrilling. The awful cannonading, the falling of the wounded and dead, the fearful pursuit of Pickett's Brigade and the retreat of the Confederates were all beautifully described. His remarks on the valor of General Mulholland were received with great applause, showing how that venerable warrior was liked by the students.

"On the eve of the battle of Gettysburg, Father Corby, chaplain of the Pennsylvania Irish Regiment, gathered the troops around him and addressed them as follows:

"'Boys, you are going into a battle, and God only knows how many will return from it. Now, kneel down and I will give you absolution, and always remember, even when in the thickest of the fight, that the Catholic Church does not recognize a man who turns his back on the American Flag.' Then standing on a rock above the men, he gave them absolution. The same rock on which he stood has been preserved and on it now stands a bronze statue of Father Corby."

Captain McGuigan confirmed Comrade Early's speech and Private McCue explained and illustrated the various bugle calls used in the Army. The singing of the Memorial Day hymn, and the "Purple and Gold" by the students concluded the exercises.

AFTERWORD

Above is the Purple and Gold *article from June, 1911 detailing the addresses by the Civil War veterans to the Roman Catholic High School students. Remarkably, thanks to some meticulous research by my cousin, Mary Lee Gallagher, I later discovered that my great-great-great grandfather's brother was Colonel Dennis O'Kane.*

WORLD WAR I BATTLE DEVASTATED U.S. FORCES, BROKE HEARTS AT HOME

(Edited version published on the September 26, 2018
WHYY.org website)

HAND-TO-HAND FIGHT IN ARGONNE FOREST

Americanss Force Germans to Yield After Stubborn Contests—Line Moves Forward as Villages Are Taken

By the Associated Press

With the American Forces Northwest of Verdun, Sept. 24.

Along the entire American front the Germans made a stand yesterday, but in spite of their determined efforts to hold their positions yielded one after another to steady hammering. The sweeping advance of the first day was region of Charpentry, which continued until late in the day. The Germans left strong detachments of machine gunners flanking the town, and it was considered wise to supplement the infantry's work with that of artillery which was placed in position at midday.

In the same part of the field bitter fighting culminated in victory for the Americans along the road between Montblainville and Eclisfontaine.

Philadelphia Evening Public Ledger - 9-28-18

On September 26, 1918, the soldiers of the 28th Division, many of them from Philadelphia, nervously glanced at their watches as dawn approached. The massive artillery fire from their gunners which had begun hours before had finally ceased. H Hour was nearly upon them, and as the men in the trenches awaited the signal to "go over the top", the macabre paradoxes of war found many shaken with fear, yet strengthened by courage while stalked by Death.

For 28th Division Lieutenant Daniel Lafferty of the 109th Infantry Regiment, and Sergeant Bernard Breen of the 108th Machine Gun Battalion, both alumni of Philadelphia's Roman Catholic High School, the moment was all too familiar as they had already experienced heavy fighting during the summer. Indeed, Lafferty was slightly wounded just a few weeks before, but had returned to his regiment. It's likely that their thoughts were for the men that they would soon lead into battle, as Lafferty and Breen were well-respected Army veterans, admired for their leadership qualities. Both had served on the Mexican border in 1915, and Lafferty had received his commission a few months prior to the battle, while Breen had just been recommended for his commission. They knew that the success of the attack, and the lives of their men, depended upon how well they would lead them into battle.

A rolling fog crept through the Argonne forest as the officers told their men to get ready. Helmet straps were tightened. Field packs, gas masks, rifles, and ammunition were checked. Fighting was expected to be at close quarters, and a final order was barked to the infantry: "Fix bayonets!"

One hundred years ago, on the morning of September 26, 1918, at 5:30am, following a 6 hour Allied artillery barrage from over 2,700 guns, the largest and deadliest battle ever fought by American soldiers began: The great Meuse-Argonne Offensive. Its primary objective was to capture the Sedan-Mezieres railroad hub, Germany's main supply and communication link, which was located between the River Meuse and the Argonne Forest. The Allies believed that capturing this crucial railway hub would result in a German withdrawal from France and force them to capitulate. It would not be an easy task. Opposing the attacking Allied soldiers along this front just north of Verdun were 40 German Army divisions.

The bitterly-fought battle lasted 47 days, and ultimately resulted in the end of the Great War. It involved 1.2 million American soldiers, and by the time that it concluded, 26,277 U.S. troops lost their lives, with another 95,786 wounded – the highest number of casualties for any battle ever fought by American soldiers. Newspaper accounts of the great battle captivated an American public anxious for news from the front lines. Worried families of the soldiers agonized as they read these dispatches which not only provided horrific descriptions of the battle, but listed the mounting casualties as well.

Perhaps the most sobering revelation of my now 7-year search for the alumni of Roman Catholic High School who gave their lives in World War 1 has been the terrible suffering that was endured by Philadelphians, both the soldiers and their families, during the Battle of the Meuse-Argonne. Newspapers from that era, such as the *Philadelphia Inquirer*, the *Philadelphia Public Ledger*, and the *Catholic Standard and Times*, have been my most valuable resource in this search, and it was while poring over these newspapers from 1918 that I noticed a gradual, yet significant, change beginning with the early days of the Meuse-Argonne Offensive. The number of names on the daily published casualty lists, as well as the number of ominous stories from the front lines, slowly began to increase. In the *Public Ledger*, pictures of the dead and wounded soldiers, with their accompanying short biographies, sometimes covered a full page. The grim casualty lists which had previously been a half-column in length, gradually expanded to 3 columns.

There were also numerous heartbreaking stories of parents receiving news that two of their sons had been killed, or that a previous notification of a son's death was incorrect. And due to the archaic communication flow of that era, there were also stories of parents receiving a letter from their son after already being notified that he had been killed in battle. My two sons are the same age as the soldiers I was reading about, and many times I had to stop reading the articles to gather myself.

My search for the names of the 32 Roman alumni who died in World War 1 has determined that many lost their lives during the Meuse–Argonne offensive. On November 1, 1918 the *Philadelphia Public Ledger* reported that Bernard Breen had been "killed in action during the fighting along the Meuse." The article noted that his brother, Joseph, was an Army Captain, also serving in France.

The December 9, 1918 *Philadelphia Inquirer* revealed that Daniel Lafferty was "killed in action in the Argonne Forest." Five days later, the *Catholic Standard & Times* reported that Lafferty was killed while "bravely leading his men in the early dawn in the advance before Petit Boureuilles, near the Argonne Forest, and edifying his men by his courage…" It also stated that a letter from a fellow soldier was sent to his widow, Mrs. Esther Lafferty, that "pays a glowing tribute to the deceased as an officer and a man."

Information traveled slowly back then, and my subsequent research found that, although their families received official notifications of their deaths in late October and early December, both men had actually died on September 27 - just one day after the start of the great Offensive.

Sergeant Bernard Breen and Lieutenant Daniel Lafferty, alumni of Roman Catholic High School, who both served in the 28th Division and lost their lives on the same day, are buried in France at the Meuse-Argonne American Cemetery. Their graves are located in the same Plot, just 2 rows apart.

CHRIS GIBBONS

AFTERWORD

Further research after the publication of this essay led to my discovery of the accompanying photo of Lieutenant Daniel P. Lafferty. When I first came upon the photo, I was struck by how young Lafferty looked, and immediately thought of the quote by Herbert Hoover: "Older men declare war. But it is the youth that must fight and die."

SPACE

DON'T LET FEAR SCRUB LAUNCH TO SATURN

(Edited version published in the October 9, 1997
Philadelphia Daily News)

Cassini launches to Saturn in 1997 (NASA/JPL photo)

On Monday, October 13, 1997, NASA is scheduled to launch the Cassini spacecraft to Saturn. Named after the Italian astronomer who studied

Saturn, it is the last and greatest in NASA's long line of "superships", so named because of their size, cost, and incredible potential for scientific return. NASA has now adopted a "better, faster, and cheaper" philosophy, and subsequent missions to the planets will reflect that approach with smaller spacecraft, narrowed scientific objectives and reduced costs.

The Cassini space probe will provide us with the most comprehensive scientific investigation of the outer solar system ever conducted. It will orbit Saturn for years, studying its moons and enigmatic rings. It will also send a robotic probe named Huygens to the surface of Saturn's moon, Titan, which has an atmosphere very much like early Earth's, and could possibly harbor primitive life.

Like its predecessor spacecraft, Voyager and Galileo, Cassini is powered by radioactive plutonium. Anti-Cassini protest groups have been lobbying President Clinton and Congress to cancel the mission on the grounds that its radioactive power supply is dangerous, untested, and presents an unacceptable risk to the population.

These arguments are misguided, exaggerated, and false. Cassini's power is supplied by a radioisotope thermoelectric generator (RTG). RTG's are proven safe. There are 22 space systems still in space, or on Mars or the moon powered by nuclear power sources, including the Pioneer, Voyager, Viking, Ulysses, and Galileo spacecraft, as well as the Apollo lunar missions.

The plutonium dioxide in RTG's is contained in 72 marshmallow-sized ceramic pellets encased in layers of iridium inside a graphite impact shell, which is then inside of an aeroshell. In the two accidents involving missions carrying RTG's since the units were redesigned in 1965, no plutonium has been released.

In order to save fuel, Cassini will swing close by the Earth in 1999 and utilize an efficient "gravity-assist" maneuver. Opponents of the mission contend that a mistaken re-entry into Earth's atmosphere is a real possibility, and the result would be catastrophic. Untrue. An accident is less than a one-in-a-million possibility, and in that extremely unlikely event, the radiation dosage a person might receive is only one millirem (unit of radioactivity). Humans receive 1,000 millirems from a series of dental X-rays.

Is there risk associated with the Cassini mission? Yes, but it is not as dangerous as its opponents contend, and the scientific gain, as well as the mission's potential for lifting the human spirit, far outweighs this risk.

AFTERWORD

This essay was my first published Op-Ed piece. In the 1990's, the Philadelphia Daily News *ran a 'Guest Opinion' column in its Editorial section, and I used it for an 'educate the public' campaign being conducted by the Planetary Society. As a member of the Planetary Society, founded in 1980 by Carl Sagan, Bruce Murray, and Lou Friedman, I was keenly aware of the growing opposition to the launch of the Cassini mission to Saturn. The Planetary Society asked its members to help educate the public on the relative safety of this mission by submitting Op-Ed articles to local newspapers that countered the numerous false arguments being touted by the groups protesting Cassini's launch. Fortunately, the voices of reason prevailed as Cassini is now regarded as one of the greatest interplanetary exploration missions ever conducted. It arrived at Saturn in the summer of 2004, and explored the ringed planet, as well as its enigmatic moons, until 2017 - incredible when you consider that its primary mission was only supposed to last 4 years. Cassini revolutionized our understanding of the Saturnian system. When Cassini finally arrived at Saturn in 2004, I published another essay in the Daily News touting this achievement and reminded readers that, way back in 1997, if "the protestors succeeded in canceling Cassini, it would have been a resounding victory for fear and ignorance."*

OUR NATION STILL NEEDS ITS SPACE

(Edited version published in the July 20, 1999 *Philadelphia Daily News*)

Neil Armstrong's bootprint on the moon (NASA photo)

Sunday, July 20, 1969, 10:50pm. My brother shook me awake as I slept in my bed. The moment we'd all been waiting for had finally arrived.

"He's coming out now," my brother shouted.

We scrambled down the stairs. My family was gathered around the television, transfixed by the amazing images on the screen. A ghostly white figure, clearly standing out against the dusky gray background, effortlessly set his foot down. And then Neil Armstrong spoke those immortal words from the surface of the moon: "That's one small step for a man…one giant leap for mankind."

We sat in stunned silence as the significance of that moment began to sink in. My brother Jerry broke the silence with the perfect word: "Wow!"

To those of us fortunate enough to be alive and witness that defining moment in human history, it will forever stand out in our minds as one of the most awesome spectacles we'd ever seen. A man had walked on the surface of another world and we were actually able to watch it on live television!

The United States, reeling from an unpopular war and widespread civil unrest, momentarily basked in the glory heaped upon it by the rest of the world. A "can do" spirit permeated the country.

"Next, it's on to Mars," proclaimed Vice President Spiro Agnew.

Unfortunately, as we all know, we never did go to Mars. We also abandoned the moon, leaving the last footprint in 1972. The Vietnam War, Watergate, budget woes, and a perceived lack of public interest effectively gutted the once-proud NASA manned exploration initiative. It remains a pathetic shell of its former self, opting instead to stay within the safe confines of low Earth orbit.

My 7-year old son, Jack, asked me why we never went back to the moon or on to Mars. I didn't know what to say. Perhaps, we lost our courage, or maybe we foolishly dismissed our innate urge to explore. I felt as if we'd let his generation down.

But there seems to be a change in the air. Private space organizations are thriving, and recent public opinion polls overwhelmingly support a human mission to Mars. Perhaps a visionary leader like JFK will commit the United States to achieving such a goal by the end of the next decade.

If that day ever arrives, I know how I'll feel, because I vividly remember how I felt on that hot July evening 30 years ago today.

AFTERWORD

As I am writing this epilogue, we just recently commemorated the 50th anniversary of the Apollo 11 moon landing. My son, Jack, is now 28 years old, and although it seems that we are no closer to a return to the moon, or a human expedition to Mars, than we were in 1999, there is a glimmer of hope. I briefly refer-enced that "hope" in this essay when I wrote that "private space organizations are thriving...", but what I never fully compre-hended in 1999 was the prominent role that private space companies such as SpaceX, Blue Origin, and Virgin Galactic would play in the future. Their role in space exploration is now so extensive that it seems likely that the first human expedition to Mars will be led by the private sector in partnership with NASA.

RETURN TO THE MOON – AND ON TO MARS

(Edited version published in the January 6, 2004 *Philadelphia Daily News*)

Gene Cernan - last astronaut on the moon (NASA photo)

On December 14, 1972, Apollo astronaut Gene Cernan paused and looked out at the magnificent vista before him, and spoke the last words heard from the surface of the moon: "America's challenge of today has forged man's destiny of tomorrow. We leave as we came, and God willing, as we shall return, with peace and hope for all mankind." Cernan often laments the fact that he has the dubious distinction of being the last man on the moon, because he knows that 31 years have passed since that day, and the furthest that humans have traveled since then has been to low Earth orbit.

"It's a little disappointing", Cernan said in a recent interview. "Apollo 17 is what I called the end of the beginning." It was the end indeed - the end of America's first phase of the human exploration of space, a phase which has not been succeeded by a second. Fueled by the stirring commitment of JFK, and the competition created by the Cold War, the U.S. met its goal of reaching the moon, and then quickly abandoned it. Since 1972, space exploration has largely been left to robots, while humans have simply stayed in low Earth orbit, either in space stations or the shuttle. NASA's dreams of lunar bases, and expeditions to Mars, were quickly dashed as the nation was distracted by Vietnam, Watergate, and a general public apathy towards the space program.

However, there has been recent widespread speculation in the media that President Bush is set to announce a bold new agenda for NASA, possibly as early as his January, 2004 State of the Union address. Early indications are that this new agenda will include the establishment of a permanent base on the moon as a possible precursor to an expedition to Mars. In addition, China, still basking in the glory of launching their first "taikonaut" in October, has publicly stated that they hope to achieve a manned mission to the moon by 2020. A second "space race" just might be developing between the U.S. and China, as a wary U.S. government is well aware that China's military is heavily involved in that country's space program.

With NASA's human spaceflight program still reeling from the Columbia disaster, an announcement by President Bush which sets a bold new agenda and direction for the space program is certainly needed. A return to the moon and an eventual mission to Mars would revitalize NASA, and stimulate the U.S. economy in the form of new jobs and efficiencies gained from spin-off technologies. Solar power stations established on the moon could beam back energy directly to receiving stations on the Earth, or to orbiting satellites. "Enough lunar solar power can be imported Earthward to supply the world's population of 10 billion people to meet all basic human needs," says advocate David Criswell, director of the Institute for Space Systems Operations at the University of Houston in Texas. The moon also has minerals, and the establishment of a permanent lunar base could help facilitate mining operations on the moon, or this base could serve as a jumping-off point for mining missions to the mineral rich asteroids. The moon is also an ideal place to set up an astronomical observatory, and discoveries made there could far surpass those made by the Hubble Space Telescope.

In addition, the lessons learned from a new lunar exploration program would serve as a technological training ground for a mission to Mars. Our robot probes have shown that the Red Planet once had large amounts of water, and possibly harbored life. We need astronauts to determine what happened to Mars that turned it into a frozen and apparently lifeless desert, so that the same fate does not befall the Earth.

We are explorers by nature, and always have been. It's time for us to leave the safe confines of Earth orbit, and begin the second phase of the human exploration of the solar system. This will stimulate the economy, fire the imaginations of our children, enhance our knowledge of the universe, and could possibly answer the question of the ultimate fate of humanity here on Earth. Let's fulfill the promise of Gene Cernan as he left the lunar surface and return to the moon, but this time, let's stay.

AFTERWORD

On March 26, 2019, Vice President Mike Pence spoke at a meeting of the National Space Council in Huntsville, Alabama and said that "it is the stated policy of this administration and the United States of America to return astronauts to the moon within the next five years." That's quite a remarkable statement when you consider that the Trump administration's budget requests to Congress do not include any substantial increases to NASA, so how this goal can be achieved by 2024 has me puzzled. In fairness to the current administration, since the 2004 publication of this essay, I have heard similar proclamations from the Bush and Obama administrations, but on a much less aggressive timeline.

I am confident that we will fulfill the promise of Gene Cernan and return to the moon someday, but I highly doubt that it will occur any time soon. I sincerely hope that I am wrong.

SPACE EXPLORATION AND THE LESSONS OF CHINA'S HISTORY

(Edited version published in the March 12, 2004 *Philadelphia Daily News*)

Chinese rover explores the far side of the moon in 2019 (CNSA photo)

President George W. Bush's recent announcement of a return to the moon and an eventual mission to Mars has stirred quite a debate among elected officials and the general public, with critics and proponents both weighing in with their opinions on the new space exploration initiative. Public opinion polls give only a slight edge to support for a manned moon/Mars expedition.

"Does he (Bush) propose to cut Medicare, education, environmental pollution, and other areas, in order to finance the space initiative? Or does he propose not to finance it and simply to allow deficits to become even larger, with adverse consequences down the road for the economy and the standard-of-living of average families?", asked Robert Greenstein, executive director of the Center on Budget and Policy Priorities. Dick Gephardt, the former House Democratic leader, recently stated that "rather than going off on some diversionary mission that may not even fit into our space program, we need to pay attention to what's going on here."

However, some advocates of Bush's plan said the United States must continue to push the envelope of space exploration to avoid falling behind other nations that are now developing their own space programs, particularly China.

"The Chinese have just recently put a man in space, and they have a goal to go to the surface of the moon within five years, or to go to at least an orbit of the moon within five years," Rep. Nicholas Lampson, a Houston Democrat, whose district includes the Johnson Space Center, said in a recent radio interview. "That's a fairly fast goal. And I hope that we are not a nation that gets to sit back and say, 'Ah, been there, done that.' Let's say, 'We're better than that, and we can be there too.'"

Clearly, we're a nation divided on this issue. However, the concerns raised here are not without historical precedence, and, coincidentally, we need only to look back through the history of our new space competitor for parallels to the current space exploration initiative debate.

In the 15th century, Zheng He, the great Chinese maritime explorer, was commander of an incredible expeditionary fleet which consisted of 28,000 men and 300 ships. Zheng He's command vessel was enormous, measuring nearly 400 feet with nine masts and 12 huge sails. It dwarfed the largest European ships of that era, which were only 1/4 the size. Comparatively, the later Columbus expedition to America consisted of 180 men and only 3 ships, with the largest being the 85 foot Santa Maria. However, just as Zheng He was set to embark upon a circumnavigation of the globe with his massive fleet, the rulers of China decided to focus exclusively upon internal affairs such as food shortages, civil unrest, and disease. The Confucian leaders dropped their support of Zheng He's fleet and forbid all further sea voyages. China isolated itself, and the Europeans took the lead in maritime exploration.

The benefits to the European community resulting from these expeditions were undeniably significant. Scientific innovations, trade benefits, land acquisition, and economic and military power were all realized by the Europeans through these ventures. China became mired in internal strife and civil war and has only recently begun to emerge from their self-imposed exile.

We find ourselves at a similar, crucial point in history. Do we focus our energies exclusively on internal issues, as advocated by Greenstein and Gephardt? Or do we finance the bold initiative outlined by Bush? The answer is clear. We should not do as China did and shrink from the challenge that space exploration presents to us. The risks that we take in undertaking this endeavor are evidenced by the Challenger and Columbia memorials. However, America has never shrunk from challenges before. The benefits to our society in supporting the new manned exploration initiative would be enormous. Indeed, a study conducted in the early 1980's by Chase Econometrics, an economic consulting firm, concluded that every dollar spent by the U.S. on the space program resulted in an eventual return of $8 dollars to the economy in the form of new jobs, new technologies, and efficiencies gained via the deployment of those new technologies.

China has boldly stated that they intend to send an expedition to the moon, possibly within the next ten years. Apparently, they have learned the lessons from their own history. The question now becomes: Have we?

AFTERWORD

Bold proclamations of achieving stupendous space exploration goals within a defined time period are not exclusive to the United States, as evidenced by the Chinese declaring in 2004 that they intended to send a human expedition to the moon within ten years. Of course, China never did achieve that goal as it's likely they realized just how difficult such an endeavor would be. However, their moon exploration ambitions since 2004 have not dimmed. As I am writing this epilogue in early 2019, China's moon exploration program achieved something that no other nation has previously accomplished: the landing of a robotic probe and rover on the far side of the moon. I still stand by my essay, and passionately believe that a strong space program is not only essential to our nation's continued growth and future viability, but our continued leadership on the world stage as well. American astronaut Leroy Chiao summed it up best in his 1-8-19 CNN editorial: "Now we have come to the moment of China's ascendency in space exploration. We must face the reality that it has, in a small but significant way, shown the world that it can be the first to accomplish things in space, too. We had better realize this soon, or we may very well wake up to find that we are no longer top dog in the space business. And if we don't learn from our complacency in space, we could end up losing our edge in other areas as well."

TO SATURN, IN SEARCH OF THE UNKNOWN

(Edited version published in the July 20, 2004 *Philadelphia Daily News*)

Image of Saturn captured by Voyager 1 (NASA photo)

"Somewhere, something incredible is waiting to be known." (Carl Sagan)

Humans are explorers by nature. We always have been. Our pursuit of knowledge, has taken us from the deepest depths of the ocean to the outer reaches of the solar system. It is this need to know, this instinctive desire to see for ourselves what's on the other side of a distant ridge or ocean that continues to resonate within us, and drives us onward in our quest. Indeed, the great explorers in our history are held in such high regard that they have achieved near mythical status in our culture. Columbus, Magellan, Cook, Lewis, Clark, and Shackleton were the physical embodiment of our exploratory spirit and they are revered for their courage and fortitude in seeking the unknown. As we read of their journeys, a part of us wishes that we could have been there with them.

However, there are too many of us today who tend to think of the great age of exploration as a bygone era whose heady days are long gone, and reverberate only in the pages of history. That couldn't be further from the truth. While it is true that humans are physically no longer at the forefront of exploration, our robot emissaries have the capability to explore places that are impossible for us to travel to. One such remarkable robot, after a 7 year voyage, finally reached its destination in the early morning hours of July 1st.

The Cassini spacecraft, a joint mission between NASA and the European Space Agency (ESA), is the largest and most complex interplanetary spacecraft ever launched. With its complex array of scientific instruments and cameras, the 6 ton probe will conduct a four year investigation of Saturn, its enigmatic rings, and numerous, icy moons. Later this year, Cassini will also release the ESA designed Huygens probe to land on the surface of the most mysterious of Saturn's moons, Titan. Titan is the only known moon in the solar system that has a substantial atmosphere which has kept its surface hidden from our view, and there is a slim possibility that it could harbor primitive forms of life. Earth based radar observations have led scientists to believe that oceans of liquid ethane and methane may exist on Titan. For this reason, the Huygens probe was designed to float and, if all goes well, it should send back some of the most stunning images from the entire mission.

Because solar power is not feasible in the outer solar system, Cassini is powered by radioactive plutonium pellets called RTG's. As a result, it was launched amid a storm of controversy as anti-nuke groups campaigned for Cassini's cancellation. Fortunately, NASA and other pro-space groups launched a counter-campaign of their own that conclusively demonstrated the safety and reliability of the RTG's. Had the protestors succeeded in canceling Cassini, it would have been a resounding victory for fear and ignorance.

On July 1st, Cassini had one more major task it had to accomplish before its primary mission could begin. A critical 96 minute engine burn worked flawlessly to place the spacecraft in orbit around Saturn. It was a white-knuckle moment for scientists and space exploration enthusiasts around the world. Had it failed, the $3 billion dollar mission would have been lost.

Cassini is not just an object of cold metal, wires, and microchips. It is a manifestation of the instinctive human desire to see the unseen, and know the unknown. Because of the technological advancements we've made, as the pictures and data come streaming across the internet, we have the unprecedented benefit of accompanying a great explorer as a new world is encountered for the first time. Past generations could only dream of such things. All of us now become the explorers. We can't be sure of exactly what we'll find in our exploration of Saturn, but of one thing we are certain: Something incredible will be discovered, and all of us will be there to see it.

AFTERWORD

Cassini successfully completed its reconnaissance of the Saturnian system, and on September 15, 2017, after NASA intentionally placed it on a trajectory to plunge into the ringed planet, Cassini burned up in the atmosphere, and thus minimized the risk of any potential contamination of Saturn's intriguing moons. Cassini revolutionized our understanding of Saturn and its moons. It deployed the European Space Agency's Huygens probe to the surface of the moon, Titan, and the pictures from its surface electrified the space exploration community. Cassini also discovered geysers of water-ice erupting from the south pole of the moon, Enceladus. Largely based upon Cassini's discoveries, many scientists now believe that both Titan and Enceladus could harbor microbial life.

It would have been an epic tragedy for science if that small group of misguided protesters succeeded in cancelling the Cassini mission in 1997.

CHASING THE DEMON

(Edited version published in the May 2, 2006 *Philadelphia Daily News*)

Test pilot Scott Crossfield (NASA photo)

"There was a demon that lived in the air. It lived at Mach 1. They said whoever challenged it would die. They built a small plane, the X-1, to try and break the sound barrier. Men came to the high desert of California to ride it. They were called test pilots. And no one knew their names."
(Tom Wolfe – The Right Stuff)

The test pilots referred to it as "the demon." To the public, it was simply referred to as the sound barrier, the hypothetical wall that would not allow planes to exceed the speed of sound (742 mph). Many scientists believed that the sound barrier would never be broken. The brave test pilots had seen the demon take the lives of their comrades whenever they challenged it. Yet, still they came by the hundreds to Edwards Air Force base in the late 1940's and early 1950's to face the demon. These were fearless young men who had flown combat missions during WW II and the Korean War, so when the demon flashed an evil smile at them, as if to say "I have you now!", it was now the demon who had reason to fear, for these men smiled back.

Scott Crossfield was one of those test pilots. Crossfield was a fighter pilot in WW II, and later became one of the best test pilots ever seen at the testing grounds of Edwards Air Force base in California. During his time there he flew nearly all of the dangerous, experimental planes, and in 1953 Crossfield became the first man to fly at twice the speed of sound. He was also the first man to fly the legendary X-15 rocket plane to the edge of space. Because Crossfield passed an altitude of 50 miles during some of his X-15 flights, he was given "astronaut" status even though he never flew for NASA. And, in one of the most remarkable aviation moments ever filmed, Crossfield was seated in the cockpit of the X-15 during a ground test of a new engine when it suddenly exploded. The engine was fully fueled at the time, so it was akin to sitting next to a bomb. Incredibly, he survived and later flew the plane again with the new engine.

The aircraft and technologies that were being tested at Edwards during this time would ultimately clear the way for America's manned space program, and eventual landing on the moon. Some of the first U.S. astronauts, like Gordon Cooper and Gus Grissom, were former test pilots at Edwards, and they became relatively famous and well known. The most famous test pilot was Chuck Yeager, but that was only due to the popularity of the book and movie, *The Right Stuff*. Yeager was largely unknown by the public until the publication of the book. Most of the test pilots who routinely put their lives on the line lived in relative obscurity. As Tom Wolfe stated in his book, no one knew their names.

Last Wednesday, during a thunderstorm in the skies over northern Georgia, the single engine plane piloted by Scott Crossfield crashed and he was killed. A resident near the crash site was sitting on his porch when he saw the plane get hit by lightning. One can't help but see the tragic irony of his death. Scott Crossfield routinely flew in some of this country's most dangerous and risky test missions. It's hard to believe he was killed while flying a simple, single engine prop plane.

Former space shuttle pilot Bob Crippen has a different perspective. "Nobody knows how he's going to exit this world, but going out flying would probably be the way Scott would have picked to exit."

Perhaps the demon had finally exacted his revenge on the man who helped relegate it to a harmless mythical status. It must have thought it would have the last laugh as it hurled a lightning bolt at the little plane. I can just imagine the puzzled look on the demon's face as Scott Crossfield shook a defiant fist and flashed a familiar smile as his plane hurtled towards the ground. How foolish of the demon to expect anything less, for it could not comprehend that Scott Crossfield and his fellow test pilots were never afraid to die.

AFTERWORD

It was sometime in 1980, and, as I sat on a crowded SEPTA bus leaving center-city Philadelphia, the man sitting next to me was reading The Right Stuff *by Tom Wolfe. I had no idea what the book was about prior to that day, but I glanced over at the page he was reading and started to read. I was fascinated, and hooked. Wolfe's prose was captivating, and I wanted to grab the book from the man's hands as he got up to leave when the bus arrived at his stop. I bought the book the next day and couldn't put it down. Apparently, the country couldn't as well. It was a N.Y. Times bestseller, praised by critics, and won the National Book Award for Nonfiction. When I read the news of Scott Crossfield's death, the voice of the narrator from the 1983 movie kept repeating in my mind: "No one knew their names." To understand why these test pilots possessed "the right stuff", as Wolf called it, he eloquently wrote in the book "…the idea here (in the all-enclosing fraternity) seemed to be that a man should have the ability to go up in a hurtling piece of machinery and put his hide on the line and then have the moxie, the reflexes, the experience, the* coolness, to pull it back in the last yawning moment—and then to go up again the next day, and the next day, and every next day, even if the series should prove infinite—and, ultimately, in its best expression, do so in a cause that means something to thousands, to a people, a nation, to humanity, to God." The poor demon. It never stood a chance, for it had no idea who it was up against.

LET'S SCRAP THE SHUTTLE NOW

(Edited version published in the June 30, 2006 *Philadelphia Daily News*)

Space shuttle Discovery launch (NASA photo)

With the space shuttle Discovery set to launch tomorrow, the U.S. now resumes its human spaceflight program after being grounded due to the dangers caused by falling foam insulation. It was a piece of falling foam that damaged the tiles of the shuttle Columbia, causing it to burn up on re-entry into Earth's atmosphere in 2003.

NASA engineers are confident that they have significantly reduced the possibility of another accident involving the foam, and this flight, technically considered a "test-flight" by NASA, will go a long way in determining how long NASA continues to use the remaining shuttles. The shuttle fleet is scheduled to be grounded in 2010 so NASA can concentrate on the development of the next-generation vehicle, which will hopefully carry astronauts back to the moon around 2018.

But such an expedition could be made much earlier if NASA were to ground the shuttle fleet now and dedicate the necessary resources to the new spaceship. The shuttle program has become a waste of money and has been plagued by cost overruns and delays since its inception. Originally hailed as an efficient and economical access to earth orbit, the program has since become a bottomless pit of taxpayer dollars.

It costs about $300 million for each shuttle launch, and NASA has spent over $1.2 billion on upgrades to the shuttle since 2003. NASA consistently cites commitments to foreign partners in the development of the International Space Station as the primary reason for continuing the shuttle program until 2010. But there is growing suspicion that the real reason is sustaining the complex internal bureaucracy that NASA has built around the shuttle. In addition, some contend that the shuttle contracts with Boeing and Lockheed have created a situation in which these large contractors now cast an ominous shadow over key NASA shuttle decisions.

The only noble and worthwhile mission left for the shuttle would be the repair of the Hubble space telescope. The aging Hubble, one of the greatest scientific instruments ever created, has revolutionized our exploration of the cosmos. But, it is in desperate need of repairs that can only be performed by space-walking astronauts. NASA is reluctant to save the Hubble because it regards such a mission as "too risky" for the astronauts. Former NASA engineer Bob Zubrin, now head of the Mars Society, believes that NASA's credibility is at stake. "The Hubble cost around $4 billion, about the same as a nuclear aircraft carrier. Imagine the captain of a navy nuclear aircraft carrier who returned with the following report: 'The ship developed a leak. We might have saved her by sending seven volunteers below to patch her up, but the odds in their favor were only 50-1. So we decided it would be best to just give up the ship.' Such an officer would be court-martialed."

If we're afraid of the risk involved in repairing the Hubble, how can we possibly have the courage to send astronauts to the moon and Mars? We have become a "risk averse" society, and our nation's future might very well be at stake if we continue to adopt this dangerous philosophy. I certainly agree that we cannot continue to put the lives of our astronauts at risk by sending them to low earth orbit for a few days to help build a space station that still has no clearly defined purpose. But history is replete with examples demonstrating that true exploration is immensely beneficial to the society that embraces it, and is well worth the risk.

The unmanned probes that NASA has sent to the planets have transformed our understanding of the solar system, and a new manned space exploration initiative will hopefully take astronauts out of low earth orbit to explore the moon and Mars. But the space shuttle is diverting space science funds, and delaying the human exploration of the solar system. We could have astronauts back on the moon by 2010, and walking across the sands of Mars by 2018 if we cut the shuttle program now. Let's scrap the shuttle program after one final mission to repair the Hubble, and get on with exploring the solar system.

AFTERWORD

Five years after the publication of this essay, the space shuttle program was finally terminated in July, 2011. It's now early 2020 and American astronauts are still reliant upon Russian Soyuz rockets to take them to the International Space Station as the U.S. has yet to replace the shuttle. However, private spacecraft built by Boeing and SpaceX are poised to end that drought in 2020 when they begin to finally ferry U.S. astronauts to the Space Station. But, I still stand by my essay. The costly shuttle needed to be scrapped, but I never thought that it would take almost 9 years to introduce a replacement.

FROM THE ASHES OF APOLLO I

(Edited versions published in the January 29, 2007 *Philadelphia Daily News*, the *History Channel Magazine*, and the January 27, 2018 *Orlando Sentinel*)

Apollo 1 astronauts (l to r): Gus Grissom, Ed White, Roger Chaffee (NASA photo)

"They gave their lives in service to their country in the ongoing exploration of humankind's final frontier. Remember them not for how they died but for those ideals for which they lived."
(Inscription on Apollo 1 memorial plaque at Cape Canaveral)

It was supposed to be a relatively easy preflight test, but things had not been going well for the crew of Apollo 1. Astronauts Gus Grissom, Ed White, and Roger Chaffee had entered the Apollo capsule at 1pm on January 27, 1967, and had been plagued by a continuous series of minor glitches. The spacecraft was in a "plugs-out" test, and the plan was to go through an entire countdown sequence without an actual launch. After numerous communication problems with mission control, a frustrated Grissom remarked, "How are we going to get to the moon if we can't talk between two or three buildings!" The communication problems forced a hold in the count at 5:40 pm.

Suddenly, at 6:31pm, something went terribly wrong. Ed White said, "Fire in the cockpit." In the next 17 seconds, television monitors showed White attempting to open the hatch, but it could only open inward and the interior pressure of the cabin made a quick escape impossible. It was also tightly secured by several latches. Garbled transmissions from the crew sounded like, "We've got a bad fire – let's get out. We're burning up." Technicians tried to get to the capsule, but were driven back by the intense heat and smoke. The final transmission from the crew was a cry of pain.

It took nearly 5 minutes before technicians succeeded in opening the hatch, and nothing could prepare them for the grisly scene it revealed. The three astronauts lay dead in the charred interior of the capsule, and the heat had been so intense that Grissom and White's spacesuits were fused together. The procedure for an emergency escape was that Grissom would lower White's headrest to enable him to un-strap his harness and open the latches, and Chaffee was to shut down the spacecraft and maintain communications until exiting. The technicians found that White was nearly out of his harness, and Chaffee was still strapped to his seat. In the last moments of their lives the men had apparently followed the protocol in trying to escape rather than thrashing around in frenzied panic. That came as no surprise to those that knew them well.

An investigation concluded that faulty wiring inside the craft had been the primary cause of the fire and, during a one year program delay, NASA implemented nearly 100 design changes. The vastly improved Apollo spacecraft that resulted eventually enabled us to safely land on the moon. Former NASA flight director Chris Kraft acknowledged the sacrifice of the Apollo 1 crew. "I hesitate to say this but I have to say it. I don't think we would've gotten to the moon in the '60's if we had not had the fire."

NASA has recently unveiled its plans for returning to the moon followed by an expedition to Mars. Initial testing of the new Orion spacecraft is expected to begin within the next few years. As we start to prepare Orion for these expeditions, it's important to remember what happened 40 years ago at Launch pad 34 in Cape Canaveral, and to accept the inherent risks of our imminent explorations. Prophetically, just a few weeks before he died, Gus Grissom said, "We're in a risky business, and we hope if anything happens to us, it will not delay the program. The conquest of space is worth the risk of life."

In the southern hemisphere of Mars, three hills were discovered by the robotic Spirit rover. NASA named them the Grissom, White and Chaffee Hills. Someday in the distant future, I'm certain that an astronaut will stand at the base of these hills. I hope that he gazes up at the tiny, blue, star-like Earth shining brightly in the Martian night sky, and gives a word of thanks to the crew of Apollo 1 before he begins his exploration of the hills named in their honor. For if he knows the story of Apollo 1, he will certainly realize that he is standing on the surface of another planet because of the sacrifice of Grissom, White, and Chaffee, and the pursuit of the ideals for which they lived.

AFTERWORD

On October 6, 2007, during halftime ceremonies of the Purdue vs. Ohio State football game, Roger Chaffee was posthumously honored by NASA with an "Ambassador of Exploration Award" for helping America attain its goal of landing men on the moon. The award was a small moon rock from the Apollo 17 expedition that was encased in Lucite and mounted for public display. It was presented to Martha Chaffee, Roger's widow, and she then subsequently donated it to Purdue for their new Neil Armstrong Engineering Hall. Martha and Roger Chaffee, as well as Grissom and Neil Armstrong, were all Purdue graduates.

I had heard about the planned ceremony about a week prior and sent a copy of this essay to Leah Jamieson, Purdue's Dean of Engineering. She informed me that she gave Martha Chaffee a copy. I hope she liked it.

RECALLING A MISSION THAT UPLIFTED A NATION

A daring moon orbit ended a tumultuous 1968.

(Edited version published in the December 25, 2008 *Philadelphia Inquirer* and an updated version in the December 21, 2018 *Orlando Sentinel*)

Earth rising above the surface of the moon, as seen by the crew of Apollo 8 (NASA photo)

"And from the crew of Apollo 8, we close with good night, good luck, a Merry Christmas, and God bless all of you, all of you on the good Earth".

(Apollo 8 Commander Frank Borman, Christmas Eve – 1968)

The astronauts in the cramped capsule of Apollo 8 were astonished by the alien landscape that lay before them. Astronaut Jim Lovell said that "we were like three school kids looking into a candy store window. Our noses were pressed against the glass." For the first time in history, human eyes were gazing down on the far side of the moon. However, it was something totally unexpected that captivated the crew even more, as the beautiful blue Earth began rising above the desolate lunar landscape. Astronaut Frank Borman said that the "most awe-inspiring moment of the flight was when we looked up and there, coming over the lunar horizon, was the Earth. The Earth looked so lonely in the Universe."

This Christmas season marks the 40th anniversary of the most daring expedition in human history: the Apollo 8 voyage to orbit the moon. In mid-1968 CIA intelligence reports indicated that the Soviet Union might attempt a manned lunar mission by year's end. NASA scrambled to devise a counter mission as the U.S. was determined to take back the lead in the Cold War space race, and beat the Soviets to the moon. The Apollo 8 crew of Borman, Lovell, and Bill Anders, all former fighter pilots, readily accepted the risky and dangerous mission proposed by NASA. For the first time, astronauts would ride the powerful Saturn V rocket and venture beyond the safe confines of Earth orbit and head to deep space. Privately, NASA Director Chris Kraft only gave the men a 50% chance of returning safely.

Apollo 8's Christmas Eve broadcast from lunar orbit was the most watched television event to date. My father and my brother Jerry skipped Midnight Mass to follow the historic mission. They listened in stunned silence as the crew read from the book of Genesis. "To hear those tinny, analog voices on our kitchen radio coming from so far away…it was daring, incredible, and just awesome," Jerry told me as he remembered that night. CBS's Walter Cronkite struggled to hold back tears as the crew signed off.

1968 was a year rocked by war, assassinations, street riots, and protests. However, it closed with a cautious message of hope and optimism from the crew of Apollo 8. "The impact of seeing the Earth as a planet, as a very small, very distant, and, apparently to the astronauts, fragile-looking ball in the blackness of space… is a moment that ranks up there with any in the human species," said space historian Andrew Chaikin. The goal of the mission was to test the hardware and techniques needed to eventually land men on the moon before the Soviets. However, its unanticipated achievement was demonstrating to the world the incredible future that might await humanity, while starkly revealing the precarious nature of our existence.

In a year marred by violence and turmoil, it's ironic that 1968 might always be remembered by our descendants for the peaceful exploration of the moon by three courageous astronauts. Borman received a telegram that summed it up best. It read simply: "Thanks, you saved 1968."

The tumultuous world we live in today is very reminiscent of 1968. The wars in Iraq and Afghanistan, the social turmoil wrought by the faltering economy, and the recent terrorist attacks in India sadly remind us that little has changed in 40 years. Unfortunately, today we have no daring space mission that can help lift our spirits, but Apollo 8 did leave us with a lasting Christmas gift: an iconic image of the rising Earth that will forever remind us of humanity's potential to achieve great things in the face of overwhelming adversity.

Take a moment this holiday season to gaze at the famous photo from Apollo 8 and remember that the blue world you see is the only one we know of that has life. In this tiny little corner of the vast Cosmos, we are alone. The beautiful, but very fragile Earth that's floating in the forbidding cold and darkness of space is the only home that we have, and it's up to each one of us to make it a better place to live. Merry Christmas and Happy Holidays to all of us, all of us here on the good Earth!

AFTERWORD

This essay was my first to be published in the Philadelphia Inquirer. *Of all of the Apollo missions to the moon, I still regard Apollo 8 as the most daring because so much was riding on its success. Had the mission failed, a landing on the moon by the end of the decade would have been very much in doubt, and a failure that resulted in the deaths of the astronauts may have cancelled the Apollo program altogether. But perhaps the most unsettling consequence of a failure was revealed by author Robert Kurson in his excellent book,* Rocket Men: The Daring Odyssey of Apollo 8 and the Astronauts Who Made Man's First Journey to the Moon, *when he recounted the words of a concerned NASA official who said, "If these three men are stranded out there and die in lunar orbit, no one – lovers, poets, no one – will ever look at the moon the same way again."*

DREAMING OF JOURNEYS STARTED BY A SMALL STEP

The Apollo 11 landing still inspires hope, not despair.

(Edited version published in the July 20, 2009 *Philadelphia Inquirer*)

*Neil Armstrong stands at the base of the leg of
the lunar lander, Eagle (NASA photo)*

I found myself gazing up at the moon more frequently as the 40 year anniversary of Apollo 11 approached. The ghostly black and white TV images from that night are still permanently etched in my mind. Along with the millions around the world, my family and I watched in amazement as Neil Armstrong descended down the steps of the Eagle and onto the surface of the moon.

It was such a triumphant moment, but as I looked up at the moon recently, I could only shake my head in frustration. Apollo 11 was supposed to be the beginning of humanity's exploration of the solar system. Instead, just a few years after that momentous day, we abandoned our exploration of the moon, and the furthest that humans have traveled since Apollo has only been to low-Earth orbit. I had such great expectations for human space exploration during the Apollo missions, and it helped fuel my passion for science fiction in the years that followed. My disappointment only grew as I looked over the old science fiction books that I'd gathered over the years.

Thousands from my generation were drawn to science fiction because of the triumphant NASA missions of the 1960's and 1970's. The stories from my books, and the incredible artwork on their covers, fired the imaginations of my generation and depicted a future that all of us were seemingly destined to see. Authors like Bradbury, Asimov, and Clarke wrote of incredible adventures set in the near future in which astronauts explored the desolate caves of the moon, the mountains of Mars, or the frozen moons of Jupiter. Illustrations by brilliant space artists graced the covers of these books, and depicted space exploration scenes so detailed that they almost looked like photographs. The NASA milestones reached during the 1960's, culminating with the voyage of Apollo 11, suggested a future very much like those depicted in the stories and illustrations. Just 12 years after Sputnik, a man walked on the moon. Imagine, I thought to myself, where we would be in 40 years!

The books now gather dust in my old bookcase. Much to my wife's dismay, I refuse to throw them out, because doing so will symbolize my reluctant acceptance of the current state of space exploration. By 2009, we were supposed to have bases on the moon and Mars, mining operations on the asteroids, and astronauts exploring the moons of Jupiter and Saturn. Instead, we have aging shuttles that occasionally transport astronauts to a small space station.

Perhaps we made naive assumptions about the future. The science fiction stories didn't focus on the enormous costs of human space flight, or the apparent loss of interest by the public. Their plot lines never revolved around the negative media response, Congressional hearings, and program delays that now inevitably follow any space related accident. Our brave astronauts are certainly willing, but the policy makers no longer believe that the conquest of space is worth the cost or the risk of life. As a result, the great space explorers of today are made of metal, wire, and silicon, but not flesh and blood. They cannot die, only cease to function. But machines cannot tell us what it feels like as the sands of Mars sift through their hands, or express their astonishment at viewing the distant Earth while slowly passing by on an asteroid. Only humans can convey these things.

I now realize that I've been quite fortunate. I actually saw men walk on the moon. Our robot probes have shown me the icy surface of Mars, the methane seas of Titan, and the frozen ocean of Europa. The only thing missing is that a human is not standing in any of those photos. The future that I imagined has simply not yet come to pass, but it will. The human spirit of exploration will once again reassert itself, it's just taking a little longer than I expected. NASA's even planning to return astronauts to the moon by 2020, and maybe Mars by 2040.

My frustration is slowly giving way to hope, and as I gaze up at the moon now, I smile as I think of another advantage that we humans have over machines. We have a way to continue on long after we've "ceased to function."

So, I'm going to dust off the covers of my books, give them to my two sons, and tell them: "I didn't get to see these things, but I'm confident that someday you, and your children, will see them for me."

AFTERWORD

Of the numerous science fiction stories that I had read as an adolescent and teenager in the 1970's, I cannot recall any that foretold a future in which space exploration would be dominated by our robots. Of course, there was HAL from 2001: A Space Odyssey (based on Arthur C. Clarke's short story, The Sentinel), but he was exploring space in tandem with the astronauts on board their doomed "Discovery" research vessel. And, although our current machines do not possess the sentience of HAL, none of the stories that I read predicted anything like the incredible discoveries and vistas that have been revealed to humanity by the Voyager, Viking, Cassini, Galileo, Huygens, and New Horizons space probes. Consequently, my initial feelings of disappointment at the pace of human space exploration have nearly diminished as our robotic probes, with their incredible, sophisticated cameras, often times make me feel as if I am on board the spacecraft with them! That being said, I do sincerely hope that I live long enough to see a human walk on the surface of Mars, which is a far cry from my expectations as a teen, when I thought, by this time in my life, I would have seen astronauts surfing the seas of Titan. Perhaps, my grandchildren will.

THE LAST OF THE GREAT AMERICAN ASTRONAUTS?

**The space program has to inspire the public again.
A mission to Phobos could do that.**

(Published in the July 8, 2011 *Philadelphia Inquirer*)

The Martian moon, Phobos (NASA photo)

On April 12, 1981, as astronauts Bob Crippen and John Young soared into a strikingly blue Florida sky aboard the Columbia for the first space shuttle flight, the hopes of NASA's manned space exploration program soared along with them as it rode a wave of public enthusiasm and support. NASA seemed to have a clearly defined 25-year plan for the exploration of the solar system: Utilize the reusable, and cost-saving space shuttle for multiple earth-orbital flights to construct a space station, which would then serve as a "jumping-off" point for flights to the moon, and finally, culminate in an ambitious manned expedition to Mars.

Unfortunately, NASA's bold exploration plans of 30 years ago never materialized. The supposedly "economical" space shuttle turned out to be anything but, the Reagan administration's grandiose space station was significantly scaled back, and plans for returning to the moon and a mission to Mars touted by both Bush administrations were eventually scrapped. Consequently, as the space shuttle era comes to an end with the final flight on Thursday, America's manned exploration program finds itself at a crossroads.

NASA's hopes now ride upon the directive of the Obama administration to rely upon Russia and the private sector to ferry astronauts to the International Space Station for the next several years while the agency focuses on development of a new heavy-lift rocket as well as a new spacecraft to take astronauts into deep space - the MPCV: Multi-Purpose Crew Vehicle. Current plans call for astronauts to explore an asteroid in 2025, followed by an expedition to Mars in the mid-2030's.

However, with the new space vehicles not anticipated to be ready until 2020, critics of the plan are wary of America's heavy reliance upon the private sector and Russia for human access to space, as well as the plan's vague, long-term exploration destinations. "NASA's human spaceflight program is in substantial disarray with no clear-cut mission in the offing", stated former astronauts Neil Armstrong, Gene Cernan, and Jim Lovell in a recent open letter to the Obama administration. "After a half-century of remarkable progress, a coherent plan for maintaining America's leadership in space exploration is no longer apparent."

While the former astronauts are correct in stating that we have had 50 years of remarkable progress in space exploration, we haven't progressed in every area, and the long sought goal of significantly reducing the cost of space exploration has been frustratingly elusive. The per-launch cost of a space shuttle is over $1 billion, a far cry from the hoped for $7 million per launch estimates touted at the program's inception. The Obama administration is trying to reduce those costs by incorporating the private sector and it's hoped for economic efficiencies into NASA's human spaceflight program. It's a huge gamble, and NASA has already committed billions of dollars to private firms such as SpaceX and its Falcon 9 rocket, which could potentially ferry NASA astronauts into space. However, critics of SpaceX and some of the other private firms are troubled by NASA's commitment and often cite the performance limitations of their rockets, as well as their questionable business plans.

As a 25 year member of the Planetary Society, the largest private space exploration advocacy group in the world, my major criticism of Obama's space exploration plan is that it lacks an achievable short-term destination that will capture the public's imaginations. Both Bush administrations set a return to the moon within 15 years, followed up by a mission to Mars within 30 years as their goals For NASA. It's easy to see why those plans were scrapped. Extended time-frames like that inevitably lead to public apathy and an eventual erosion of Congressional support.

Lately, the debate over the next space destination generally breaks down among three possibilities: a return to the moon, a mission to an asteroid, or a mission to Mars. But there is another potential mission that would capture the imagination of the public, could be achieved within the time-frame of an eight-year presidency, and would incorporate aspects of all three of the other possible destinations: the Martian moon Phobos.

Phobos is believed to be a captured asteroid, and a comprehensive study of its origin and composition by astronauts could help develop effective methods for deflecting an asteroid on an earthbound trajectory. Also, Phobos' low gravity and lack of an atmosphere mean a landing there would be much easier and cheaper than a Mars landing.

In addition, its proximity to Mars would enable astronauts to conduct detailed studies of the Martian atmosphere and surface. Current technology makes such a mission achievable, and it would require only a small increase in NASA's budget, which amounts to a miniscule 0.6 percent of the overall federal budget.

As we look back on the legacy of the space shuttle, it's important to remember the hope that surrounded the first launch of Columbia back in 1981. We need to rekindle that optimism with an achievable destination that will capture the public's support and imagination. Phobos is just such a destination.

AFTERWORD

A CNN.com *news article from April 3, 2019 stated that* "NASA wants to accelerate its timeline for the next moon landing while keeping its eyes on a bigger prize: Mars. The space agency aims to send astronauts to Mars by 2033, NASA administrator Jim Bridenstine said at a Tuesday congressional hearing. "We can move up the Mars landing by moving up the moon landing (to 2024)," Bridenstine told the House Committee on Science, Space and Technology. "We need to learn how to live and work in another world. The moon is the best place to prove those capabilities and technologies. The sooner we can achieve that objective, the sooner we can move on to Mars." Despite the current proclamations of the NASA administrator, I still believe that the first expedition to Mars, whenever that finally occurs, will not include a landing on the Martian surface, but will either be an orbital mission (like Apollo 8), or a landing on Phobos. We shall see.

THE IMPACT OF A SKILLED TEACHER CAN GO DEEP INTO THE COSMOS

(Edited version published in the January 15, 2012 *Philadelphia Inquirer*)

Carl Sagan and Viking lander (NASA photo)

"The size and age of the Cosmos are beyond ordinary human understanding. Lost somewhere between immensity and eternity is our tiny planetary home. In a cosmic perspective, most human concerns seem insignificant, even petty. And yet our species is young and curious and brave and shows much promise. I believe our future depends powerfully on how well we understand this Cosmos in which we float like a mote of dust in the morning sky." (Carl Sagan)

The recent news of NASA's incredible discovery streamed across the internet on December 20th: *The First Earth Sized Planets Found Beyond Our Solar System*. I have to admit that I wasn't surprised because my former teacher predicted that discoveries like this would be commonplace someday, but I thought it was ironic that this announcement was made on the 15th anniversary of his death. That night I thought about him as I gazed up into the sky. The clouds had finally broken, and the stars shimmered like jewels in the clear, crisp winter air. They reminded me of a tapestry of Christmas lights adorning the velvety- black background of space. It was an awe inspiring sight, and as I gazed up, I could still hear the familiar and distinct voice of my former teacher: "The Cosmos is all that is or ever was or ever will be."

The simplicity and power of his words still rivet me, and it's during moments of great scientific discovery that I especially miss him. Although he's been gone now for 15 years, his impact on my life, as well as the lives of millions around the world, continues to resonate to this day.

Considering that I never met Carl Sagan or sat in one of his Cornell University classrooms, some people might find it odd that I refer to him as my former teacher. But when the groundbreaking PBS series *Cosmos* premiered in September of 1980, I became a student in a Sagan classroom that had dramatically expanded to encompass millions of American living rooms. Although he was a relatively well known public figure prior to the series, primarily due to his books and frequent appearances on *The Tonight Show*, Sagan's popularity soared through *Cosmos*.

The critically acclaimed 13 part series featured Sagan as both narrator and presenter of a diverse range of topics, such as philosophy, religion, history, astronomy, and physics. Sagan's skills as a teacher were clearly evident as he helped the general public understand such complex scientific concepts as time dilation, quantum mechanics, and the theory of relativity. But the heart of the series was Sagan's unique ability to effectively communicate why these various subjects were important to humanity's understanding of, and future within, the Cosmos.

Inspired by Sagan and *Cosmos*, I finally enrolled at Drexel University, something I'd been putting off for over 2 years. I pored over the *Cosmos* companion book, acquired a telescope, and joined Sagan's newly-formed Planetary Society. Although my career path gravitated to financial services, I felt that I could still make a difference by becoming an outspoken advocate for space exploration. I wrote several Op-Ed articles which rigorously defended NASA and espoused the need to continue our exploration of space. After Sagan died, the Planetary Society posted a wall on their website where members could comment on the impact that Sagan had on their lives. I was amazed to find that there were hundreds of stories like mine, and as I read them, I couldn't help but think of the Henry Adams quote: "A teacher affects eternity; he can never tell where his influence stops."

Unfortunately, Sagan's influence, while extensive, was limited, and lately it seems that other voices are growing louder. I'm hearing the familiar cries to curtail space exploration, or prohibit the teaching of evolution in our schools. There are the loud rants of the religious fanatics who declare that God personally told them the date of the world's end, and the shouts of the pseudo-scientists who claim that the Apollo moon landings were faked. When the voices of ignorance become too loud, I know what I have to do – I'll gaze up at the Cosmos and listen for the voice of my former teacher rising above the din. The numerous stars will remind me that millions of my classmates continue to hear his voice as well, and we're prepared to defend the ideals that Carl Sagan taught us.

AFTERWORD

I received numerous e-mails from teachers in response to this essay. Perhaps the most poignant was from an 8th grade Physical Science teacher who wrote the following: "What a fine tribute you penned for your educational muse. I am a middle school physical science teacher who tries desperately to channel the engaging narrative of Carl Sagan when I see my student's eyes glaze over as I introduce the periodic chart. I do my best to explain the life cycle of stars and how essential supernovas were to arriving at our conscious state. Usually this engages a core group and they want to extrapolate on black holes, parallel universes, string theory, and the possibility of other life forms. I too worry about the influence of creationists, and do my best to quietly inform the students that science and religion are not at odds but different intellectual disciplines." I wrote back to all of them and let them know that I was heartened to find that many of my "fellow classmates" had become teachers who now pass along to future generations what all of us had been taught. Our teacher, Carl Sagan, would be proud.

NASA'S CURIOSITY ROVER: A $2.5 BILLION BARGAIN

(Edited version published in the August 3, 2012 *Philadelphia Inquirer*)

Curiosity rover captured this image of "Mount Sharp" on Mars in 2015 (NASA photo)

On Monday, August 6th, shortly after midnight, the greatest pay-per-view event in history will begin its broadcast around the globe on all of the major television news stations, as well as streamed across hundreds of internet websites. Incredibly, despite the fact that this event cost approximately $2.5 billion to produce, it has the distinction of being one of the least expensive for viewers to purchase. In fact, most of the world will get to view the event for free, courtesy of the U.S. taxpayers.

No, it's not the long awaited Manny Pacquiao vs. Floyd Mayweather boxing showdown, or a UFC 15-fight extravaganza. It's not even *WrestleMania 500*, or a *Live-Aid/Woodstock* style mega-concert. And, no,

Geraldo is not going to open another one of Al Capone's vaults. It's not taking place in Las Vegas, or Atlantic City, or in the Superdome.

As a matter of fact, this event will dramatically unfold over 142 million miles from the Earth, and its ultimate outcome could have profound implications for humanity and its place in the Cosmos. For in the early morning hours (EST) of August 6, NASA's car-sized Curiosity rover will begin its daring plunge through the atmosphere of Mars and modern technology will enable millions around the world to anxiously follow its perilous descent and subsequent extensive explorations of the Red Planet's surface.

You may be wondering – what does this NASA mission have to do with pay-per-view? Well, in reality, that's essentially what it is. Actually, it's the greatest pay-per-view bargain ever. The Curiosity rover cost U.S. taxpayers approximately $2.5 billion to develop. Now, before you cringe at that figure and join the tired chorus of critics who contend that space exploration is too expensive, let's take a look at what each of us is really paying and getting in return. Using a recent estimate of 143 million individual U.S. taxpayers, Curiosity has roughly cost each U.S. taxpayer a very modest $17.48 (it's probably less than that as the U.S. government collects taxes from other sources, such as corporate taxes). And since the rover's development costs have been spread out over 9 years, the cost per taxpayer over that time period has been about $1.94 per year. What a bargain! Sitting in the comforts of our homes, watching the mysteries and wonders of an alien planet unfold on our TV's or computer monitors for less than $2.00 per year! Heck, I once paid $50.00 for a pay-per-view boxing match only to have it end after 3 rounds because Mike Tyson bit off a piece of Evander Holyfield's ear.

According to NASA associate administrator David Weaver, the Curiosity rover is "the most sophisticated scientific system ever sent to another planet." With its nuclear power source, it has the potential to last several years and travel hundreds of miles over the Martian surface. Curiosity's suite of scientific instruments will study the climate and geology of Mars, and transmit stunning, panoramic images back to Earth. But the rover's primary goal will be to determine if the Red Planet could have ever had an environment suitable for life. If the chemical building blocks of life, or "biosignatures", are discovered, it will be one of the most profound moments in human history. If our tiny solar system has at least two planets that supported life, then it's likely that the Cosmos is teeming with life.

The success of the mission is by no means assured. The entire landing sequence, dubbed by scientists and engineers as the "Seven Minutes of Terror", is the most dangerous part. They're hoping that NASA's innovative, but entirely new "sky-crane" will successfully lower the rover onto the surface. The tension-filled wait for a positive landing signal will certainly be heart-stopping moments, full of drama.

So, if you happen to be awake after midnight on August 6, just turn on your TV or logon to the internet, and get ready for a truly exhilarating experience. Remember, if you're a taxpayer, you've already paid for it, so take this opportunity to enjoy it. Whether the mission fails or succeeds, it'll be the best $2.00 you've spent this year.

AFTERWORD

Not only did the Curiosity rover successfully land on Mars just three days after the publication of this essay, but, it's now nearly 8 years later, and it continues to rove across the surface of the enigmatic Red Planet. With its suite of scientific instruments, Curiosity has revolutionized our understanding of Mars. The mobile robot has not only found evidence of an ancient streambed, but also confirmed that the Red Planet could have supported microbial life billions of years ago. All of that at a cost $2 per taxpayer – what a bargain! And, as I am writing this in April, 2020, a new NASA Mars rover, named Perseverance, is being readied for a July, 2020 launch. Perseverance, largely built from the spare parts of Curiosity to save money, will attempt to land on the Martian surface in February 2021, and once again, it will be another "must watch" pay-per-view bargain!

A YEAR OF COMETS AND MARVELS

(Edited version published in the March 6, 2013 *Philadelphia Inquirer*)

Comet Hale Bopp captured in an image from the Ulysses
space probe (NASA photo)

"You lift your children onto your shoulders that they may better see a comet and, in so doing, join a chain of generations that stretches back far beyond the reach of written memory. There is no cause more important than protecting that ancient and most precious continuity." (Carl Sagan and Ann Druyan from their book, Comet*)*

To the ancients, the enigmatic celestial visitors that suddenly appeared in the skies were omens of doom, or warnings that the gods were angry. Many had tails that stretched across the heavens, reminiscent of a mane of hair flowing from the head of some angry, omnipotent messenger and they called them comets (from the Greek/Latin *cometes* meaning "long haired").

For thousands of years humans cowered in fear at the sight of these phenomena, and blamed them for wars, disease, earthquakes, and animal mutations. The most famous recurring comet in history, Halley's Comet, was believed to be responsible for Europe's Black Death pandemic, and Pope Callixtus III contended that the comet was an ominous message from Satan himself. As recently as Halley's appearance in 1910, gullible citizens consumed "comet pills" to save them from the poisonous Cyanogen gas streaming from its nucleus.

Indeed, the recent meteor explosion over Russia reminds us that our innate fear of certain celestial phenomena is sometimes still justified. However, humanity's gradual embrace of science and quest for knowledge over the years has determined that unless a comet is on a trajectory to crash into the Earth we have nothing to fear. Comets visible to the naked eye, while relatively rare, can be the most beautiful and stunning of all celestial events, and 2013 has the potential to be the greatest year in comet-watching history.

In early March, Comet PanSTARRS should become visible in the Northern Hemisphere's evening sky, possibly as bright as the planet Venus (the Evening Star) and trailing a long, spectacular tail. But the comet that has the entire astronomical community buzzing with excitement is Comet ISON, which will closely approach Earth in November. Current calculations indicate that ISON has the potential to be the brightest comet ever seen by humans, and could even be visible during daylight! Unfortunately, the words "could" and "possibly" often accompany discussions regarding an approaching comet's potential brightness because there are numerous factors contributing to it, such as comet size, nucleus-activity, and distance from the Earth and Sun. But based on current estimations of these factors for ISON, astronomers are cautiously optimistic that it will live up to its "once in a lifetime" billing.

Recent Earth-based and robotic probe analyses of comets have confirmed earlier assumptions that they are primordial remnants of the early solar system. In 2005, NASA's *Deep Impact* spacecraft shot an 820 pound projectile into comet Tempel 1 and analyzed the material ejected by the impact, and NASA's *Stardust* spacecraft returned dust samples to Earth of Comet Wild 2 in 2006. Surprisingly, both probes revealed lower than expected amounts of water ice, but also discovered that they were not loosely cemented rubble piles, which conflicted with the generally accepted "dirty snowball" theory of comet composition first espoused by astronomer Fred Whipple in 1950. More surprises are expected next year when Europe's *Rosetta* spacecraft will rendezvous with a comet and dispatch a lander to study its surface and composition.

Astronomers believe that ISON's composition is similar to Tempel 1 and Wild 2, and will likely survive its close swing around the Sun. They also surmise that it must be a relatively large object (maybe 2 miles across) because it was discovered while still extremely far from Earth. Both of these factors, in addition to its close approach to the Earth and Sun in November, are the primary reasons why it has the potential to be as bright as a full moon. Incredibly, two months prior to our encounter, we may get a preview of what we'll see when NASA's Mars rover *Curiosity* attempts to take a picture of ISON as it moves across the Martian skies in September. The ancients could not have imagined achieving such things!

All of us are fortunate to be living in a time when two bright comets could illuminate our skies in the same year, with one of those comets having the potential to be the brightest ever seen by human eyes. Like our ancestors, we will lift our children onto our shoulders so that they may better see these ancient celestial visitors. But unlike previous generations, we will teach our children to marvel, and not cower, at the sight of these comets and, in so doing, reinforce humanity's continuing triumph of science over superstition.

AFTERWORD

Forecasting the expected brightness of a comet is difficult and not an exact science. Early observations of Comet ISON by astronomers led to predictions of a steady increase in brightness that could eventually exceed the brightness of a full Moon. Unfortunately, Comet ISON's gradual increase in brightness dramatically slowed as it neared its closest approach to the sun (perihelion). On November 28, 2013, under great stress from the sun's energy, the comet broke up. Sky-watchers around the globe were dismayed. As for Comet PanSTARRS, it was bright, but for Northern Hemisphere observers, the setting sun often obscured it from view. However, the media hoopla surrounding Comet ISON reminded me of seeing Comet Hale-Bopp in the night skies of early 1997. It is still one of the most awe-inspiring sights of my life. And, although I feel fortunate to have witnessed such an event, I am still hopeful that I'll see another "comet of the century" within the next 20 years.

VOYAGER STILL CARRIES OUR HOPES OF FINDING THAT WE'RE NOT ALONE

(Edited versions published in the October 27, 2013 *Houston Chronicle*, and the September 5, 2017 *Philadelphia Inquirer*)

Artist rendition as Voyager 1 enters interstellar space (NASA/JPL image)

On Sept. 5, 1977, humanity stood at the shoreline of the ancient cosmic ocean that had been beckoning for generations, and with a massive, rocket-propelled heave, we hurled a kind of message in a bottle out into the vast sea of space. That "bottle" was Voyager 1.

Within its spindly metal framework was a gold-plated audio-visual disc filled with photos, music and messages from the people of Earth. Although its primary mission was to conduct a scientific reconnaissance of Jupiter and Saturn, scientists also knew there was a good chance that the probe would eventually leave our solar system someday and enter the great void of interstellar space.

Consequently, a team of scientists and engineers, led by Carl Sagan, viewed Voyager as a unique opportunity for humanity to send a greeting card into space - a cosmic message in a bottle.

And, like children on a beach, we have patiently watched our bottle slowly drift farther and farther from shore. Last month, we learned that it finally has dipped below the horizon, and we can do nothing more now than simply hope that, someday, our bottle may be found.

Voyager 1 is one of the most successful and remarkable space probes ever launched. It conducted the first detailed studies of Jupiter and Saturn, and its discoveries electrified planetary scientists. As Voyager 1 encountered the Jovian moon Io, it discovered the first active volcano outside of the Earth. It also revealed the ice-covered surface of Jupiter's enigmatic moon Europa, as well as the complex structure of Saturn's rings.

Scientists spent years poring over the trove of data transmitted back to Earth by the probe. And although they initially thought that Voyager would cease providing any valuable scientific information after its Saturn encounter in 1980, the rugged probe soldiered on.

Ten years later, Voyager took its final photo - the first "family portrait" ever of the solar system - from a record distance of 6 billion kilometers. The image became famous because the Earth appeared as nothing more than a small "pale blue dot," inspiring the title of the seminal book by Sagan.

In 1998, Voyager passed another milestone as it surpassed the distance traveled by Pioneer 10, and last month, NASA confirmed that the intrepid probe has become the first man-made object to enter interstellar space.

Voyager 1 is now heading in the general direction of the star Gliese 445 and will pass within 1.6 light years of it in about 40,000 years.

The likelihood that another space-faring civilization will someday retrieve Voyager 1 is truly remote. In that extremely unlikely event, it will probably be millions of years from now, when humanity is long gone.

But if Voyager 1 is ever found, we can only hope that those who come upon it will somehow decipher the messages we've placed within our bottle. Perhaps they will conclude that on a blue planet orbiting a very ordinary star, there once lived a society of sentient beings whose curiosity and innate desire to explore eventually led them to wade into the mysterious cosmic ocean that surrounded their home.

Perhaps they will also decipher that although the beings from the blue planet recognized that they were a deeply flawed species, one that was prone to violence and a dangerous embrace of superstition, they were also determined to overcome their demons by trying to understand the cosmos and their place within it.

What the retrievers of Voyager 1 could never comprehend is that one of humanity's primary motivations in sending this message in a bottle was something that couldn't be placed on a gold-plated disc or etched into the metal chassis of our robot emissary. It is a certain longing that has been troubling us for decades, and it chills our souls whenever we contemplate the size of the universe and the incredible number of stars and planets contained within it.

For each time we have shouted out into the deep, infinite expanse of space and listened for a reply, the only response we've received has been a disturbing silence. The bottle couldn't possibly convey that we have always felt so very alone and desperately hoped that we were not.

AFTERWORD

There are many people who proclaim that the discovery of other intelligent life in the Universe would be the single most profound moment in human history. If that were to ever be confirmed, I would have to agree. However, if through some miraculous means we were able to decisively conclude that we are the only sentient beings in the Cosmos, it would not only also be the most profound moment in human history, but, in my opinion, the most disturbing as well.

AFTER NINE YEARS, A CLOSE ENCOUNTER WITH PLUTO

(Edited version published in the July 14, 2015 *Philadelphia Inquirer*)

Photo of Pluto captured by the New Horizons space probe (NASA photo)

"The challenge of the great spaces between the worlds is a stupendous one; but if we fail to meet it, the story of our race will be drawing to its close."
(Arthur C. Clarke, Interplanetary Flight, 1950)

The tiny planet at the edge of our solar system has always eluded me. Despite the fact that I've always known that it was extremely unlikely that I would ever be able to view Pluto through my modest back-yard telescope, I have continually tried. Although it was officially reclassified as a "dwarf planet" and a "plutoid" in 2006 by the International Astronomical Union, Pluto will always be the ninth planet to me. Unfortunately, it's also still the only one of the nine original planets of our solar system that I've never viewed through my telescope. Frustrated by this inability, I have often gazed up at the area of the night sky where I knew Pluto was wandering and marveled at the immense distance that prevented its reflected light from reaching my eyes. During those moments, I've also wondered if Pluto and its secrets would ever be revealed to me, and if humanity would someday venture to the cold, distant region where this little world resides.

The secrets of this mysterious planet have not only eluded me, but the greater scientific community as well. Discovered by 23 year old Clyde Tombaugh in 1930, Pluto is about 1/3 smaller than Earth's moon, and so distant that it's been nothing but a fuzzy point of light to even the largest Earth based telescopes. The powerful Hubble Space Telescope has only been able to provide a highly pixelated smudge-image of the tiny planet that reveals very little. Fortunately, over the last several weeks, a robotic probe speeding towards Pluto has been transmitting images of this enigmatic world, and the veil of mystery shrouding it is gradually lifting. And on July 14th, after a 9 year, 3 billion mile journey, NASA's New Horizons probe will conduct a close encounter with Pluto, which will reveal this world and its moons in unprecedented detail. This mission will complete humanity's initial reconnaissance of the original nine planets, which began with NASA's Mariner 2 successful fly-by of Venus in 1962 and now culminates with the New Horizons fly-by of Pluto. There are currently no plans for another mission to that region of our solar system after New Horizons.

As expected, the tired chorus of negativity that inevitably surrounds the arrival of a space probe at another world has already begun. It was especially loud during New Horizons' recent communication glitch, so the now familiar rants of "Do we really need to spend billions on space exploration with the problems that we have here on Earth?" and "Who cares about a hunk of ice and rock in space?" are starting to circulate. Of course, I could simply respond, as I often do, with the numerous studies that have concluded that every dollar that's been spent on space exploration has resulted in an eventual $8 dollar return to the economy, or that certain hunks of ice and rock in space on Earth-bound trajectories could destroy civilization. But there is a deeper, more fundamental reason why our exploration of space must continue.

Humans are explorers, and always have been. But although it is in our nature to explore, history is still replete with instances of collapsed or stagnated cultures whose deterioration can be traced to a rejection of science and exploration. The burning of the great Library of Alexandria in ancient Egypt, and the 15th century Chinese rulers dropping their support of the great maritime explorer, Zheng He, are just a few examples. If we turn away from our exploration of the Cosmos it will not only amount to a summary denial of who we are, but could also foretell our eventual demise.

New Horizons bristles with scientific instruments that will image Pluto and its moons, map their surfaces, and determine their composition. However, it also carries a small container with some of the ashes of Clyde Tombaugh with the inscription: *Interned herein are the remains of American Clyde W. Tombaugh, discoverer of Pluto and the solar system's 'third zone'.* And thus, on July 14th, this intrepid robot explorer will not only reveal the secrets of the mysterious planet that have long eluded me, but because the craft carries a small piece of humanity, it will symbolically confirm that if we choose to do so, we can meet the challenge of the great spaces between the worlds.

Hopefully, our exploration of Pluto will represent the continuing saga of a curious and brave civilization that's trying to understand its place in the Cosmos, and not the final chapter in the story of a race drawing to its close.

AFTERWORD

Fortunately, the New Horizons probe's reconnaissance of Pluto and its moons in 2015 was a huge success. Incredibly, the probe continued its reconnaissance of the outer solar system after Pluto, and, in January, 2019, it sent back stunning images of the strange Kuiper Belt object named "Ultima Thule". However, following the publication of this essay in the Inquirer, *I received an email from a reader who was not a big fan of space exploration expenditures, particularly this mission to Pluto, and wrote:*

"With the $$$$$ 18+ trillion dollar debt, don't you think all of this money could be used for high priority issues?? The infrastructure is obsolete. Bridges are suspect. Roads and overpasses, questionable. California has no water!!! Any suggestions?? And why go to Pluto????? What can be done there?? I'm looking at America, what are you looking at today??? I demand that my tax dollars be used in a positive way. I live in the real world, not Disney World !!!!!"

I responded: "Ok...let's pull down all of the weather satellites that provide warnings of typhoons, hurricanes, and tornadoes and save thousands of lives each year, right? They were developed as a part of space exploration. You sent your communication to me via an infrastructure whose origins can be traced to space exploration and development. Electronic miniaturization, medical technologies that save lives, smoke detectors that save lives, and the improvements to computers over the last 40 years are just a few of the technology spin-offs attributed to NASA. Remove them all now and focus on solving our problems here on Earth? That would be foolish. You are short-sighted, and what you fail to realize is that in the pursuit of the exploration of space, new technologies are gained that lead to resolutions of problems here on Earth. And these new technologies lead to better ways to grow crops to help feed the hungry, and to new businesses that employ people, among many other things. Solve Earth's problems? Absolutely. But don't eliminate the programs that help resolve some of those same problems."

I never received a response.

THE PILOT WHO SAVED APOLLO 11

(Edited version published in the July 20, 2019 *Orlando Sentinel*)

Neil Armstrong next to the X-15 rocket powered aircraft (NASA photo)

"...(Werner) von Braun...would stand for eight hours a day soliciting money beside a display on interplanetary exploration. As part of his 1930 pitch, von Braun would bark, 'I bet you that the first man to walk on the moon is alive today somewhere on this Earth.' That very year, future moonwalker Neil Armstrong was born on a farm near the small town of Wapakoneta, Ohio." (From American Moonshot: John F. Kennedy and the Great Space Race *by Douglas Brinkley)*

On July 20, 1969, thirteen hundred feet above the moon's surface, Apollo 11's lunar landing vehicle, *Eagle*, entered the final stage of its powered descent. Aboard the spacecraft, Commander Neil Armstrong and Lunar Module Pilot Edwin "Buzz" Aldrin, both steel-nerved Korean War fighter-pilot veterans, monitored the rapidly changing telemetry data streaming through *Eagle's* landing radar.

As chronicled in Jay Barbree's biography, *Neil Armstrong: A Life of Flight*, Armstrong then looked out the window to survey the emerging rugged landscape below him, and gradually realized that something was terribly wrong. He knew from the countless hours he'd spent studying the lunar reconnaissance photos that *Eagle* was off-course, and the spacecraft's auto-pilot was steering them towards a crater strewn with boulders. Armstrong would have to take manual control of *Eagle*. The success of the mission, and the lives of the astronauts, were now dependent upon the piloting skills of the kid from Wapakoneta.

The millions back on Earth who were tuned in to the television and radio broadcasts of Apollo 11's historic descent to the lunar surface were unaware of the perilous drama playing out above the moon's Sea of Tranquility. But if there was any American who was born for this moment, it was Armstrong. During the Korean War, he survived a dangerous, high-speed ejection from his heavily damaged Panther jet, and later piloted the powerful X-15 rocket-plane. But it was a near fatal mishap during the Gemini 8 space mission in 1966, when Armstrong heroically succeeded in stabilizing the wildly spinning spacecraft, that he likely solidified his selection by NASA for the crew of the first mission to attempt a landing on the moon.

As Armstrong flew the spindly *Eagle* spacecraft over the rugged lunar surface, he spotted a smooth, flat area, safely distanced from the boulder-strewn crater. Armstrong then fired *Eagle's* thrusters to maneuver towards it.

Despite their now precarious situation, Buzz Aldrin remained calm as he continued to call out the telemetry data, "Okay, 75 feet. There's looking good."

Mission Control in Houston was now racked with tension. "60 seconds", CapCom Charlie Duke radioed to the crew, meaning that there was only 60 seconds of fuel left in *Eagle's* tanks. The unanticipated change in the flight path resulted in precious fuel being used up in the maneuvering thrusters. If they ran out before landing, *Eagle* would then have to attempt a very risky abort procedure. "CapCom, you better remind Neil there ain't no damn gas stations on that moon", said Flight Director Gene Kranz.

The tension in Mission Control intensified when Buzz Aldrin told Armstrong "Lights On," as the low-fuel signal began to blink, indicating that they were down to 30 seconds left of fuel.

Seconds seemed like hours. Mission Control could now only monitor the data, and listen to Armstrong and Aldrin as they descended. Finally, at 4:17:42 PM EDT, the historic words from Armstrong confirmed the data the engineers were seeing: "Houston, Tranquility Base here. The *Eagle* has landed."

In the applause that then erupted in Mission Control, many eyes turned to the 57 year-old rocket scientist with the German accent, and controversial Nazi past, that they regarded as the man most responsible for this stupendous achievement. Werner von Braun beamed with pride.

In the months leading up to this 50th anniversary of the Apollo 11 moon landing, I've heard the familiar proclamations from NASA, as well as from private space organizations, that a return to the moon and a human mission to Mars are in the planning stages. Although I am skeptical of their optimistic timelines, I do believe that the first man or woman who will walk on the surface of the Red Planet is alive today somewhere on this Earth. But my advice to those who will determine who the Commander of that mission will be is this: choose wisely. For, it is distinctly possible that the crew of that mission will face a perilous moment very much like that encountered by Apollo 11, and it would be prudent to remember that pilots like Neil Armstrong only come along once in a lifetime.

AFTERWORD

In the days prior to the 50th anniversary of the Apollo 11 moon landing, I read a number of interesting articles about the mission in various newspapers and magazines. One of the most fascinating was an article in The Atlantic *by Marina Koren (The Moment That Made Neil Armstrong's Heart Rate Spike - July 15, 2019) which focused on the heart rates of the 3 astronauts during their historic mission. Just before Armstrong and Aldrin began their descent to the lunar surface, Neil's heart rate was a remarkable 75 beats per minute! Koren wrote that "an adult's normal resting heart rate is between 60 to 100 beats per minute." What is even more incredible was the crew's heart rates at launch, one of the most dangerous phases of the mission: Armstrong - 110, Buzz Aldrin - 88, and Michael Collins - 99. Equally telling was Armstrong's heart rate as he took manual control of the landing - 150. I was somewhat relieved to read that. It seems that one of the heroes from my youth was human after all!*

STORIES
OF LIFE

THE FIGHT OF THE CENTURY

(Edited versions published in the March 13, 2006 *Philadelphia Daily News* and the July/August 2006 edition of the *History Channel Magazine*)

Joe Frazier vs. Muhammad Ali fight poster (Chris Gibbons photo)

The year was 1971, and the priest stood at the front of the Church and looked out among the elementary school students of Immaculate Heart of Mary School. He had just read a story from the New Testament which recounted a miracle Jesus had performed, and he wanted to engage the students during his homily by asking a question of them. "Who was the most powerful man who ever lived?", he asked the students. A hand immediately shot up among the first graders. The delighted priest, surprised that such a young child wanted to answer, called on the young boy, and he stood up. I looked over and saw that it was my little brother Pat. "Tell us young man.", the priest proudly intoned. Pat confidently replied, "Joe Frazier!"

That story is now legendary in my family, and we always have a good laugh when we recall it. However, those that know my family well certainly understand Pat's response. Just a few years prior to that day, my Uncle Joe's friend had given me and my five brothers each a photo of an up and coming young Philadelphia heavyweight standing in a classic boxers pose. Handwritten on the photos were the words: "Keep on smokin' - Joe Frazier". We all believed that "Smokin' Joe" had personally written those words just for us, and the heroic status he achieved in our home was unmatched by any other athlete. We celebrated when he defeated Jimmy Ellis to win the title, but we also all knew that there was one fighter that Joe had to defeat before he was universally recognized as the true heavyweight champion.

35 years ago, on March 8, 1971, what many regard as the greatest fight in boxing history took place in Madison Square Garden. For the first time, an undefeated champion, Joe Frazier, faced an undefeated ex-champion, Muhammad Ali. It was billed as "The Fight of the Century", and legendary boxing announcer Don Dunphy called it the greatest night in the history of sports. Luminaries from the entertainment, sports, and political worlds were seated at ringside. Ali and Frazier received record purses of $2.5 million each, the Garden was sold out a full month in advance, and an estimated 300 million watched it on closed circuit TV.

The pre-fight build-up was also racially charged as Ali shamefully referred to Joe as an "Uncle Tom" and "The white man's champion." These statements were particularly painful to Frazier who was raised as the dirt-poor son of a South Carolina sharecropper. If anyone embodied the impoverished, discriminatory experience of many African Americans of that era, it was Frazier.

On the night of the fight, as they stood in the center of the ring to receive the referee's instructions, Frazier and Ali continued their bitter war of words that had started nearly two years before. Ali said, "Don't you know that I'm God and can't be beat?", and Joe replied, "Well, God's gonna get his (butt) kicked tonight!"

The fight lived up to its billing. Ali danced behind a piston-like jab while continually landing punishing right crosses, but Joe doggedly pursued the former champion in his familiar crouched stance, and frequently rocked Ali with his trademark left hook.

The fight became a dramatic war of attrition and the battered faces of both fighters were a testament to its ferocity. Frazier was staggered by Ali in the 9th, and Ali was nearly out on his feet in the 11th. As the fight moved into the 15th and final round, Frazier was ahead on all scorecards, and he punctuated his performance by landing his vaunted left hook and flooring the former champion. Astonishingly, Ali got off the canvas and finished the fight. Frazier was awarded a unanimous decision victory.

Throughout the night, television shows were periodically interrupted with news of the fight, and our house erupted in joy upon hearing of Joe's victory. My brother Mike was fortunate enough to see the fight via closed-circuit broadcast, and he captivated us for hours with a blow-by-blow description when he returned. He was better than Howard Cosell.

Joe used to live a few miles from our Roxborough neighborhood, and sometimes we would see him driving alongside of us on Henry Ave. He would always flash a big smile and wave if he noticed us frantically trying to get his attention, and I often wonder if he ever knew that so many Philadelphians regarded him as their hero, especially six white kids who didn't care if he was black, white, blue, or green. Joe was from Philly, and he signed the photos tacked on the walls above our bunk-beds – that's all that mattered.

I've watched that fight numerous times on tape over the years, and I don't think that anyone could have beaten Joe Frazier that night. Well, maybe Jesus could have…maybe.

AFTERWORD

It's difficult to convey to people who didn't grow up in the Philadelphia area during the 1970's the heroic and iconic status that Joe Frazier had in the Delaware Valley. When the news of his stunning loss to George Foreman in 1973 reached our home, my brothers and I were in tears. My brother Pat was so distraught that my mother kept him home from school the following day! But, that incredible night in 1971 when he defeated Ali in the "Fight of the Century" is still indelibly burned within my memory, which is remarkable when you consider that I didn't actually see the fight until a year later when it was finally broadcast on TV by ABC Sports. Until that day I had relied upon the descriptions provided to me by my brother Mike, and the brilliant sportswriters of the Philadelphia Inquirer, Philadelphia Bulletin, *and the* Philadelphia Daily News. *I recently read a clipping from the issue of the* Daily News *on the day after the fight. Sportswriter Stan Hochman's prose from his article is pure gold as he poetically described the epic left hook from Frazier that floored Ali in the 15th round: "It came whistling out of Beaufort like the Suncoast Limited, screeching on invisible tracks, sending sparks into the night. Only the wail of the whistle was missing. And it crushed into Ali's handsome head just like the locomotive it resembled."*

SEARCHING FOR DON MCLEAN

(Edited version published in the August 30, 2006
Philadelphia Daily News)

(l to r) Mark Gibbons, Mike Gibbons, me, and Don McLean - 2006

*"A long, long time ago, I can still remember, how that music
used to make me smile."*
(Lyrics from American Pie)

I rummaged through the drawers of my brother's dresser, not really sure
of what I was looking for. I guess I just wanted to touch something that I
knew he had touched, or hold something that he had held. I don't really

know. The things that he left behind were all that remained, and I naively thought that if I could just hold his things and smell his clothes and stare at his picture, then maybe he would seem closer and the pain would go away. My big brother Jack had tragically drowned just a few weeks prior to that, and I was searching for something, anything, that would alleviate the sadness. I found a 45 rpm record in his top drawer. It was *American Pie* by Don McLean, a huge hit during that summer of 1972 when he died. I stared at the record, and vividly remembered how Jack would smile that half-grin of his whenever that song came on the radio and sing along. For the first time since he had died, I smiled.

American Pie is legendary in the annals of music industry history. Originally released in November, 1971, it moved up the charts faster than any other song in the history of United Artists. It reached number one in January, 1972 and stayed on the hit parade for nearly four months, a remarkable achievement for a song 8 ½ minutes in length. It sold more than three million copies as a single, five million as an album. The song is dedicated to Don's boyhood hero, Buddy Holly, who tragically died in a plane crash in 1959. The song has long been interpreted as McLean's social commentary on the chaotic state of America in the years following Holly's death.

As a young man, Don lamented the loss of many things he believed in while growing up. "In a sense, *American Pie* was a very despairing song. In another, though, it was very hopeful. Pete Seeger told me he saw it as a song in which people were saying something. They'd been fooled, they'd been hurt, and it wasn't going to happen again. That's a good way to look at it -- a hopeful way."

For me and my family, the song is now indelibly linked to my brother Jack. Every time we hear it we think of him, and we agree with McLean that the song can be both hopeful and despairing. Sometimes we'll laugh when we hear it, and sometimes we'll cry. We have strange stories associated with the song as well. One time, I was driving in the car with my wife and infant son. We stopped at a red light and I mentioned that the street in front of us was the last one my brother had walked on. A few minutes later we pulled into a parking space. I pointed to a man walking a few feet from our car and said, "This is weird. See that guy over there? He was with Jack when he died." At that same moment, *American Pie* came on the radio. I was momentarily shaken as I looked in the rear view mirror at my son in the back seat. His name is Jack.

For a few years now, I've been searching for Don McLean. I'll frequently check his website for local appearances, and on October 7th he's perform-ing in Carlisle, Pa. I've heard that Don will sometimes talk to his fans after his shows and my family and I think that this might be a good opportunity for us to let him know about the special connection that exists between his song and our brother Jack. We don't know if we'll ever be able to tell him in person, or how he'll react if we do. He probably gets stories like this all of the time. But, we feel we owe it to Jack to let McLean know that the only record he owned when he died was *American Pie*, and how that music used to make him, and now all of us, smile.

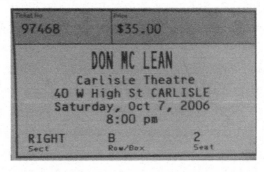

Ticket stub from the 10-7-2006 show at the Carlisle

AFTERWORD

On a summer night in 2005, my brother Mike and I sat in my parent's backyard in Cape May Courthouse, NJ, and listened to 70's music playing on the radio as we looked up at the stars. American Pie came on the radio, and we sang along. When the song was over, I turned to Mike and said, "I've had this idea in my mind for the last few years. I think we should track down

Don McLean and let him know about Jack and his song." Mike brushed aside tears and said, "I think we should too."

Our search finally culminated in Carlisle, Pa. in October of 2006. I made it to Don's show that night, along with my brothers, Mark and Mike. Prior to the start of the show, Mike asked one of the guys helping backstage if he could give McLean a copy of the article. The guy took the copy backstage to Don. To our surprise, he returned with the copy of the article and said "Don's been eager to meet you…he'll see you after the show." It turns out that he has old friends in Philadelphia and someone had already sent him a copy of the article.

We met Don after the show, and he turned out to be one of the nicest guys we've met! He wanted to know all about Jack and our family (it turns out that Don went to Villanova for a year in the 1960's and also had friends at Temple University as well). We took a photo with Don, and he told me before we left, "That was a beautiful article and I've kept a copy of it." It was a really special night for all of us.

THE VETERANS OF THE DOMINO

(Edited version published in the November 8, 2006
Philadelphia Daily News)

It was just a neighborhood bar in the Philadelphia neighborhood called Roxborough. Its actual name was The Domino Lounge, but we always simply referred to it as the Dom. It was nothing fancy really, just the kind of place you could go to in the neighborhood and have a beer with a familiar face.

It smelled of stale smoke and food, and a perpetual haze seemed to hover at the ceiling, but it was the bar that my friends and I adopted as our own. It had previously been the exclusive domain of a group of guys that were part of what came to be known as "The Greatest Generation", but because some of our fathers were regulars, we were quickly accepted into their company. An intriguing dynamic soon developed as two generations frequently rubbed elbows at the same bar. Although they were 20 to 30 years older than us, these men became our friends. They tolerated our screaming at the Eagles and Flyers on the TV, and we tolerated them singing Sinatra tunes or old Irish ballads. Oh, how I used to hate when they would start singing those songs when the Flyers were on TV!

As we got to know them, one of the most notable things that became apparent to all of us was that most of these men were veterans of World War II or the Korean War. There was Tony Consolo, John McHugh, Ralph Roberts, Jack Kerwood, and Vince Hopkins, who were WW II veterans. Russ Becker, Ken MacDougall, Harry Barr, Bob Morrissey, and my father were Korean War veterans. Remarkably, another veteran, Harry Rogers, fought in WW II, Korea, and Vietnam!

They rarely ever spoke of what they experienced during the war. We'd try to prod it out of them, and every once in a while, when the alcohol washed away the locked gate where they stored the memories better left unspoken, they would tell us bits and pieces. I remember a WW II vet that we affectionately referred to as "Uncle Ben" tried to tell me of a battle he was in, but he couldn't finish the tale, as his red-rimmed eyes filled with tears. I pretended that I didn't notice, and tried to change the subject. "How 'bout those Phillies, Ben?", I sheepishly asked, hoping to break the awkward silence that followed and ashamed of myself for making him go there.

There were hundreds of bars like the Dom throughout the neighborhoods of Philadelphia, and there's still quite a few of them left. But, neighborhood gentrification, population flight to the suburbs, and generation aging resulted in many of these places closing for good. My friends and I no longer have a neighborhood bar like the Dom. We'll occasionally get together at one of the many suburban Sports Bars, with their ten TV's, spicy mozzarella sticks, and micro-brewed $7.00 beers. I never feel very comfortable in those places. At the Dom, I used to feel welcome, like I belonged. These Sports Bars have no character, and everyone looks, dresses, and acts the same. There's not even a smoky haze hovering near the ceiling, for God's sake!

Time eventually caught up to the Dom. At the spot where it stood is now a hair-cutting joint. Unfortunately, many of the veterans of the Domino are gone as well. I'm thankful that my Dad is still around, and sometimes we'll go to his local VFW. I like it there, and in many ways it reminds me of the Dom, but it's not the same.

I wish that I could walk into the VFW and see Harry, Jack, Ben, Tony, and all of the veterans of the Domino just one more time. I'd do what I should have done while they were still here, and tell them how much I respected all of them. I'd ask the bartender to turn the off that Flyers game, and I'd sing along with them as a Big Band song played on the jukebox. And if they tried to tell me what happened on those battlefields so long ago, I'd quickly change the subject. I already know what happened, and because of that, I'd like to buy the next round and wish them all a Happy Veterans Day.

That's what I'd like to do, but unfortunately I can't, because most of the veterans of the Domino aren't around anymore.

AFTERWORD

In June of 1984, as I watched the national news segments of the various ceremonies in Europe commemorating the 40th Anniversary of D-Day, I made a mental note to myself that I was going to sit down with some of the veterans of the Domino and interview them about their war experiences while recording it on cassette. I knew that someday they would no longer be around, and when that inevitable day came to pass, I also knew how valuable these recordings would be. But, I thought to myself at the time, these veterans were in their 50's or 60's, and I had time to do it, so I kept putting it off. As the years slowly passed, and my life priorities dramatically shifted to marriage, work, buying a house, and raising a family, I continued to put the "Veterans of the Domino Project", as I called it, on the back-burner. Whenever I thought about it, I kept reassuring myself that I still had time. And then one day I sadly realized that my time had run out - the Domino and its veterans were gone. Although I did not get to record their personal experiences, the bits of information that I gleaned directly from them back-in-the-day, as well as my own knowledge of World War 2 and the Korean War, has enabled me to gain a good understanding of what they endured. Unfortunately, their personal recollections would have been much more compelling and meaningful. Although I knew that the veterans of the Domino were not unique, I was still quite surprised at the number of e-mails that I received from Daily News readers who revealed similar stories of the veterans who frequented the corner bars of their Philadelphia neighborhoods. I feel privileged and lucky to have known the veterans of the Domino, and I'm proud to say that they were my friends.

IN THE SHADOW OF THE TITANIC

(Edited version published in the April 6, 2007 *Philadelphia Daily News*)

Jack Thayer (photo courtesy of the Thayer family)

The young man from the Philadelphia area was preparing for bed when he felt a slight swaying of the great ocean liner. Seventeen year old Jack Thayer then noticed that the engines had stopped, and he could hear the sound of running feet and frantic voices just outside his cabin. Jack and his father went up on deck to find out what the commotion was about, and they ran into one of the ship's designers, Thomas Andrews. The ship had struck an iceberg, and Andrews told them that "he did not give the ship much over an hour to live." The unthinkable was happening: the RMS Titanic was sinking.

The ship stewards soon passed the word that women and children were to proceed to "B" deck and board lifeboats on the port side. In the commotion, Jack and his new friend Milton Long were separated from Jack's parents as the surging crowd pushed between them. "I never saw my father again", Thayer would later write.

Jack and Milton desperately clung to the side rails of the ship as it began to sink into the freezing waters of the North Atlantic. Long turned to Jack and said good-bye, then slid down the side of the ship, never to be seen again. Jack jumped in soon thereafter, and was pulled down by the suction of the sinking ship. Just when he thought he could hold his breath no longer, he suddenly surfaced near an overturned lifeboat and was pulled aboard. Five hours later he was rescued by the RMS Carpathia, where he was reunited with his mother and 703 other survivors. Lost at sea were 1,503 people, including his father. Although it had been a moonless night, the Titanic had still cast a shadow, and it fell across the life of Jack Thayer.

In the years following the Titanic tragedy, Thayer served as an artillery captain in World War I, and he eventually became financial vice president of the University of Pennsylvania. He married and had five children, but his memory of that night never faded. In 1932, Thayer wrote a riveting personal account of the sinking for *The Philadelphia Bulletin*, and he later wrote a 30 page booklet that was published in 1940. He dedicated it to the memory of his father.

Unfortunately, during the latter years of World War II, Thayer's life began to unravel. In October, 1943, his son Edward, an army bomber pilot, was reported missing in action after his plane was shot down. His body was never found. Jack Thayer was never the same again. His father was lost at sea, and now his son was lost at war. Six months later, in an eerie coincidence, his mother died on the 32nd anniversary of the Titanic's sinking. Friends said he seemed forgetful and despondent in the waning summer days of 1945.

On Tuesday morning, September 19, 1945, Jack Thayer unexpectedly left his office at Penn, and drove the sedan registered in his wife's name to a destination known only to him. His family reported him missing on Wednesday. A few days later, they found the car parked near the south-side trolley loop on Parkside Ave. Although it had been there for a few days, neither the trolley passengers nor a group of neighborhood boys playing football nearby took any particular notice of it. However, two curious Philadelphia Transportation Company employees decided to check out the apparently abandoned vehicle. Inside the car, they found the body of Jack Thayer slumped down in the front seat. He had slit his wrists and neck with a razor and bled to death. "He just couldn't deal with my uncle's death", his grandson Edward told me.

Did the relentless shadow of the Titanic contribute to gradually dimming the life from Jack Thayer? Did his suppressed emotions and horrific memories of that night, his final glimpse of his father, Long's last good-bye, and the agonized cries of the dying as he sat helpless on the overturned boat, come back to haunt Thayer as the realization that his lost son would never be coming home again slowly chipped away at his anguished, fragile psyche? The coroner listed the cause of death as self-inflicted "knife wound", but he shouldn't be faulted for doing so. Professional protocol would never have allowed him to list it as a "broken heart", even though he knew that's what killed Jack Thayer.

"I still have fond memories of sitting on his lap as he cut the roast before Sunday dinners. He was a very loving person, and I still miss him", his daughter Lois told me. As we spoke, I sensed a certain nostalgic longing and sadness in a bitter-sweet voice that was tinged with traces of regret and sorrow. It seems the ominous shadow of the Titanic still has the power to dim the light even to this day.

AFTERWORD

My interest in the tragic story of the Titanic dates back to my early teens. During that time, my Uncle Joe Baird (my mother's brother), a priest in the Philadelphia Archdiocese, was living in a stately rectory in the Chestnut Hill section of Philadelphia. The rectory was actually a mansion, donated to the Archdiocese that had abundant grounds with a large, beautiful in-ground pool. It was the site of many Baird-family gatherings and reunions throughout the 1970's. We were told that the mansion was the former home of a survivor of the Titanic, who was rumored to have dressed as a woman in order to board one of the lifeboats. In 2019, I decided to research the history of the mansion, and discovered that it was the former home of Thomas Cardeza, who, along with his mother, did indeed survive the Titanic disaster. However, unlike Jack Thayer and his father, the then 36 year old Cardeza simply boarded one of the lifeboats and, apparently, did not dress as a woman, seemingly dispelling the rumor we had heard. His secretary stated in the April 23, 1912 Philadelphia Inquirer that "Mr. Cardeza told me that he entered the fifth or sixth lifeboat that was launched from the side of the liner. He said that there was no objections to him entering the boat, nor was there any rush to board the craft."

THE LIFEGUARD

(Edited version published in the August 7, 2007
Philadelphia Daily News)

Photo - Derick Adame

I recently walked along a deserted beach, momentarily lost in my thoughts until I suddenly came upon a lifeguard stand. It was unoccupied, but as I looked up at the empty wooden seat my thoughts drifted back in time, and in my mind I could still picture the lifeguard.

It's been nearly thirty five years, but my memory of him hasn't faded. I can still see him sitting on top of his lifeguard stand, white sunscreen on his nose, and slowly twirling a tethered silver whistle around his finger.

I will also never forget what the lifeguard did, and when I think about that day I am flooded with the memories of that summer.

For a young boy growing up in the Roxborough neighborhood of Philadelphia, summer was the smell of a freshly mowed lawn, or the squeaking sound of high-top Chuck Taylor Converse skidding on the hot asphalt during a game of wire-ball. Summer was the taste of an old, hand-me-down leather baseball glove as you chewed on one of its frayed laces. It was throwing rocks in the creek, playing wiffle ball games in the drive-way, and burning cap-gun ammo with a magnifying glass. It was looking up at the stars every night and wishing that life would always be this good.

To many Philadelphians, summer also meant the Jersey shore. The small coastal resort towns of southern Jersey were inundated with vaca-tioning families from the neighborhoods of Philly.

In 1972, my family vacationed in Ocean City, N.J. I can still remember running down to the beach as soon as we arrived. The sweeping expanse of ocean that greeted me as I ran on to the beach that day was overwhelming. I was one of eleven children and our home was crowded. But the ocean represented room, and freedom, and possibilities to me.

That was also the day that I first saw the lifeguard. His incessant whistling, and arm waving was the beginning of my disdain for him. He reminded me of my school teachers as he continually interrupted the fun with his shrill whistle, and orders to move over, or come in closer, or stop throwing wet sand at your little brother.

One particular day, my little brother Pat and I were bodysurfing. The surf was unusually rough, and the two of us were frequently getting tossed around by the waves. After getting pounded by a huge wave, I stood up, cleared the water from my eyes, and noticed that I couldn't find Pat. I was surprised because he had been right next to me before the wave hit. Finally, I saw him. He was further out than he should have been. I quickly realized that he was in water that was well above his head, and he was definitely struggling. I started to swim out towards him, but the water was too rough, and my frail, skinny body wasn't making any headway. Pat was being pulled out into deeper water, and he must've been caught in a rip-tide. I began to panic and started to scream for help. I was wildly thrashing around, and swallowed some salty seawater. Pat was clearly in trouble, continually going under and resurfacing. I was trying to scream, but was gagging so badly that I couldn't. I looked out again, and for the first time during the ordeal, I didn't see Pat. My God, I thought to myself, my little brother has drowned!

Suddenly, something shot over my right shoulder, as a dripping shadow flitted across my face. It knifed into the water just ahead of me, barely making a splash. It quickly emerged out of the water, with arms and feet rapidly flailing, like a powerful machine, with synchronous, chopping movements in the water. It was the lifeguard, and he was moving like a torpedo towards my brother. I will never forget how quickly he got to Pat.

The lifeguard got Pat out of the water and back to the beach. Pat was OK, but he was kneeling down and spitting-up seawater. I knelt down next to him. We looked at each other and didn't say anything. We both had tears in our eyes, but for different reasons. He was a pain in the neck, but he was my little brother and I loved him, and he came within a few seconds of losing his life. You're supposed to look out for your little brother, but I failed. I looked up at the lifeguard and hoped that he could somehow understand what I wanted to say, but couldn't articulate. I think he did.

In a heartbreaking twist of fate, just a few days after we returned from our vacation, my oldest brother Jack drowned in the Schuylkill River while swimming with some friends. Nothing would ever be the same again for me and my family. A house in a Philadelphia neighborhood wailed in sorrow that night, and the awful sound of it drifted across the hills of Roxborough. It was during that terrible night that a wishful image first came to my mind and continues to haunt me to this day. It's an image of a lifeguard stand. It sits on the banks of the Schuylkill River. Sitting atop the stand is a young kid, with white sunscreen on his nose, slowly twirling a tethered silver whistle around his finger on a hot August day in the summer of '72.

AFTERWORD

I received a lot of e-mails from Daily News *readers following the publication of this essay, and many were from people who had also experienced the tragic loss of a brother. The following is an excerpt from one of the most touching among them:*

"Dear Chris, Let me first say that I am very sorry for your loss and the memories that haunt you. The parallels between your family experience and mine are unbelievable. You may even hear from my younger brother…I cried when I read your article and when I called (my brother) to tell him to read it, he cried too. We also lost a brother some years ago to tragic circumstances. It hasn't been nearly 35 years, but 30…Nothing was ever the same after that night in a VERY cold and snowy February, 1978 for my family either, and the howls of pain from my father in that house in Torresdale echo in my ears to this day. I have been attending lifeguard training and final testing is tomorrow. The last test is to swim a mile. When I want to quit, (believe me when I tell you the thought WILL cross my mind - at 49…I'm not the stud I once was) I will think of your brother, my brother, my father…That wishful image of a lifeguard stand on the banks of the Schuylkill - I can't man that post, any more than I can bring back those we both know who died WAY too early, but I will man a real lifeguard stand somewhere. I'll probably earn the disdain of some young turks. I PROMISE you, I'll do my best to keep anyone from getting in over their heads. And if they do, I'll get them back. Rest easy, my friend."

THE BLIND GUY FROM IVY RIDGE

(Edited version published in the December 21, 2007
Philadelphia Daily News)

It was bitterly cold that Christmas Eve. I can't remember whether it was 1968 or 1969, but I do remember how cold it was. The late afternoon darkness of the early winter was ushering out the day, and my house was filled with excitement and anticipation as we prepared to decorate the Christmas tree. My mother had to get some last-minute things at the deli, and wanted to get there before it closed. I decided to tag along with her because I had a quarter (a rarity for me in those days), and I wanted to get some licorice and a Milky Way bar. My kids always laugh when I tell them this, but a quarter was big money in those days. Life couldn't be better: it was Christmas Eve, Santa was on his way, and I had a quarter in my pocket!

My Mom parked the car in the Ivy Ridge Shopping Center in Roxborough, and I ran down towards Al's Deli to escape the cold. I slowed down when I noticed the blind guy sitting in his usual spot next to the soft pretzel stand. It seemed like he was always there. Nobody knew his name, so we all just referred to him as "the blind guy from Ivy Ridge." He was overweight, with thick black hair, dark Roy Orbison sunglasses, and a bristly stubble of whiskers across his multiple chins. He just sat in his usual spot, pathetically shaking a tin cup that always sounded as if there was nothing more than a few coins rattling within it. I always felt sorry for him, but on this particular night I was stunned to see him out in the bitter cold.

The blind guy was shivering badly, and he wasn't really shaking the cup as much as he was simply extending his arm and letting his quivering body do the rest. I asked my Mom, "Doesn't he have anywhere to go?" She said she didn't know, and I could see by her expression that the sight of him in the cold was beginning to bother her too. She reached into her purse, and gave him what she could before we both headed into the nearby deli.

I watched the blind guy through the window of the deli with my hands in my pockets. I rolled the quarter around in my hand as I eyed the blind guy and the candy display next to the cashier. I remembered some of the things the older kids used to say about him - that he wasn't really blind, and he just shakes that cup to get extra money. Besides, I thought to myself, my Mom just gave him some money, so that counts as coming from me as well. Proud and satisfied with my reasoning, I bought my candy, and Mom and I headed out the door. The blind guy heard us passing, and he said "Merry Christmas." As I sat in the car and stared at the shivering blind guy, I regretted my decision. He looked very lonely as we drove away, and I felt as empty as his cup.

Christmas came and went, and I promised myself that the next time I saw the blind guy I was going to drop a quarter in his cup. But each time I saw him, I convinced myself that I'd give the next time. When I finally did, it was mid-spring and the sound my quarter made as it hit the bottom of his tin cup was as hollow as the gesture itself. I thought that I would feel better, but I didn't. I knew I should have done it on that cold Christmas Eve night a few months prior, but I missed my chance.

I don't know whatever happened to the blind guy. As the years went by, I saw him less frequently until eventually I never saw him again. I guess life is like that sometimes.

Christmas truly is a wonderful time of year, and it still has a certain magic about it that captures the imaginations of young and old alike. But, it's also a time of year to try and help those in need. It doesn't have to be money or a gift, maybe it's just a helping hand, or spending some time with a lonely senior citizen, or calling an old friend to tell them that you were thinking about them. Try and do these things while you can, because, as we all know, there might not be a next time.

Remember, it truly is better to give than it is to receive at this time of year. Even the blind guy from Ivy Ridge could see the truth in that sentiment.

AFTERWORD

Shortly after I published this essay, a former grade-school classmate told me that he heard that the "blind guy" was actually the father of another one of our former grade-school classmates. I had never heard that before, and was shocked. And, although this may still turn out to be just a rumor, somehow my recollections of the "blind guy" are now tinged with a bit more sorrow.

BACK THE 'CRICK'

(Edited version published in the March 28, 2008
Philadelphia Daily News)

The Wissahickon Creek in Philadelphia (Chris Gibbons photo)

"And perhaps across his mind there'll flit a little errant wish, that a man might not have to become old, never outgrow the parks and the merry-go-rounds of his youth. And he'll smile then too because he'll know it is just an errant wish". (Rod Serling from the Twilight Zone *episode "Walking Distance")*

As I walked through a Sporting Goods store recently, I noticed a small sign stating that "Opening Day" for trout season in Philadelphia is Saturday,

March 29. I smiled as I read it, because it conjured up pleasant memories from my youth of trout fishing, and opening days spent "back the crick" with my buddies.

The Wissahickon Creek (pronounced "crick" in Philly-speak) snakes through the northwest neighborhoods of Philadelphia, and it was an annual rite of spring for the young boys of Roxborough, Manayunk, and East Falls to prepare for opening day of trout season. I'm told that it was very much the same thing in the NE Philly neighborhoods surrounding Pennypack Creek.

My fellow fishermen in those days were the boys that I had grown up with, most of whom I'd known since I was 6 years old. We hung out under a Henry Avenue bridge, and called ourselves "The Bridge." Other guys in the neighborhood mockingly called us "The Trolls." It seemed as if our major goal in life back then was to make each other laugh, and we were pretty good at it, too. We made up amusing nicknames for each other, most of which were references to some unique anatomical feature we possessed. There was Curly, Freckle, Hair, Fly, Gut, and Chalk (because of his pale complexion). A lot of these nicknames centered on head sizes or shapes, so we also had Brick Head, Pineapple Head, Bucket Head, Globin, and Boulder.

We used to make up bawdy songs, with indecent lyrics that we would sing as we walked along the trails of the Wissahickon. We thought of ourselves as being great outdoorsmen simply because we knew how to light a fire with a magnifying glass and cook minute steaks in old pans we confiscated from our kitchens. Our plan was to cook the fish that we caught and pretend that we could "live off the land" if we had to, but most of us weren't very good at fishing. Bucket Head and I once grabbed a dead trout that was floating downstream and fried it. Of course, we had no idea what we were doing, and didn't gut and bone the fish. I can still remember my poor mother struggling to scrape the mysterious foul-smelling gristle from that old black pan. But, that was nothing compared to what I had to scrape the day after I ate it.

One of my buddies was really quite good at fishing, and we used to call him "Fisherman." He could easily catch 25 trout in a single day. He was also smart enough to get as far away from the rest of us as possible. While we were busy un-snagging our lines, pushing each other into the creek, or throwing rocks in the water, Fisherman was 50 yards downstream catching trout and laughing at all of us. We didn't care though, and in the naïveté and exuberance of our youth we thought those days would last forever. But, our fishing days together, and our adolescence, slowly began to fade with the passage of time.

I still enjoy hiking along the old trails of the Wissahickon Creek. Whenever I'm there, I am always amazed by its beauty, and thankfully, it has changed very little over the years. Walking along the banks of the Wissahickon is like stepping back in time. I'll often stop and listen to the wind as it whispers through the towering trees. If I listen carefully, sometimes it carries with it the sounds of my past, and I can hear the laughter and singing of familiar young voices as an errant wish momentarily crosses my mind. Perhaps the past can sometimes be within walking distance.

I've decided I'm going to get my fishing gear together, and call Bucket Head, Fly, Hair, TK, Fisherman and some of the others from the old crew. So, if you happen to see some middle aged guys with fishing rods walking across Henry Avenue in the early morning hours of some Saturday this spring, and they happen to be laughing while singing a crazy song in unison, don't be alarmed. It's just the boys from The Bridge, and we'll be heading "back the crick".

AFTERWORD

Whenever I tell people who are from outside of the Philadelphia area my old neighborhood trout-fishing tales, I'm invariably met with a puzzled look, followed by, "I thought you grew up in Philly?" What they don't realize is that the Wissahickon Valley, which I regard as one of our country's best kept secrets, is a unique pastoral oasis in our large Northeastern metropolis. As a result of Roxborough's close proximity to the Wissahickon Creek, it resulted in "Opening Day" of trout fishing season being one of the big annual events in our neighborhood. I received quite a few e-mails from Daily News readers in which they fondly recalled their trout fishing days along the Wissahickon. I also have many other fond memories of the Wissahickon, which include hiking with my father and siblings, and feeding the ducks with my young children, but one memory in particular is not so pleasant. When I was about 8 or 9 years old, I was fishing "back the crick" with my older brothers and my cousins. While we were leaving and climbing a steep hill, I slipped and badly sprained my ankle. I couldn't walk or put any weight on it, and was in so much pain that I thought it was broken. My cousin Mickey, several years older than me, put me on his back and carried me all the way home – a 2 mile journey that was frequently uphill over rugged terrain. I remember thinking at the time that he was the strongest guy in the world. At his father's funeral in 2019, Mickey told me that he has this article framed and displayed in his home.

THE GREEN RADIO

(Edited versions published in the July 28, 2008 *Philadelphia Daily News* and the July 24, 2018 *WHYY.org* website)

"The world is a bad place, a bad place,
A terrible place to live, oh, but I don't wanna die.
All my sorrows, sad tomorrows, take me back, to my old home."
("Reflections of My Life" by the Marmalade)

It was just a little green radio with a big, clear, plastic tuning dial. In the late 1960s, my big brother Mike found a small piece of wood paneling and used it as a shelf for the green radio, and he placed it on the wall above his bunk-bed.

There were four of us in that bedroom, and every night we would fall asleep with the radio on. We would listen to Philadelphia radio stations

WFIL and *WIBG* (or "WIBBAGE" as we used to call it), and the songs that the DJ's played became the soundtrack of our childhood.

Sometimes we would sing along to the songs, and my brothers would laugh when I imitated Frankie Valli's falsetto voice in a mock rendition of "Big Girls Don't Cry." My parents would hear the laughter and tell us to get to bed, and turn the radio off.

Unfortunately, we also heard the news broadcasts drift up to our room as my parents watched television downstairs. Unlike the green radio, those television broadcasts were much more serious and ominous. We tried not to listen, and instead focused on the music emanating from the green radio. In a world apparently gone mad, the green radio helped to restore some sense of sanity and safety.

Fifty years ago, in the summer of 1968, the world did seem like it was a very bad place. The war in Vietnam was still raging; Martin Luther King and Bobby Kennedy were recently assassinated; protesters and police battled in the streets of Chicago during the Democratic National Convention; and riots erupted across the urban areas of some large cities. America's cities were burning.

Although I was just a child at the time, I do remember some of the disturbing images from the television, and the concerned, sometimes incredulous, looks on my parents' faces as they watched the evening news.

"What in the world is happening," I can remember my mother questioning on numerous occasions. My older brothers were a few years younger than the dead soldiers and the beaten, bloodied protesters who filled the television screen that summer. But one of the older boys on our street would soon be off to Vietnam, and my parents were justifiably worried.

Our country seemed to be falling apart, and the spirit of rebellion that it spawned eventually seeped into our home as my brothers battled with my Dad over the length of their hair, going to church on Sundays, and the "hippie" music they liked to listen to. Sometimes, if the arguing got too loud, I would escape to the bedroom and turn on the green radio to drown out the noise.

Of course, to my Dad, anything coming from *WFIL* or *WIBG* back then was "hippie" music, but to all of us, the music seemed to serve as a way in which our generation bonded and distinguished itself from the older generation. This was "our" music, and the variety and quality of it in the late '60s was stunning.

On one radio station, you could hear the psychedelic sounds of the Jefferson Airplane, the hard rock of Steppenwolf, the pop music of the Monkees, the soul music of the Temptations, or the beautiful ballads of the Carpenters.

The music of the Beatles, the Turtles, Smokey Robinson, the Rascals, the Supremes, and the Beach Boys filled our bedroom that summer, and we sang along as we forgot about the violence and turbulence that was rocking the country.

The DJs on *WFIL* (Boss Jocks) and *WIBG* (Good Guys) became local celebrities, and we quickly came to recognize the voices and distinct personalities of Hy Lit, Jim Nettleton, "Long John" Wade, Dr. Don Rose, Bob Charger, and Duke Roberts. I always looked out for the *WFIL* "Prize Patrol" whenever I was in the car, but I never did see the bright red Mustang following us. Even if I had, my Dad would have never stopped the car to collect the prize. I could just hear him now, "Just a bunch of hippie-crap for a prize, anyway!"

The green radio, along with the old *WFIL* and *WIBG* radio stations, are long gone. Fortunately, the music still lives.

Before my parents sold their home in Cape May Courthouse several years ago, my brother Mike and I would sometimes get together there and sit in the yard at night with the satellite radio tuned in to the '60s and '70s stations. We'd look up at the stars and reminisce about those summer days of 1968 when, though the world seemed to be falling apart, the music emanating from the green radio in our bedroom helped to shelter us from the chaos enveloping the world. A familiar song from that era would often come on the radio, and Mike and I would look at each other and say, "That's a 'green radio' song!"

It's been 50 years since that tumultuous summer of 1968, and, unfortunately, the world still often seems like a terrible place to live. Our country is once again starkly divided, American soldiers still die in war zones, terrorists (American born and foreign) continue to threaten us, and the possibility of global nuclear annihilation has not abated.

Rather than tacitly accept this endless cycle of violence, those of us who lived through it have an obligation to try and break it by teaching our children what we have learned.

The songs of the green radio once preserved the innocence of our youth, but the words of some of those songs now also serve as a reminder of our responsibility to the next generation:

"Wake up, all the teachers
Time to teach a new way
Maybe then they'll listen
To what'cha have to say
'Cause they're the ones who's coming up
And the world is in their hands
When you teach the children
Teach 'em the very best you can"

— *"Wake Up Everybody" by Harold Melvin & the Bluenotes*

AFTERWORD

Since I was a child, not only have I had a love of rock-n-roll music, but I've also been fascinated with radios. I have quite a collection of vintage wood-cabinet and Bakelite tube radios, including a beautiful, large 1940's-era RCA Victor console radio in my living room. Recently, I've also begun to collect vintage transistor radios from the 1950's and 1960's. As any collector knows, half of the fun is in the search. But there's one radio in particular that has eluded my internet and flea-market search efforts. It's a 1960's-era little green radio with a big, clear, plastic tuning dial made by the now defunct Jade Transistor Radio Company. However, this one's not for my collection, for, if I'm fortunate enough to find one, it will go where it belongs. I'm sure that when I give it to my brother Mike, he'll make a small, wood-paneling shelf to place the green radio upon the wall of his home.

THE MUSIC COULDN'T DIE

(Edited version published in the February 3, 2009 *Philadelphia Inquirer*)

Buddy Holly publicity photo - circa 1957

"I can't remember if I cried,
When I read about his widowed bride,
But something touched me deep inside,
The day the music died."
(Lyrics from "American Pie" by Don McLean)

The cold February wind cut through Clear Lake, Iowa that fateful night 50 years ago, and temperatures plummeted down into the single digits. Inside The Surf Ballroom, the *Winter Dance Party Tour*, starring Dion & The Belmonts, J.P. Richardson (The Big Bopper), Richie Valens, and Buddy

Holly, was finishing its show. Although the 1,200 in attendance that night were whipped into a wild frenzy, the members of the tour were weary, and dreaded another ride on their freezing tour bus. The bus heater had broken, and one tour member was suffering from frostbite. Holly couldn't bear the thought of riding the bus to the next city, and he leased a small plane that could only hold three tour members.

A young Waylon Jennings, playing bass guitar for Holly's tour band, gave up his seat to an ill Richardson. Richie Valens won a coin flip with guitarist Tommy Allsup for another seat, and Buddy Holly took the last seat. Before they left for the airfield, Holly jokingly said to Jennings, "Well, I hope your old bus freezes up again!" Waylon playfully responded, "Well, hell, I hope your old plane crashes!" On February 3rd 1959, just after 1am, the plane crashed in a cornfield shortly after take-off, killing all aboard. Despite it being said in jest, Waylon Jennings was haunted by his remark to Holly for the remainder of his life. Holly's grieving widow, Maria, would suffer a miscarriage two weeks later. America's youth had lost their heroes to tragedy, a pattern that would become all too familiar in the tumultuous decade that followed.

Buddy Holly was a unique talent almost without equal in those early days of rock-n-roll. Hailing from a musical family in Lubbock, Texas, his rise to stardom is now legendary. In 1955, at the age of 18, Holly attended an Elvis concert in his hometown and from that moment on he wanted to be a rock star. He formed a band called Buddy Holly and the Crickets, and in 1957 they had their first number one hit with "That'll Be The Day." Numerous hits followed: "Peggy Sue", "Maybe Baby", "Rave On", "It's So Easy", and "Not Fade Away." Millions across the U.S. watched when the band performed on *The Ed Sullivan Show*. They followed their appearance with a highly successful tour of Australia and the United Kingdom.

When you consider that his career as a popular entertainer spanned only 18 months, Holly's accomplishments are remarkable. His innovations and style shaped the future of rock-n-roll and still resonate today. Unlike nearly all of the early rock artists, Holly sang and wrote most of his songs. He could play piano, violin, guitar, and drums. Holly's concept of a self-contained band with a lead guitar, bass, rhythm guitar and drums became the prototype for all rock bands that followed. He pioneered the use of double tracking, used various stringed instruments in his compositions, and wrote songs with sophisticated harmonies and melodies. Fans loved his unique "hiccup" style of singing, but perhaps Holly's most endearing quality was that he appealed to the ordinary guy. With his signature black-rimmed glasses, he let it be known that you can wear glasses and still be cool.

Holly's influence on the giants of rock-n-roll is readily acknowledged by the artists themselves. The Beatles (whose name was inspired by The Crickets), Rolling Stones, Dylan, Springsteen, and U2 are just a few of the numerous artists who recognize the profound influence that Holly had on their careers. Paul McCartney even acquired the publishing rights to all of Holly's songs. *Rolling Stone Magazine* ranks him at #13 on their list of the "100 Greatest Artists of All Time." Many would argue that he's in the top 5.

Don McLean's famous ode to Holly's death, *American Pie*, described February 3, 1959 as "the day the music died." However, that's somewhat of a misnomer. That date is the day Buddy Holly died, but his music and spirit still lives. Holly is there whenever you turn on the radio. He's there when an aspiring rock band performs at a local bar, or when a group of kids decides to form a garage band with dreams of hitting it big. I hear Buddy Holly now, as the sounds of my son's guitar-playing drift up from our basement. While I close my eyes and listen, in my mind I can vividly see the lanky kid from Lubbock with the black-rimmed glasses and rapidly flailing guitar hand. The kid who tragically died, yet still triumphantly endured. Rave On, Buddy Holly…Rave On!

AFTERWORD

As I write this during the summer of 2019, I am thoroughly intrigued by a fascinating new technology that is being used for an upcoming "virtual" concert tour starring Buddy Holly and Roy Orbison! Well, it's actually hologram depictions of the two rock legends performing with a live band and back-up singers. Can you imagine the possibilities as this technology matures, and a hologram eventually becomes indistinguishable from a living person? Buddy Holly – the kid who tragically died, yet still endures through his music, his influence, and......his hologram!

FAREWELL TO THE KING OF HILL ROAD

(Edited version published in the April 24, 2009 *Philadelphia Inquirer*)

Peanuts Kerwood (Photo courtesy of Tom Kerwood)

He wasn't like the other dogs I had known. Peanuts, a lab-terrier mix with a lean yet powerful build, somehow seemed to sense the uneasiness and fear that I always had around dogs, so he treated me differently than the other kids. He would run up to the others, and put his paws on their thighs, looking for a back-scratch. With me, he would slowly stroll up and look up at me with his big brown eyes while gently bowing his head. He was the only dog I would scratch on the head.

One of the many wonderful things about John Grogan's *Marley and Me* is that it brought back the memories I have of Peanuts Kerwood. My friends and I respected him so much, that we still refer to him with a surname. Technically, he was my friend Tom Kerwood's dog, but we all thought of him as our own. In reality, Peanuts didn't believe he had an owner because he was so fiercely independent. I had the impression that he thought the Kerwoods lived with him, but was content to have them believe otherwise.

The 7300 block of Hill Road in the Roxborough section of Philadelphia was a remarkable street for the baby-boom generation. Despite the fact that it was only about 250 yards long, there were some 85 kids (18 and under) living on that street in the early 1970's. We always include Peanuts in that total because we thought of him as one of the gang. He would play tag with us in the summer, jump in leave piles with us in autumn, and pull us on our sleds in the winter.

Peanuts was also very protective of his friends and I welcomed his companionship along my paper route, especially after dark. There was one mean dog on my route that constantly harassed me whenever Peanuts wasn't around. Peanuts took him on one day, and I wasn't bothered again after that. I looked down at him after that scrap, scratched his head, and said, "You're the King of this street, Peanuts."

As my adolescence gave way to young adulthood and college, Peanuts was still patrolling Hill Road. I remember after one particularly rowdy night of drinking beer "back the woods" I was struggling while taking a zigzag path home, when Peanuts suddenly appeared ahead of me. He turned and gave me a look that said "Better follow me". I closed one eye, focused the other on Peanuts and said, "Lead the way old buddy."

Wild stories floated around about Peanuts. People claimed to have seen him all over town, at City Hall, or down at Veterans Stadium after a Phillies game. Others said they saw him driving a car, or leisurely drifting down the Schuylkill River in a canoe. It was rumored that he had a job in construction. His legend began to grow, especially among the female dogs, and I wouldn't be surprised to learn that he had sired hundreds during his reign as King.

I eventually married and moved away, but I was always glad to see Peanuts during visits to my parent's house. He limped a little and was getting a bit slower and rounder as the years went by, but he would still greet me the same way: head down, eyes looking up, waiting for a head scratch.

During a visit in the late 1980's, my brother Pat and I heard a commotion outside the house. Someone was saying that Peanuts was hurt. We noticed that a small crowd had gathered on the Kerwood's lawn. We hurried up the street, and there, laying on the lawn, was Peanuts. "We've put him here so that everyone can say good-bye", Tom's sister Kathy cried. "He has to be put to sleep. Some no-good bum shot him." The vet couldn't determine when he had been shot. The limp we had noticed over the last few years was probably the result of the .22 caliber bullet that slowly deteriorated the muscle in his hind leg. Peanuts just lived with the pain, until he couldn't anymore. Kathy was right. Whoever shot him was a no-good bum.

I knelt down next to Peanuts. He looked at me with sad brown eyes and gently bowed his head. Tears filled my eyes as I scratched his head for the last time. I noticed that the crowd behind me was growing, and I wasn't surprised. The loyal subjects were gathering, for they had come to pay their respects and bid a final farewell to the King of Hill Road.

AFTERWORD

Although I embellished just a bit about Peanuts driving a car, and having a job, he truly did seem like one of us. His death hit me much harder than I initially thought it would. Over the years, whenever I'd meet another dog, I would often look for those same characteristics that Peanuts possessed. I eventually realized how futile that was, and have since stopped, for I now know that there will never be another like Peanuts. In the words of William Shakespeare, "I shall not look upon his like again."

THE MAGIC UP ON THE ROOF

(Edited version published in the September 7, 2009
Philadelphia Inquirer)

The backyard porch roof of the author's childhood home

"When this old world starts getting me down,
And people are just too much for me to face,
I climb way up to the top of the stairs,
And all my cares just drift right into space."
("Up On The Roof" – The Drifters)

I used to hear them up on the porch roof in our back yard on those summer nights back in the late '60's and early '70's. Sometimes I would look up and see their cigarette smoke slowly curling up into the moist, humid air. My older brothers, Jack, Jerry and Mike, used to climb up onto the porch roof, lie on their backs with their legs crossed, and look up at the stars in the summer sky, without a care in the world. They would smoke my parent's cigarettes, drink my Dad's beer, and talk about the things that really mattered in their world: the Phillies, rock'n'roll, girls, and their big plans for the future. Their voices, laughter, and cigarette smoke would float up into the night, mix in with the hum of the air conditioners, and briefly cling to the moist summer air, before slowly drifting down into the yard and across the rolling, hilly streets of Roxborough.

Nearly inseparable since they were toddlers, the three of them had often been mistaken as triplets, but 25 months actually separated oldest from youngest. They made each other laugh like only brothers can, the kind of laughter that comes from knowing each other as well as you know yourself. Mike did a hysterical imitation of my Irish grandpop. When his neighborhood in North Philly (known as "Swampoodle") started to get a bit rough in the late 1960's we would ask grandpop if we could go outside and play when we visited on Sundays. He would reply in his thick Irish brogue, "Well…can ya fight?" Mike would do that routine (among many others) up on the roof, and I could hear my other brothers laughing whenever he did. I would laugh as well, but not too loud. They would've chased me away if they knew I was down in the yard. I often wished that I could go up there with them, but little brothers weren't allowed.

Over time, the voices and laughter emanating from the roof gradually diminished. Jack tragically died, Mike joined the Navy, and Jerry became occupied with college. I started going up there myself with my brother Pat and my friends, but it wasn't the same. The roof just didn't have the same magic that it seemed to have for Jack, Jerry, and Mike.

The night before my parents finally moved out of the old house, I stood in the yard and looked up at the roof. I don't know what I expected to find there, but I wondered what happened to its magic. Perhaps, if I closed my eyes and listened closely, I would hear the laughter and smell the smoke just one more time. But there was only silence and the sad feeling that something cherished, yet quite elusive, used to be up there, and had long since faded away.

A few weeks ago, Mike and Jerry stopped over at the house I was renting in Sea Isle. I wasn't home, but I told them I'd meet them up on the 2nd floor deck. When I arrived I started to walk up the steps, but then I stopped because I heard a familiar sound coming from above. Mike was imitating my grandpop, and Jerry was laughing. They were drinking beer, and looking up at the stars, and talking about their big plans for the future. At that moment I realized that the old porch roof never held any magic after all, but it had always been in my three older brothers all along. I sat on the deck, and I let them do most of the talking. I made sure that the beer kept flowing and the '70's music kept playing. Their laughter floated up into the night, and mixed in with the hum of the air conditioners, before slowly drifting down onto the streets of Sea Isle below. I laughed along with them, but not too loud. I really just wanted to take it all in because after all of these years I had gotten my wish, and finally made it up on the roof with them.

AFTERWORD

All throughout my life, whenever I've informed new acquaintances that I am one of eleven siblings, they are usually startled to hear it. But when I tell anyone that I am one of sixty grandchildren of my mother's parents, Jim and Mary Baird, they are dumbfounded. You read that correctly – I have 59 first cousins on my mother's side of the family. My mother was one of twelve, eleven of whom survived into adulthood. Many of her siblings had large families themselves. When this story was published, one of my cousins, Jimmy Baird, who was the same age as my older brothers and was very close to them when he was younger, sent me a text message. He told me that this was his favorite of all of my stories, that he remembered sitting up on that roof in our backyard, and that he laughed and cried as he read it. Jimmy died from cancer in 2015 at the age of 60, well before he should have. He was a good man who would often check in on my aging parents while they lived in Cape May Courthouse, NJ as he lived only a few miles away in Wildwood, NJ. When I heard that he died, I remembered that text he sent me, and I smiled as I imagined him up in heaven as a young teen sitting with my brother Jack on the old backyard roof.

JOURNEY OF THE MIND BEGAN 50 YEARS AGO

"Twilight Zone" remains one of the best TV shows

(Edited version published in the October 2, 2009 *Philadelphia Inquirer*)

Publicity photo of Rod Serling for the premiere of The Twilight Zone

"You're traveling through another dimension, a dimension not only of sight and sound but of mind; a journey into a wondrous land whose boundaries are that of imagination. That's the signpost up ahead – your next stop, the Twilight Zone!" (Rod Serling's opening narration to The Twilight Zone)

I was just about 10 years old at the time, and my older brothers were setting me up, but I didn't know it. Their bedroom was only lit by the eerie illumination of their black and white TV as we watched a *Twilight Zone* re-run. I had never seen the episode before and I was shivering in fright. In the now famous episode, a doctor was about to remove the last bandages from the unseen face of a hideously disfigured woman. My brothers told me that her face was the most frightening thing they had ever seen, and it might be better if I didn't look. My hands covered my eyes, and my heart raced from fear as the final bandage was removed. I couldn't resist and I peeked through my trembling fingers as her face was revealed, but, to my astonishment, the woman was beautiful! "We were only kidding", my brothers said. Relieved, I put my hands down, but wondered what the point of the episode had been. Suddenly, the camera revealed the faces of the doctors and nurses, and THEY were the ones who were hideously ugly! The blood drained away from my frightened face as my brothers roared with laughter. Although Rod Serling's ending narration conveyed a moral lesson of beauty being in the "eye of the beholder", it did very little to help dry my wet pajamas. I couldn't sleep for 3 days.

October 2nd marks the 50th anniversary of the premiere of one of the greatest television shows ever: Rod Serling's *The Twilight Zone*. Despite tepid ratings during its 5 year run, the show's popularity surged in re-run syndication and it gradually entrenched itself into American pop culture. Its influence is such that Serling's unique voice and delivery are still commonly imitated, people will often mimic the show's iconic opening theme music ("dee-dee-dee-doo") whenever a strange coincidence occurs, and the term "twilight zone" is now widely used to describe anything ambiguous or unknown.

Serling, a paratrooper in WW II, used his GI Bill benefits to enroll in Antioch College, where he began writing radio and TV scripts. In 1957 his *Playhouse 90* teleplay, *Requiem for a Heavyweight*, garnered him a Peabody Award. However, he often clashed with television executives over stringent program censorship. "I think it's criminal that (television drama) is not permitted to make dramatic note of social evils…in our society," he said in an interview.

TZ enabled Serling to mask his social commentaries under the guise of "fantastic fiction" in an anthology format. He presented a different story each week, many with strange settings, but with the familiar human themes of courage, fear, jealousy, sacrifice, and greed. Issues that would later epitomize the social upheaval of the 1960's were also dramatized: racism, communism, nuclear war, and civil rights.

Although Serling wrote most of the scripts, *TZ* also employed other brilliant writers, such as Charles Beaumont and Richard Matheson. The show was an inspiration to budding writers, and future Hollywood icons like Steven Spielberg. But, *TZ's* lasting legacy was that it touched the imaginations of its numerous fans with thought provoking and chilling episodes, many with twist endings that would leave viewers stunned. A few of the most memorable: an airplane crew dismisses a passenger's bizarre claims of a creature damaging the wing of their plane, a former Nazi Concentration Camp guard is put on trial by the ghosts of the inmates he murdered, a troubled executive travels back in time to deliver a message to the boy he used to be, and an old man outwits Mr. Death to save a little girl's life, but at the cost of his own. These are just a fraction of the numerous *TZ* gems, and it won 3 Emmy's and 3 Hugo Awards during its run.

I never forgave my brothers for setting me up that night, but I also never thanked them. They introduced me to one of the most wondrous television shows ever produced, and I now have nearly every episode on DVD. I often watch them with my sons, and the show's legion of fans continues to grow across generations. The old saying is true. Beauty is in the eye of the beholder, and *The Twilight Zone* truly is a national treasure to behold.

AFTERWORD

After reading this essay, Rod Serling's daughter, Anne, sent me an e-mail expressing her appreciation. However, despite my best search efforts, I couldn't find it in my files. Such is life. As I wrote this afterword in January of 2020, The Twilight Zone continues to make news. Season 2 of Jordan Peele's TZ revival series on CBS All Access has just announced the list of actors that will be appearing in the upcoming episodes of 2020. I enjoyed season 1, and I'm very happy that a true TZ fanatic, like Peele, is at the helm of the new series. Sadly, it was also just reported that Rod Serling's wife, Carol, passed away at the age of 91. Rod died nearly 45 years ago of a heart attack. In 2013, TV Guide ranked TZ #5 on its list of the 60 greatest TV shows of all time, and #4 on its list of greatest TV dramas.

AN OLYMPIC MEMORY, RED, YELLOW, AND WHITE

A young Austrian's bravery and skill got the crowd behind him – even in Philadelphia.

(Edited version published in the February 12, 2010
Philadelphia Inquirer)

Franz Klammer, Innsbruck - 1976 (Photo courtesy of Fischersports)

The television images of him from that winter-day broadcast in 1976 are still permanently etched in my mind. Wearing a blazing yellow ski suit with bright red boots and helmet, the fearless young Austrian cemented his legendary status not only in the annals of Olympic history, but also in the memories of those who witnessed it. My brothers and I watched in awe as he careened down the snow covered mountain, at times airborne and seemingly out of control, with his arms wildly gyrating in a desperate attempt to maintain his balance. We didn't know it at the time, but what we were watching is now regarded as one of the greatest moments in Winter Olympics history: the 1976 gold medal winning downhill skiing run by Franz Klammer at Innsbruck, Austria.

Although I've often tried to convey to my two teenage sons the thrill of watching Klammer's electrifying downhill run, they glance at me with skeptical expressions on their faces that expose their true thoughts: "C'mon Dad...he was just skiing!" However, to understand why it is so memorable to the "over-40" generation, one has to understand television in the mid-1970's. This was an era before cable and satellite TV, and the program choices were limited to just 7 or 8 channels. Consequently, ABC's *Wide World of Sports* and the Winter Olympics were eagerly anticipated, especially in the sports-crazy home where I was raised. As a result, we all gained an appreciation for just how difficult, exciting, and dangerous downhill skiing can be.

The 22 year old Klammer was favored to win the gold in his home country, and nearly 60,000 were in attendance. But as he crouched down in the starting gate, Klammer was faced with a seemingly impossible task. He was the last of the 15 competitors, and the condition of the course had deteriorated with each skier. Switzerland's Bernhard Russi, the 3rd skier that day, was the leader with an amazing time of 1:46.06. If Klammer was going to win the gold medal, he would have to post a time that was an astonishing 2 seconds better than his previous best time on that same course. He later commented that he felt that he had no other choice but "to go all out."

Klammer's daring style nearly cost him as he luckily avoided crashing at the top of the course. At the halfway point, he trailed Russi by a fraction of a second and Klammer sensed that he was behind and "had to do something". In a desperate and dangerous gamble to pick up speed, he decided to ski closer to the boundary gates where the snow wasn't as "chopped up". The voices of *ABC* commentators Frank Gifford and Bob Beattie became noticeably tense. His coach couldn't bear to watch, frequently closing his eyes in fear as Klammer repeatedly and miraculously escaped catastrophe. My brothers and I began to cheer him on because he was no longer just another foreign skier, but he had suddenly become the living embodiment of the human spirit fighting to overcome insurmountable odds. On our old "pre-HD" console color TV, Klammer became a streaking bright yellow and red blur against a snow-white background, as he attacked the course with reckless abandon. Again, near the bottom of the course, he almost fell, precariously teetering on one ski. I held my breath while staring at the time clock as Klammer raced down the final straightaway. When he crossed the finish line, Frank Gifford exclaimed, "Klammer has done it! This crowd has gone crazy!" Our living room erupted!

On New Year's Day, I watched hockey's *Winter Classic* with my sons and my good friend Bill. During a commercial about the upcoming Winter Olympic Games, Bill said, "How 'bout that run by Franz Klammer that time?" Our faces lit up and we shook our heads in amazement as the memories came flooding back. My sons glanced at us with those same skeptical expressions and I actually felt sorry for them because they weren't alive on that memorable day in 1976 when a fearless young skier from Austria transcended sports with a remarkable demonstration of courage and skill. My eyes momentarily glazed over as the vivid images of a blazing yellow and red figure with wildly gyrating arms streaked across my mind. "I'll never forget it...incredible", I replied to Bill, and I thought I noticed the looks of skepticism on my sons faces change to looks of envy.

AFTERWORD

It really can be difficult to fully express the sheer excitement of witnessing Klammer's remarkable downhill run to those, like my sons, who were not alive when it happened. Every Winter Olympics telecast since 1976 always conjures up images of the streaking Austrian daredevil dressed in yellow and red. In

January of 2016, to commemorate the 40th anniversary of that incredible moment, The Guardian's Richard Williams brilliantly described Klammer's fearless battle against the course: "Within the first 15 seconds it became apparent to anyone watching from the warmth and safety of their front room that here was a man willing to go beyond the limits of control. The course was being attacked head-on and it responded by biting back, forcing Klammer into lurid feats of last-ditch recovery. Old-timers, taught to lock their skis together in neat parallel turns, recoiled at the way all the rules of style and balance were abandoned in one man's juddering, flailing battle with gravity and centrifugal force."

IT TOOK OUR BULLIES TO BEAT THEM

Remembering the Philly team that bested Boston, Buffalo – and Russia.

(Edited version published in the May 4, 2010 *Philadelphia Inquirer*)

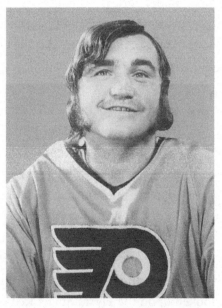

Rick MacLeish - Philadelphia Flyers - 1973

"The Flyers salvaged Canada's pride in her nation's sport with a near perfect hockey masterpiece." (Tim Burke – Montreal Gazette)

As Rick MacLeish took the pass from Ross Lonsberry, he used his exceptional speed to skate in alone on the great Russian goaltender, Vladislav Tretiak. My brother Jerry leaped out of our living room chair. "He's gonna go high to the glove side!" he yelled. My brothers and I stood, and inched closer to the television, our hearts pounding in anticipation. Although the Flyers were leading 1-0, the game was far from over as this Russian team was known to strike quickly and often. We collectively held our breath as MacLeish closed on Tretiak, but I already knew what was going to happen.

―――――

On Tuesday night, HBO Sports premieres *The Broad Street Bullies*, the story of the legendary Philadelphia Flyers teams that won two Stanley Cups in 1974 and 1975, as well as beat a seemingly invincible Soviet Red Army team in the 1976 "Super Series."

The documentary reveals the tight bond that developed between the Flyers and its growing fan base in the early 1970's. The Phillies, Sixers, and Eagles were mediocre at best, but the Flyers steadily improved since their inception in 1967, and by 1972 they were regarded as one of the better teams in the NHL. In a short period of time Philadelphia became enamored with hockey and the Flyers. Kids all over Philly's neighborhoods played endless hours of street hockey. My friends and I made goalie pads out of old couch foam, and nets out of wood and chicken-wire. The old Gold Medal sporting goods store in Andorra couldn't keep enough Mylec hockey balls and sticks in stock, and I still vividly remember the wild celebrations on Ridge Ave. that followed their two Stanley Cup victories.

But the 1976 "Super Series" of games between NHL teams and two touring Russian hockey teams holds a special place in my memory, as the hockey world looked upon the Flyers-Soviet Red Army game as the unofficial World Championship. I remember being as pumped for that game as I was for any of the Flyers playoff games, including the Stanley Cup clinching games against Boston and Buffalo. This Russian team had easily defeated the New York Rangers (7-3) and the Boston Bruins (5-2), and tied a powerful Montreal team in the days leading up to the showdown with the Flyers.

The fans and sportswriters of the other NHL teams had angered me because prior to the Super Series, they had unfairly categorized the Flyers as a team of thugs who never deserved to hoist the sacred Stanley Cup above their heads. But now they suddenly looked upon "their" Flyers to salvage the NHL's pride. No thanks, I thought to myself, this is our team and always has been, and we'll take on the Russians alone without your shallow support.

MacLeish did beat Tretiak on that breakaway, and the goal seemed to break the Red Army's spirit. It turned out to be the game winner as the Flyers won 4-1, and were recognized as the unofficial World Champions of hockey.

One day last year, as I sat at the VFW bar in Sea Isle, NJ with my Dad and my brother Mike, I was surprised to see Rick MacLeish sitting across the bar. "Oh, he likes it here", the bartender told me.

Life can be so strange sometimes. Here was a guy I idolized as a kid, the guy who scored two of the biggest goals in Flyers history - one clinching a Stanley Cup, and the other a world championship. And he wasn't at a swanky Atlantic City lounge or the Stone Harbor Country Club bar, but he was in the Sea Isle VFW, with the old veterans, retired cops and firemen, and the rest of us. I shouldn't have been surprised, though. After all, one of the reasons why our city had embraced these tough, working-class guys from small towns across Canada was because, as we often said, "they're just like us."

I wanted to tell MacLeish how those Flyers teams lifted the spirits of our city, and showed us what a bunch of blue collar type guys could do if they stuck together and believed in themselves. So, I let him know my appreciation in the time honored way it's been done in bars like the VFW for years. I bought him a beer, and he nodded in thanks as I tipped my bottle towards him.

MacLeish didn't know it, but he once again made my day, much as had more than 30 years earlier, by beating one of the greatest goalies ever with a wrist shot that went high to the glove side - just as I knew he would.

Me, my wife, and Bernie Parent

AFTERWORD

Shortly after this story was published, my brother Mike told me that his father-in-law ran into MacLeish at the VFW in Sea Isle and gave Rick a copy of my article. I truly hope that he liked it, and I felt like a bit of my childhood died when MacLeish passed away in the spring of 2016. So many of those Flyers from that era made Philadelphia and the South Jersey shore towns their homes, and I wasn't surprised to run into Hall of Fame goaltender Bernie Parent a few months after MacLeish died at a restaurant in Avalon N.J. – just a few miles south of the Sea Isle VFW. Bernie was great as he heartily greeted me and my wife when I recognized him, and took several photos with us – one of them is shown here. What a moment that was for me and my wife! I often wonder if those Flyers really comprehend what they meant to so many Philly kids who grew up in the '60's and '70's.

THE END OF A SUMMER, AND WITH IT MUCH MORE

This year would bring a new school, new friends, and an irreplaceable loss.

(Edited version published in the July 25, 2010 *Philadelphia Inquirer*)

Vincent "Vinnie" Hopkins (Photo courtesy of the Hopkins family)

"I never had any friends later on like the ones I had when I was twelve. Jesus, does anyone?" (Narrator from the movie "Stand By Me")

My friend Vinnie and I would often sit on the red brick wall in front of my house on those warm summer nights in 1975. We would talk long into the night about our upcoming freshman year at Roman Catholic High School, the long SEPTA bus ride into Center City, and the changes in our life that we knew would soon be upon us. The little world we had known was about to get a whole lot bigger, and we both sensed that the innocence of our adolescence was slowly fading as the long, lazy shadows of the summer twilight slowly crept across our street each evening to eventually merge with the darkness of the inevitable night.

Vincent "Vinnie" Hopkins was my next door neighbor and classmate since 3rd grade, and our summers during that time were filled with endless hours of wiffle-ball, kick-ball, running through lawn sprinklers, eating Good Humor popsicles, playing line-tag, hammering caps, and long talks into the night that only ended when our mother's called us in. Vinnie had a hearty, infectious laugh that actually made others laugh when they heard it, and if I ever felt down about something he would be the first one to try and cheer me up. I liked talking to him on those summer nights of '75 because although he was experiencing the same apprehension that I was, he was handling it with that same easy sense of humor that I had come to admire, and he put me at ease.

We would often take the bus together to Roman, but we also slowly began to drift apart during our freshmen year. We hung out with different groups of guys, and my crew was extremely mischievous, and frequently in trouble. We smoked, drank, cursed like sailors, and thought we were "too cool" for everyone else. Consequently, I was a frequent early morning guest at Roman's detention classroom, but Vinnie seemed to maintain some of the innocent qualities of our youth that in many ways I wished that I still had, but was afraid to admit, especially in front of my "cool" friends.

One night, Vinnie and I had an argument after my friends and I had squirted a school's fire extinguishers on the basketball court where he was playing. We didn't speak to each other for weeks.

On a blustery Sunday in March 1976, Vinnie asked me if I'd like to head over to a local public high school's parking lot to play street hockey. I told him that it might rain, so I would pass, but his invitation gave me the impression that our little rift was over. It was so typical of Vinnie to extend a hand of friendship even though I was the one who was wrong. Sadly, that was the last time I saw him alive. A few hours later, a freak windstorm blew through our neighborhood. Broken glass and debris from the school's rooftop was violently hurled down upon the boys playing in the parking lot below. Vinnie's neck was badly cut by the flying debris and he was rushed to the hospital. He valiantly fought for his life for several days, but his injury was too severe. Vinnie died on March 25th.

The pallbearers gathered at my house the morning of the funeral. The first one to arrive was a good friend of Vinnie's from his other crew named Ed. Although Ed Delaney and I had known each other throughout grade school, we never talked as much as we did that day. We started to talk that morning about Vinnie and the tragedy, and life in general, and we didn't stop until the day had ended. Ed and I became the best of friends and have remained close ever since. We often say that we think Vinnie would be happy to know that.

I've come to realize that you never really do have friends like the ones you had when you were twelve, and I guess that's why most of those guys from my old crew are still my friends. But there is one friend that I wished that I still had, and I often think about that freckle faced kid with the infectious laugh who always seemed to lift my spirits. I know that as this summer winds down and I watch my son walk down the street to catch the SEPTA bus to Roman to begin his freshmen year, I'll remember two boys who once did the same thing together nearly 35 years ago, and left their innocence in the fading shadows of the summer twilights they used to know.

AFTERWORD

I received a lot of e-mails from Inquirer readers regarding this essay about Vinnie, and the most touching was from a young lady who was inspired to reach out to a friend who had drifted from her life. She wrote: "I'm not entirely sure if you remember me, but I attended your son, Jack's graduation party in June... I recently read your article in the Philadelphia Inquirer and I can honestly say it was one of the most touching articles I have ever had the pleasure to read. It caught my eye in the newspaper because I have quite a few friends who attend Roman Catholic, and after reading it, I couldn't help but shed a few tears. My closest friend lives across the street from me, and she and I have remained closest of friends since we were born. We are now sixteen, and though we have always attended separate schools, we have still remained very close. She is like a sister to me. Your article reminded me of the summers we used to spend together, either playing ball in the street, chasing after ice cream trucks, or sitting on the steps in front of her house after a long day of summer camp, just talking and enjoying each other's company. We have since drifted during the summers, no longer going to summer camp together. I am now a lifeguard at the local pool, and she can be found as a counselor at a sleep away camp. However, after reading this, I think I will call her up and see if she's up for a little street volleyball and we can maybe even chase after an ice cream truck or two. As you can tell, your article really spoke to me, and the last few lines were especially powerful... "I know that as this summer winds down, and as I watch my son walk down the street to catch the SEPTA bus to Roman to begin his freshman year, I'll remember two boys who did the same thing together nearly 35 years ago, and left their innocence in the fading shadows of the summer twilights they used to know. " I guess I never realized it, but we really do leave our innocence behind in the summer before freshman year; it tends to get lost in the shadows. We are all so intent on fitting in, and testing the limits, and shedding our old childhood skin, that we tend to forget those old summer nights spent with the neighborhood kids. When it comes down to it, you are absolutely right. You never really have friends like the ones you had when you were twelve and that is why I am giving Leah a call as soon as I finish this e-mail. Thank you so much, for your incredibly inspiring article. It really touched me. I hope to read more of your articles in the future."

LOSING AND FINDING, THE OLD NEIGHBORHOOD

A crime reveals what has and hasn't changed.

(Edited version published in the September 15, 2010
Philadelphia Inquirer)

Vince Poppa (Photo courtesy of Nick Poppa)

"The old neighborhood's changed," my friends from West Catholic often told me during their annual reunion in North Wildwood. I would shrug it off as the cliché lament of former city dwellers who had fled to the suburbs.

But when I heard about what happened to Vince Poppa, I was shocked at just how much the old neighborhood had changed.

On March 13, around 9 p.m., some kids at James Finnegan Playground in Southwest Philadelphia were playing a new game they called "catch and wreck." Its objective was to catch and mercilessly beat someone they assumed to be homeless. They cornered Poppa, 73, who was not homeless, outside his senior citizens' apartment complex, struck him in the back of the head with a gun, and kicked him when he fell. He suffered a heart attack during the beating, which was so savage that hospital personnel found sneaker marks all over his body.

A week later, the kids beat 42-year-old Belinda Moore, who was not homeless either, after finding her walking through the playground. They told police they did it "for fun."

In the section of Southwest Philly surrounding Finnegan playground, there was a time when the neighborhood children loved and respected Vince Poppa. He owned "Vince's," a mom-and-pop convenience store at 65th Street and Dicks Avenue. The store was a veritable neighborhood institution where local kids would buy candy, gum, and trinkets. In the late afternoon, it was common to see a crowd of girls from West Philadelphia Catholic High School, in their green blouses and knee-high socks, milling around outside the store.

Finnegan playground is just a few blocks from Vince's, and many fondly recall it as the place where they learned to swim, hit a baseball, or shoot a jumper. Playground violence at the time was limited to an occasional fistfight; pistol-whipping people for fun never entered anyone's mind.

Although I was from Roxborough, my wife was from this working-class neighborhood of mostly Irish and Italian heritage. Several Catholic parishes dominated the area and were broken down by ethnicity: St. Barnabas and Good Shepherd were primarily Irish; Our Lady of Loreto was mainly Italian; St. Clement and St. Irenaeus were mixed.

I always felt safe and welcome among the neighborhood's narrow, rowhouse-lined streets. I often stopped at Vince's for a pack of cigarettes or gum and was greeted with a friendly smile and a "How ya doin'?!" The neighborhood adopted me as one of its own, and some of the people who grew up there became my best friends.

I learned early on that it was a proud place, much like my own neighborhood. Punishment for unruly kids was meted out by parents and nuns, not police officers. Honor and respect were not just words.

One night, a buddy from Roxborough and I were in one of the neighborhood's numerous corner bars, Sullivan's Café, when two tough-looking guys walked in and sat down. Each downed a shot of whiskey. One looked at the other and said, "You ready?" "Let's do it," the other replied, and they stepped outside.

My friend and I looked at each other, puzzled. We asked the bartender why they had gone outside. "To fight," he said. "To fight who?" we asked. "Each other." We noticed that none of the other patrons went outside to watch; to do so would have violated some unspoken neighborhood protocol. The men soon reentered the bar with cuts and bruises and sat down next to each other as if nothing had happened. Nobody was seriously hurt and, in a way some might not understand, an issue was privately resolved.

Vince spent 39 days in the hospital and is still struggling to recover. Last month, a large group of his friends, family, and former classmates gathered at a South Philly restaurant and presented him with a plaque marking their friendship. "We just wanted to let him know that we love him and care about him," Vince's close friend Matt Senior told me. Many wiped away tears during the emotional evening.

It is true: The old neighborhood has changed. But when I heard about the people who rallied around Vince Poppa, I was heartened that those who grew up there haven't changed. They've shown that the old neighborhood is a place that exists not only within the confines of your memories, but also within the hearts and souls of those who used to call that place home.

AFTERWORD

Following the publication of this essay, to say that I received a lot of e-mails in response to it would be an understatement. In reality, my inbox was "crushed", predominantly with e-mails from those who grew up in the old neighborhood. The great majority of them expressed anger, shock, and frustration over what happened to Vince, Ms. Moore, and their old neighborhood. The following e-mail expressed the feelings of the former neighborhood residents the best: "Just read your article in today's Inquirer, and although this is not something I typically do I just had to write to comment. In about an hour I am leaving for the shore - I am meeting a group of women (my sorority sisters) that I have been friends with for over 40 years, and we are all from the old neighborhood. Some of us have been together since the playpen, some grade school, all of us starting hanging out before entering high school. The majority of us are good ole Catholic girls and attended - St. Clements and then West Catholic - we do have one publican in the group. I lived at 73rd and Wheeler - near the intersection of Island Rd. and Elmwood Ave. - we all hung out at 74th Street. The majority of my friends did live near Finnegan Playground and have glorious memories of it - and were frequent customers of Poppa's. I had not heard of the violent attack on Mr. Poppa. I am very saddened by it, and the pain he must have suffered - he is lucky to be alive - how nice there was an event to honor him - I'm certain that helped to heal his spirit.

My sorority sisters and would I tell you that we grew up in the best neighborhood in the world - where everyone knew your name - where if you were in need of help all you had to do was yell loud enough or go to someone's door - where we would go out in the morning and besides coming home to eat or use the bathroom - no one thought of watching TV. For fun we played games - sang songs - listened to music and danced up a storm. Our lives were centered around our neighborhood, our church, or families and friends. It saddens me to read about the violence

- to think that the spirit of our neighborhood has been diminished in this way - I would love to be able to go back and reclaim it, but would be too afraid. I feel sorry for the people who think it is okay to confuse violent acts with fun - it makes you wonder just how horrible their lives must be to think this is acceptable. Our old neighborhood deserves better than that! I have packed your article in my suitcase - believe me it will be the center of our discussion this evening. Thank you for honoring our neighborhood - for letting people know that it used to be a wonderful place to live. You may have grown up in Roxborough, but you seem like a good ole Southwest Philly boy to me."

GHOSTS OF CHRISTMASES PAST

As children grow up, nostalgia suffuses the holidays.

(Edited version published in the December 24, 2010
Philadelphia Inquirer)

Jack and Ryan Gibbons - Christmas, 1996

It was a few days before Christmas, 2001, and a light snow was steadily falling outside that morning as my two young sons and I were rushing out the door. Trailing behind the two of them, I closed the door, but they suddenly stopped as they were momentarily startled by the sight of something at the end of our driveway. "What're you guys looking at?" I said impatiently as I emerged from the doorway. Standing motionless in the swirling snow some 15 yards away were three deer. One was a buck with an impressive set of antlers and steaming breath that billowed up from his nostrils as he struck a majestic pose. Humans and deer faced each other in the near silence of that moment as the soft patter of the laying snowflakes was barely audible above the sound of our beating hearts. My 5 year old son, Ryan, perfected the picturesque moment when he softly whispered: "Reindeer!"

I noticed my wife gazing out our kitchen window recently, a bit misty eyed and seemingly lost in her thoughts. "I miss them", she said in a melancholy voice. I glanced out the window to see what she was looking at. My two teenage sons, Jack and Ryan, were teaching our neighbor's little boy, 3 year old Cohen, the finer points of street hockey. "You miss who?" I replied. "I miss Jack and Ryan," she said, but she quickly noticed my puzzled expression. "I mean, I miss when they were little like Cohen". As the street-hockey ball rolled into one of the neat piles of leaves lining the curbs on our street,

I remembered that when my boys were Cohen's age they would joyfully jump in the piles of the autumn leaves. We were both now gazing out the window and vivid memories of them came flooding back. I saw them again as little boys throwing snow-balls, and wildly waving at Santa Claus as he rode through our neighborhood on a fire-truck, and happily bounding down the stairs on Christmas morning. "I miss them too", I said as a bittersweet smile ran across my face.

The Holiday season, more so than any other time of year, prompts many of us to fondly recall, and sometimes yearn for, the past. This innate human tendency has spanned the generations and has often been reflected in popular culture through books and film. From Charles Dickens' *A Christmas Carol*, through Frank Capra's *It's A Wonderful Life*, and even up to today with Jean Shepherd's *A Christmas Story*, we find the recurring theme of revisiting Christmas past, either through fictional fantasy or vivid childhood recollections. Many of us readily identify with this yearning and for those of us with grown children, the desire to once again experience Christmas morning with them as little girls and boys can sometimes be overwhelming and often lead to feelings of regret and lament.

Although most of us at one time or another wish that we could somehow revisit our past, to either change an outcome or to relive special moments like Christmas, there is a certain risk in dwelling upon it too much. Rod Serling brilliantly addressed this theme in his classic story, *Walking Distance* in which a harried executive's desire to live in the past is so powerful that he is miraculously transported 25 years back in time. In the story's most poignant moment, the man's father asks him why he has come back. "I've been living in a dead run and I was tired" he responds. "And one day I knew I had to come back here. I had to get on the merry-go-round and listen to a band concert. I had to stop and breathe, and close my eyes and smell, and listen." "I guess we all want that", his father says. "Maybe when you go back, you'll find there are merry-go-rounds and band concerts where you are. You've been looking behind you. Try looking ahead."

Like the man in the story, I often wish that I could revisit my past. But this Christmas I'm determined to recognize that the best days of my life are now and not in the past. The key is not to wish that my kids and I were young again, but it's to be young at heart and approach life with the same wondrous spirit that I had as a child. So, if I get the chance, I might jump in a pile of leaves, or maybe even have a snow-ball fight with Cohen. And if I'm lucky, there just might be another snowy morning when I'll see a buck standing in a majestic pose in front of my house. A voice will once again softly whisper "Reindeer", but this time, the voice will be mine.

AFTERWORD

One of the things that I could always count on following the publication of one of my essays in the Inquirer *was an e-mail from my neighbor, Tony. He always wrote how much he enjoyed reading it, and that he looked forward to reading more from me. Tony's feedback was a great source of encouragement for me because I could tell from his e-mails that he was a wonderful writer himself. Of this essay he wrote: "Your article was especially poignant for Bea and I who have looked out onto the* same circle at our children, and other children growing up for these 38 years…we've found the nostalgia for the past with our own boys growing up has been dimmed considerably by the arrival of grandchildren. So hold onto the "wondering spirit" and be patient."

Tony Schiavo, Korean War Veteran, passed away on July 30, 2019 at the age of 87. At his viewing, one of his sons pulled me aside and said he had something he wanted to give me. It was a beautifully written essay by Tony. In the essay, Tony recounts a day that he was watching the neighborhood boys play street-hockey in our circle, which then prompts recollections of the street-games of his youth while growing up in South Philadelphia. He closed his essay with a beautiful, poignant message to the boys: "I'm not going to try to persuade the boys outside that I'm one of them, me playing in their games is too grotesque to imagine – especially after my spectacular flop on the first pass I had them throw me. But if I could get a message through the age communications barrier, it would be this: enjoy playing, but also take it all in – the games, the plays, and especially the faces – not to tell others, they won't care, but to recall how good it was when they are old men watching new boys play."

THE BOXER

A tough guy fallen on hard times

(Edited version published in the June 1, 2011 *Philadelphia Inquirer*)

Image - Jean Beaufort

"In the clearing stands a boxer, and a fighter by his trade,
And he carries the reminders, of ev'ry glove that laid him down,
Or cut him, 'till he cried out, in his anger and his shame,
"I am leaving, I am leaving", but the fighter still remains."
(Simon and Garfunkel - "The Boxer")

The two thugs had jumped me in the Philadelphia subway concourse that night over 30 years ago, but I had managed to break away and was running towards the steps that led to Market Street. I never turned my head to see how close they were, but I could hear the clap of their sneakers behind me echoing off the concourse walls, and I remember fearing that a knife blade would pierce my back at any moment. I ran up the steps and raced down a seemingly deserted Market Street, towards 18th. Fueled by fear and adrenaline, I had no idea where I was running to, or what I was going to do, I was just hoping to outrun the two thugs. A lone car was stopped at the red light on 18th Street, and as I raced towards it, I couldn't believe my eyes - it was my good friend's older brother Anthony!

I opened the car door, and dove in. "Jesus Christ", he screamed. "What the f***?! You look like you seen a ghost, brother!" I was breathing so heavily that I could barely speak. "I just got jumped!", I finally managed to blurt out. "They were running after me, but I don't know where the hell they are now!'

Anthony, or "Antny" as he was known by everyone in the neighborhood, didn't blink an eye, and said, "I got two baseball bats in the trunk. Let's go get 'em!" I was still pretty shaken from the whole incident and said, "No, let's just get the hell out of here." We drove off, and Antny took me home.

Over the years, as I've gotten to know people who grew up in Philadelphia, we will often talk about the memorable characters from our old neighborhoods. Anthony was my very good friend's older brother, and one of the tough guys in our Roxborough neighborhood. He wasn't very tall, but he was broad-backed and muscular, and his build reminded me of former lightweight boxers Ray Mancini and Vinny Pazienza. As a matter of fact, the night that Anthony rescued me, he was on his way home from a South Philly boxing gym where he worked out. At one time, Anthony had dreams of becoming a pro, and I always believed that if he had stuck with it and received the right training, that he could have made a bit of a name for himself as a boxer. While he was training, he once put on a remarkable demonstration of his hand speed for me and my friend Paul. He snatched a buzzing house-fly out of the air with his right hand, then let it go, and quickly snatched it back out of the air with his left hand!

Unfortunately, Anthony's boxing career never materialized, but he did have his share of memorable street fights. Among them, my friends and I vividly recall Anthony and his buddy in their blood-stained prom tuxedos following a street fight with two other neighborhood guys, while others often recollect Anthony and another guy throwing haymakers at each other during a softball game dispute.

Time eventually caught up with all of us, as it does with every generation. The old neighborhood that I knew, and the characters that used to inhabit it, now only live within the confines of my memories. Jobs, marriages, kids, and just moving on in life were inevitabilities that we never really thought about "back in the day", but they ultimately claimed most of us. Sadly, some were taken by the ravages of drug addiction. That's what happened to Anthony.

A few months ago, rumors had been swirling that Anthony was homeless and living under the Ben Franklin Bridge. One night, as I sat in my car while stopped at a red light at the base of the bridge, I remembered the rumor, and my eyes scanned the darkened corners under the bridge looking for the familiar face of Anthony.

The baseball bats that I had in my trunk couldn't scare off the demons that now chased Anthony, but for a brief, naive moment, I thought that if I saw him, maybe I could help him escape his troubles, and drive him home like he had once done for me. But unfortunately, the simplicities of our youth gradually elude us, and the harsh realities of life sometimes dictate that the road to get back home is one that must be traveled alone. His brother has since told me that Anthony's battling back, like the fighter that he is, but the struggle is difficult.

I never saw Anthony that night and I drove away. As I watched the bridge recede in my rear-view mirror, my thoughts drifted back to the night when I was rescued, and I hoped that the boxer had somehow managed to find his way home.

AFTERWORD

After this essay was published, Anthony called me. During a highly emotional call in which we both shed a few tears, he thanked me for the kind words in the essay about him, and I thanked him for saving my life. He told me about his difficult struggles, and I let him know that I had confidence in him because of the fighter that he is, and always was. His daughters sent me e-mails after reading the essay, as well – excerpts from them are below.

"Hi Chris.....I am Anthony's middle daughter. I wanted to write to say thank you for that article about my father. I was told about this article.... and it brought me to tears remembering the old Dad I grew up with. To this day when people find out who my father is I still get told those old fighting stories or about his generosity. He does know about the article and I bet you he would also say thank you. Things have gotten a little better with him, and he is trying every day... So from my family, and myself, thank you for those old happy memories from the good old days!"

"Hi Chris.... I am Anthony's youngest daughter. I saw the article you wrote and I just wanted to say thank you. The article was amazing and it brought a smile to my face. I was happy to read the fond memories you have of my father. Your piece hit home because everyone who knows my Dad and knows that I am his daughter always tell me stories of the tough guy they once knew. Hopefully the boxer you once knew does find his way home...... Again, thank you so much for the article."

THE MAN WHO SAVED THE WORLD

(Edited version published in the September 25, 2011
Philadelphia Inquirer)

Mushroom cloud over Nagasaki

*"We have not yet experienced a global thermonuclear war --
although on more than one occasion we have come tremulously
close. I do not think our luck can hold forever."*
(Carl Sagan)

Try to remember, if you can, what you might have been doing shortly after 4pm EST on Sunday, September 25, 1983. Perhaps you were enjoying Sunday dinner with your family, or visiting friends, or maybe just taking in the beautiful early autumn day in the Delaware Valley. Some of you were still in diapers, or not even born. The Phillies and Eagles both played the St. Louis Cardinals in their respective sports that afternoon, and many in the Philadelphia area were shocked and saddened to learn that popular *WPVI-TV* weatherman Jim O'Brien had died in a skydiving accident.

Return of the Jedi, Trading Places, and *War Games* dominated the box office. *MTV* was airing 300 videos per day, and Michael Jackson, the Police, and the Eurythmics topped the music charts. Our country was in the 3rd year of Ronald Reagan's first term and the previously stagnant U.S. economy was improving, but tensions with the Soviet Union were alarmingly high. Just a few weeks prior to that Sunday, the Soviets had shot down a South Korean passenger plane that had mistakenly strayed into Russian airspace, killing all 269 aboard. Cold War anxieties were so prevalent that 10 year-old American schoolgirl Samantha Smith achieved overnight fame when she wrote to, and received a reply from, Soviet Premier Yuri Andropov asking him if his country would start a nuclear war.

Try to recall what you were doing around 4pm that Sunday, because half a world away, in a secret military bunker just south of Moscow, warning alarms were ominously sounding, and what you were doing could have wound up being the very last thing that you did on this Earth if not for the level-headed decision made by 44 year-old Soviet lieutenant colonel, Stanislav Petrov.

Although it is cited by CIA analyst Peter Pry as "the single most dangerous incident of the early 1980's," the tense drama that played out in the bunker that night is largely unknown by the general public. A Soviet early-warning satellite had signaled to the bunker that the U.S. had launched 5 nuclear armed Minuteman missiles at the Soviet Union. Petrov, in charge of a military staff that monitored these satellite signals, told the Washington Post that he was initially in "a state of shock."

Computer consoles and maps were flashing in the bunker indicating that the Soviet Union was under attack, and a red "START" button was blinking on Petrov's console. By pressing the button, Petrov would have informed Jurij Votincev, the Commander in Chief of the Russian missile defense, who then would have informed Andropov. Because of the heightened tensions between the U.S. and the Soviet Union, many military analysts believe Andropov would have ordered a counterattack, which would have prompted a full U.S. retaliation. The resulting nuclear exchange would have likely destroyed civilization.

The tension in the chaotic bunker reached near-panic levels as Petrov held a phone to his ear. A military officer on the line shouted at him to "remain calm and do his job." The protocol, which Petrov had written himself, was clear: he must push the red button. The pressure on Petrov mounted as his staff of 120 military officers and engineers awaited his decision. But Petrov told the Post that he "had a funny feeling in my gut." Soviet ground radar had not picked up a missile attack, and Petrov said that "when people start a war, they don't do it with five missiles." He finally faced his staff and told them to do nothing - it was a false alarm. Humanity's greatest catastrophe had been averted.

Investigations later revealed that the satellite had misinterpreted sunlight reflecting off cloud tops as missile launches. The Kremlin was embarrassed by the flaws exposed by the incident, and severely reprimanded Petrov for not properly detailing the event in his activity journal. Believing he was a scapegoat, Petrov retired a year later. He now lives on a paltry $200 per month pension in a small village near Moscow.

Although I've tried to recall, I can't remember exactly what I was doing on that Sunday in September of 1983, but I know what I'll be doing shortly after 4pm this Sunday. I'm going to take a moment to admire the beautiful fall foliage, or just breathe in the air, or maybe think about all of the wonderful things I've experienced in my life over the last 28 years. I know that my thoughts will eventually turn to a man who lives half a world away in relative obscurity, but whose courageous decision enabled all of us to live to see this day. And then I'll silently thank Stanislav Petrov, the man who saved the world.

AFTERWORD

I was heartened to learn that in 2013 Petrov was awarded the Dresden Peace Prize in Dresden, Germany, which included €25,000. In 2014, Petrov also became somewhat of a celebrity as a result of the release of the award winning documentary, The Man Who Saved The World. *He died on May 19, 2017.*

In a bizarre twist of irony, I eventually did remember exactly what I was doing on Sunday, September 25, 1983 – the day the world almost came to an end. I had attended a Baird family (my mother's side) reunion. The only reason that I remembered that was because on the Sunday that this essay was published, one of my cousins reminded me of that fact as I arrived at another Baird family reunion.

SEEING WHAT MATTERS MOST AT CHRISTMAS

(Edited versions published in the December 24, 2011 *Philadelphia Inquirer* and on the *WHYY.org* website on December 21, 2018)

(Photo courtesy of Rich Murray)

"In the darkest corner of the night,
Only dreams illuminate their eyes,
And they see all the colors that we cannot,
And theirs' is the most beautiful Christmas on the block."
(From "Christmas On The Block" by Alan Mann)

Our good friends Bill and Maryellen host an annual Christmas Eve gathering at their home in our Lafayette Hill neighborhood, and it's one of the highlights of the holiday season for me and my family.

With a varied assortment of family, friends, and neighbors, we'll gather around Bill's outdoor fire, reminisce about Christmases past, and sing along to the Christmas songs playing on his boom-box. Traditional songs by Nat King Cole, Brenda Lee, and Bing Crosby are favorites, as well as classics by Elvis, the Carpenters, and The Beach Boys.

Even relatively newer Christmas songs by millennial artists are starting to become popular among the gathering's largely baby-boomer crowd.

Inevitably, though, as the music is playing and the fire is roaring, I'll gaze out into the street to admire the Christmas lights decorating the houses in our neighborhood, and the words to one of the most beautiful Christmas songs ever will echo in my mind. I always look forward to hearing it played on the radio every year. Its poignant lyrics, along with the uplifting story behind the song, exemplify the true meaning of Christmas.

Alan Mann's *Christmas on the Block* is largely unknown outside of this region, but many Philly-area residents consider it their favorite song of the season. They often cite the song's powerful, emotional impact, not only because it evokes childhood memories of Christmas lights illuminating the neighborhood blocks of their youth. It also conveys a message of selfless giving that resonates during the yuletide season.

In the mid-1980s, rising Philadelphia rock star Alan Mann heard of a group home for the blind on a street in Upper Darby. Every Christmas, the residents would decorate a tree in front of their house, and neighbors considered it the most beautifully decorated tree on the block. Although they could not see, the residents wanted to give an annual Christmas gift to those who could.

The story inspired Mann to visit the house and write the song, which features a chorus sung by second-graders that often moves listeners to tears.

"I can never hear this song and not have a tear or three," a listener wrote on YouTube.

Aspiring Temple University film student Richard Murray made the video — his first — for the song. It received extensive airplay on *MTV* during the 1986 Christmas season, and it was the only video by an unsigned artist to ever play in regular rotation on *MTV*.

Mann seemed poised to follow The Hooters and Robert Hazard in breaking out of the 1980s Philly rock scene onto the national stage.

But it was not to be. In October of 1987, Mann died when he jumped or fell from the second floor of his burning South Philly apartment building.

For over 30 years, *WMMR* DJ Pierre Robert has kept alive the memory of Mann and his iconic Christmas song with regular plays during the Christmas season.

Murray continued his passion for music videos and filmmaking with a long list of feature film credits. He is currently working on a documentary about the life of Alan Mann titled, *No Deal, No Sleep*. He called it "the story of a classic underdog, a perpetual contender who vowed to never give up until he got a record deal."

For me, *Christmas on the Block* embodies the true spirit of Christmas. Despite their lack of sight, the residents showed all of us that Christmas is a time when we should focus on what we can give, rather than focus on what we don't have. A line in the song prompts listeners to wonder if maybe all of us are the ones who are truly blind: "They cannot see the lightning, and they cannot see the thunder, they know what no one understands."

On Christmas Eve, as we gather around the fire at Bill's house, I'll think about the words to *Christmas on the Block* and try to imagine what it would be like to be blind by momentarily closing my eyes. Surprisingly, the music always seems livelier, the fire seems warmer, and the voices and laughter of everyone around me seems heartier.

It's during those moments that the true meaning of the song becomes apparent. Although my eyes are closed, I'm still able to see the things that really matter during Christmas.

AFTERWORD

Richard Murray, the director of the Christmas on the Block *video, sent me an e-mail after reading this essay. He updated me on the documentary he was working on about Alan, and* wrote: "I would love to interview you for this project. It would be great to have your perspective on Alan, and the song in the film." Needless to say, I was thrilled, and Rich eventually conducted a filmed interview with me in a downtown Philly office building. I hope that I make the final cut for the film! As of late 2019, Rich wrote on his Facebook site that the documentary "WILL be finished in 2020". I am really looking forward to seeing it and hope that it brings some long overdue recognition for a great, forgotten Philly artist.

WHAT MADE THE MONKEES "REAL"

(Edited version published in the March 6, 2012 *Philadelphia Inquirer*)

The Monkees - NBC TV publicity photo

"Another pleasant valley Sunday,
Charcoal burning everywhere,
Rows of houses that are all the same,
And no one seems to care."
(The Monkees – Pleasant Valley Sunday)

When I heard the sad news that the Monkees' Davy Jones had passed way, I thought of the drive I took through my old neighborhood in Roxborough just a few months ago when the band was scheduled to appear at the Tower Theater in Upper Darby. The red brick twin homes streamed past my car windows as I drove through the familiar hilly streets of my youth. Like giant red picket fences lining both sides of the road, the houses seemed to enclose me, but in a familiar, comforting way. The Monkees song *Pleasant Valley Sunday* was playing on the stereo, and the lyrics couldn't have been more appropriate. Those red-brick twins really are all the same, I thought to myself, and when we were growing up, no one really cared. I noticed that the spindly-metal TV antennas that once adorned all of those roofs were now all gone.

Perhaps it's better today, but I still cringe when I see my monthly $200 cable bill. My thoughts drifted back to a very different and simpler time, and as the Monkees continued to play on my stereo, I remembered laughing hysterically while watching their goofy TV show on Saturday mornings in the early 1970's. At that moment, I wouldn't have sold the tickets I had for their upcoming concert at The Tower Theater for a thousand dollars.

The Monkees incomparable story began in September, 1965, as television producers Bob Rafelson and Bert Schneider were hoping to capitalize on the success of the Beatles movie, *A Hard Days Night*. They ran an ad in the show-business weekly *Variety* that simply read: "Madness. Auditions. Folk & Rock Musicians Singers For Acting Roles in New TV Series."

Incredibly, the ad was answered by over 400 young men. Among them were future rock stars Harry Nilsson and Stephen Stills, but television producers Bob Rafelson and Bert Schneider eventually selected two unknown folk musicians (Mike Nesmith and Peter Tork), a former child-actor (Mickey Dolenz), and a diminutive British pop-singing wannabe (Davy Jones) for the roles. The television show was given the go-ahead by *NBC* in early 1966, and the improbable success story of the Monkees was about to begin.

Benefiting from the popularity of their hit TV show, and backed by producer Don Kirschner's stable of talented songwriters (Carol King, Gerry Goffin, Boyce & Hart), the Monkees rocketed to the top of the pop music charts in 1966 and 1967. Their first 4 albums were released in a one year span and each went to # 1. *I'm A Believer* was the top single of 1967, with *Daydream Believer* tied for 3rd. Their songs, *Stepping Stone, Last Train To Clarksville, Pleasant Valley Sunday,* and *Valleri,* were huge hits and they became the first music artists to win two Emmy Awards.

But the group came under heavy criticism when it was revealed that, although they played their own instruments while touring, they largely relied upon studio musicians for their recordings, and they didn't write the majority of the songs on their first 2 albums. This was particularly sting-ing to Nesmith and Tork, the two true musicians in the band, and they angrily insisted to Colgems Records that they play and write much of the music on their 3rd album, *Headquarters.* Over the vehement objections of Kirschner, The Monkees got their way, and *Headquarters* shot to # 1 on the charts. The group viewed it as a victory and a validation of their claim of being a "real" band.

Unfortunately, despite the fact that other popular groups of the era routinely used studio musicians for recordings (such as the Beach Boys, the Turtles, the Byrds, the Who, and the Kinks, among many others), the Monkees could never escape the criticism. *Headquarters* was soon bumped out of the # 1 spot by *Sgt. Pepper's Lonely Hearts Club Band,* and it not only heralded the "rock as art" era, but it also signaled the demise of the Monkees brand of bubble-gum pop. Despite various futile attempts to remain relevant, the band's TV show was cancelled in 1968 and they eventually split up by 1970.

A scheduling issue forced the Monkees to cancel the final 9 dates of their 45th Anniversary Summer Tour, which included The Tower on August 31st. I guess I shouldn't have been surprised because turbulence always seemed to follow the band. Apparently, their agency booked shows without the band's approval. It's too bad too, because Rolling Stone maga-zine wrote that their New York concert "was an excellent show from a legendary pop band...It's hard to imagine anybody disappointed by this show unless they just plain hate life."

I'm glad that I did get to see Jones perform with the Monkees once. It was at old Veterans Stadium in 1986, after a Temple football game and during the band's 20th anniversary tour. It was a great show, and I'll never forget the exuberant Temple students dancing up and down the Vet's steps as the band played their greatest hits.

To some, the Monkees are nothing more than a fabricated fake band with no relevance in rock history. But to me, they are the quintessential American rock band, one that succeeded despite the obstacles. Their story and accomplishments are legendary and they deserve to be in the Rock Hall of Fame. Their music represents an era when rock-n-roll wasn't the "high-art" some insist it should be, but was just plain fun. The Monkees embody a simpler time and place where the smell of burning charcoal filled the air, the rows of houses were all the same, and no one seemed to care.

AFTERWORD

Based upon the e-mails that I received in response to this essay, apparently the Monkees still have their supporters and detractors. Nearly all of the e-mails were positive, with the exception of one. It's reprinted here along with one of the positive ones, but I did feel somewhat vindicated when, in the summer of 2016, nearly 50 years after their formation, the Monkees released their 12th studio album, Good Times!. It was critically acclaimed (Ultimate Classic Rock declared that "The fact that there is a new Monkees album in 2016 is miraculous enough, but that said album, Good Times!, is nothing short of a masterpiece is astounding."), and it reached the # 14 position on the U.S. Billboard 200 chart, and # 1 on the U.S. Billboard Vinyl Albums chart. How many bands currently in the Rock Hall of Fame can claim that they had hit albums 50 years apart?

Not-so-positive email: "I have always respected the Philadelphia Inquirer, however, they wasted a lot of space on the ramblings of an ageing baby boomer. You cite the Monkees! Maybe read some good books, poems, and essays. Am astonished they published that nonsense."

Positive e-mail: "Well said about the Monkees. Of course they belong in the Hall of Fame..... I understand that one of the editors of Rolling Stone has been blocking their entry. It's ridiculous the criticism they took for practicing what bands routinely continue to do to this day. Shoot, all labels back in the day depended on a coterie of house writers and studio musicians. And the Monkees are raked across the coals for this? Snobbish hypocrisy! Yes, the music was fun. But Head *was art, and Nesmith had a hand in it. Old story, huh? Band reaches new artistic heights, then splits up. Of course, they followed that with the baffling 33 1/3 Revolutions. Dolenz approached art with* Randy Scouse Git, *and* Going Down, *and Nesmith approached art on practically every album - and absolutely achieved it with a highly consequential output after he left the band. I'm 47. When I was growing up it was The Beatles and The Monkees. Alpha and Omega. I saw the Monkees at the Mann in the 80s during their MTV-led revival. It was one of the best shows I have ever seen, with absolutely every generation in attendance. I have not seen the like since. Nice article, Chris. Maybe one day soon we'll see them inducted to that big hall in Cleveland."*

BRADBURY'S BUTTERFLY EFFECT

(Edited version published in the June 13, 2012 *Philadelphia Inquirer*)

Some of the Ray Bradbury books on my bookshelf (Chris Gibbons photo)

"It fell to the floor, an exquisite thing, a small thing that could upset balances and knock down a line of small dominoes and then big dominoes and then gigantic dominoes, all down the years across Time. Eckels' mind whirled. It couldn't change things. Killing one butterfly couldn't be that important! Could it?

Eckels moaned. He dropped to his knees. He scrabbled at the golden butterfly with shaking fingers. "Can't we," he pleaded to the world, to himself, to the officials, to the Machine, "can't we take it back, can't we make it alive again? Can't we start over? Can't we-"

He did not move. Eyes shut, he waited, shivering. He heard Travis breathe loud in the room; he heard Travis shift his rifle, click the safety catch, and raise the weapon.

There was a sound of thunder."

(From "A Sound of Thunder" by Ray Bradbury)

As I read the final words of the story, my mouth was agape in astonishment as a chill ran up my spine. The written word had never had so profound an impact upon me. Although I was just 11 years old at the time, I knew that what I'd just read would somehow stay with me forever. The story was *A Sound of Thunder,* and I still regard it as one of the greatest science fiction short-stories ever written. It tells the tale of time travelers hunting a Tyrannosaurus Rex, but an arrogant hunter carelessly steps on, and kills, a butterfly with dire consequences for humanity. I read the story's chilling ending over and over - at least a hundred times. I stared at the cool sci-fi cover art on the little paperback book for hours, and its title and author were permanently carved into my mind: *R is for Rocket* by Ray Bradbury.

To most, it was just another one of my big brother Jerry's numerous $1.50 sci-fi paperbacks from the rotating book-display rack at Woolworth's department store. But, to me, it was pure gold. I eagerly tore into the book's other short stories and they captivated my imagination: astronauts fight for their lives after crash landing in the swampy jungles of Venus, an ancient sea creature rises from the depths of the ocean, drawn to the sound of a lighthouse fog horn, and astronauts come to the realization that the paradise planet they discovered has hidden dangers they never anticipated. These were just a few of the brilliant stories written in Bradbury's unique poetic prose - a wondrous mix of science fiction, fantasy, suspense, and horror.

After that day, I was hooked, and if Jerry couldn't find his other Bradbury books in his bedroom bookcase, he knew where they'd be. I read Bradbury's other short story collections found in *S is for Space, The*

Illustrated Man, and *The Golden Apples of the Sun* so many times that I cracked the spine of the books. Over the years, Jerry and I would often talk about our favorite Bradbury stories, and whenever he had a new book released we would make sure we let each other know about it.

Although I had always liked to write, and would often tell my family and friends that "one of these days I'm going to write about that", I never took it seriously until I read Bradbury's book on writing, *Zen in the Art of Writing.* In it he wrote, "What are the best things and the worst things in your life, and when are you going to get around to whispering or shouting them? You fail only if you stop writing." I remember feeling that he was speaking directly to me. I started to write on a regular basis shortly after I read that.

When I heard the news that Ray Bradbury had died, I felt like I had lost an old friend. I knew who I had to contact first, and I thanked Jerry for introducing me to Ray.

In his seminal novel *Fahrenheit 451,* Ray Bradbury wrote, "It doesn't matter what you do...so long as you change something from the way it was before you touched it into something that's like you after you take your hands away."

A Ray Bradbury paperback book is such a small, exquisite thing, and it can change things all down the years and across time. And the stories within that book can touch and change lives forever – including the life of a kid for whom those stories resonated like a sound of thunder.

AFTERWORD

When my son, Jack, started his freshmen year at Roman Catholic High School in 2010, his English teacher handed out the reading list for the class. It listed the short stories and books that they were going to focus on for the upcoming school year. "A Sound of Thunder" was on the list, and I smiled at the thought that the story just might resonate with one of the kids in the class in the same way that it had for me nearly 40 years before.

GAMES OF CHESS

(Edited version published in the October 26, 2012 *Philadelphia Inquirer*)

Chess pieces (Photo by George Hodan)

"When the world and I were young, just yesterday,
Life was such a simple game, a child could play,
...but today there is no day or night, today there is no dark or light,
Today there is no black or white, only shades of gray"
(Shades of Gray – The Monkees)

My brother Mike and his buddy Dennis would often play chess until 3 am in our bedroom-basement during that summer of 1977. It was the five year anniversary of the epic 1972 World Chess Championship between Bobby Fischer and Boris Spassky, and the two of them would jokingly refer to themselves as Fischer or Spassky as they took big swigs from their Budweiser quart bottles between chess moves.

Dennis would volunteer to teach me how to play chess, but I had the attention span of a goldfish back then, and I would always decline his invitation. I tried to learn by watching them play, and it always seemed so easy at the beginning, but as the game wore on, it became more difficult for me to follow and understand. You had to anticipate and plan several moves ahead, and I struggled to apply that concept in the game. Dennis would notice the bewildered look on my face when a game ended and say, "What the heck are they teaching ya down there at Roman, son? If you would just concentrate a little, you'll understand."

While they were playing, Mike and Dennis would often tell me and my brother Mark funny stories about the guys they hung out with. Their nicknames alone made you laugh – Head, Mole, Nit, Gob, Gumby, Clang, and Shan, just to name a few. Because a lot of these nicknames were derived from an evident physical characteristic, I would simply laugh at the sight of them as they entered our room. "What are YOU laughing at?" Head would say. "Nothing", I'd sheepishly reply as I wiped the grin from my face while trying to avert my eyes from the obvious.

After their chess games ended, we would watch re-runs of *Highway Patrol* through the smoky haze of our burning Marlboros on a tiny 12 inch black and white TV. We would often talk into the early morning hours about sports, music, politics, or just life on general. It was a crazy summer that year, so there was plenty to talk about. The Sixers lost the NBA Championship to Portland, Son of Sam was still terrorizing New York during a massive blackout, *Star Wars* was a stunning box-office smash, and Elvis died. Although they welcomed my input, I was usually content to just listen to their stories and their outlook on life. I remember Dennis heading home quite a few times that summer as the darkness of the night gave way to dawn.

I didn't see Dennis too often after that summer. The guys from Mike's crew were turning 21, so they started hanging out at the local bars. Drinking quarts of Bud and playing chess in our basement-bedroom started to lose its appeal as they got older. As the years went by, anytime that I saw or heard of anything related to chess, I would always think of Dennis and Mike playing until the wee hours during that summer of '77. A few years ago, I gave Mike a new chess set for Christmas. And this past summer marked the 40th anniversary of the famous Fischer vs. Spassky chess match. I thought about those games of chess in the old basement-bedroom as I read about the anniversary in the paper.

Mike's text message to me last week caught me off guard. I read it several times, but still couldn't believe it: "Dennis McCauley died yesterday. Heart Attack." He left behind a wife, a son, and two step-daughters.

I guess the complexities of life often seem like a game of chess to me. It's so simple and easy to understand in the beginning when you're still so young, but becomes more difficult as time goes by and you have to anticipate, and try to plan for what might happen down the road. Shortly after hearing the news about Dennis, I looked up at the gray twilight sky as it slowly darkened above me, and I could still hear his voice: "If you would just concentrate a little, you'll understand." Unfortunately, when I think about Dennis, those games of chess, and life in general, there's still quite a bit that I don't understand.

AFTERWORD

Dennis's niece, Maureen, graduated with me from I.H.M. grade school. Following the publication of this essay she sent me this email: "I wanted to thank you on behalf of my family for the article you wrote today. My Uncle Dennis was so full of life and we are all struggling with this loss. Dennis was like a brother to me, just 5 years older than me. I have so many fond memories of all of the guys hanging at my grandmom's house on the "other" Hill Road. Your article reminded me of those great times. My mom said to tell you what a wonderful writer you are as well. I am saving the article and know that Dennis's little boy will appreciate it someday. I know his family does very much. Hope life is good to you and your family. Please thank your brother Mike for me again, for coming to Dennis' services. I can't express how much the article has helped us in this difficult time."

IN 1902 ROMAN TEAM STOOD UP AGAINST RACISM

(Edited version published in the February 20, 2015 *Philadelphia Inquirer*)

BASKETBALL
TEAM (1902)

Roman Catholic High School 1902-03 Basketball Team (Photo courtesy of RCHS)

It was the late autumn of 1902, Patricia Corkery remembered her Uncles telling her, and twenty-four year old coach William "Billy" Markward gathered his Roman Catholic High School basketball team together at the imposing gothic school building at Broad and Vine streets in Philadelphia.

Markward, a Spanish-American War veteran, was starting his first year of coaching at Roman and had just received a disturbing letter from the scholastic league that Roman played in during that era. Although his initial reaction may have been to respond to the league on his own without discussing with the team, Markward also recognized the importance of teaching life lessons, as well as basketball, to his players.

The team was primarily comprised of poor Irish-Catholic boys from the inner-city neighborhoods of Philadelphia, and most were probably the sons of immigrants. But there was one boy among them whose background was very different. John "Johnny" Lee was the son of a former slave, and he was one of the first African Americans to play basketball in that scholastic league.

As the boys sat, Markward, a former pro basketball player himself, towered over them and began to read the contents of the letter. It stated that the league was notifying Roman that they would be banned from the league if Lee, a "Negro" player, remained on their roster. Sadly, considering the racial discrimination that was common for that era, this stance was not unusual, but how the team responded definitely was.

In a letter to Roman's Alumni Association detailing the incident, Patricia Corkery wrote that her uncle and team captain, John Corkery, was the first to stand up and speak: "If Johnny Lee doesn't play, then I don't play." One by one, each of the players, including her other uncle, Maurice, stood up and said that they wouldn't play as well. As he watched each of the boys pledge to stand with their teammate, Billy Markward, the coach who always stressed the importance of how to live over how to play, must've beamed with pride. "Roman stood with Johnny and the league backed down", Patricia Corkery wrote.

From that moment on, a special bond formed between John Corkery and Lee. Through the years, both men remained active in Roman's Alumni Association, and their friendship grew. Lee would never forget the courageous stand that Corkery and his other teammates took for him, and when John Corkery died in 1929, Johnny Lee was heartbroken. Patricia fondly remembers the touching scene that took place at her home every year on the anniversary of her uncle's death. "Growing up in the Port Richmond area of Philadelphia in the late 20's and early 30's, my world was white-mostly Irish Catholic," Patricia Corkery recalled in the letter. "Only one African-American crossed my path. It was once a year (John Lee) came to our house and I had to be on my best behavior. Always, I had to be dressed up and with my best manners for this visit. John Lee came to our house on the anniversary of my Uncle John's death…and paid a tearful visit to the pictures of Roman's team still on our walls."

Over the ensuing years, Billy Markward would consistently turn down numerous college coaching offers and remained at Roman from 1902 to 1942, winning an incredible 20 championships. He achieved legendary status not only at Roman, but in the entire Philadelphia region, and the prestigious Markward Awards are presented annually to the Philadelphia area's top high school basketball players.

As for Johnny Lee, breaking down racial barriers became something of a family trait. Johnny's granddaughter, Sister Cora Marie Billings, became the first African American to enter a community of nuns in Philadelphia, and the first to join the Sisters of Mercy. She also became the first African American in the U.S. to serve as the leader of a Church parish as pastoral coordinator for St. Elizabeth's in Richmond, Va. "My great-grandfather (George Lee)…worked as a slave, owned by the Society of Jesus", Cora wrote in the July 7-14, 2014 issue of *America Magazine*. "I know that our church and our world are not as they once were and they are not where I want them to be. But my hope is things will continue to get better."

Another of Lee's lasting legacies at Roman is readily evident when reviewing the success that the school has achieved in basketball since 1968. Largely due to the contributions of many great African American players during that span, Roman won an unprecedented 18 Catholic League championships, and their current team is nationally ranked.

When we look back upon this incident from 1902, we can appreciate just how far our nation has progressed in eliminating discrimination. However, the social unrest resulting from the recent incidents in Ferguson and New York are sobering reminders that far too often our society has a troubling tendency to split opinions along racial lines. Our inability to determine the reason why we continue to divide this way leaves us angry and frustrated, and we blame each other for this failure. Perhaps, before we can find an answer and move forward, we need to look back and remember the pledge that was made in the school at Broad and Vine streets over 110 years ago. For what the Roman Catholic High School basketball team understood back then, but what many of us fail to realize today, is that the primary reason for our failure is ignorance, and the first step in defeating it is to stand together and confront it.

1902-03 RCHS Basketball Team - 1942

*(l to r) Frank Corkery - great nephew of John Corkery, Del Markward -
great nephew of Billy Markward, and Curtis Cockenberg - grandson of
Johnny Lee, at the March 30, 2016 Markward Club Awards Dinner.*

AFTERWORD

In March of 2016, Dennis Hill, Executive Director of the William H. Markward Basketball Club of Philadelphia, asked me to give a speech about this essay at the upcoming Markward Club Awards Dinner. The club, which is the oldest basketball club in the country, was founded in 1946 and was created to honor Philadelphia area scholastic basketball players. Dennis also invited living relatives of Billy Markward, John Corkery, and Johnny Lee. It was a memorable night for me because as I gave my speech, I couldn't help but notice that seated in the audience were many African American athletes who were recipients of Markward Club awards that evening. At that moment, I realized the true impact that the 1902-1903 Roman basketball team had, and I was filled with pride for being a graduate of a school that has not only embraced diversity since its founding, but was willing to courageously stand up against those who sought to stop it.

THE PREACHER ON MARKET STREET

When needed, comfort from an unexpected source

(Edited version published in the February 8, 2016 *Philadelphia Inquirer*)

The Market Street Preacher (Chris Gibbons photo)

"And the sign said 'The words of the prophets
Are written on the subway walls and tenement halls'
And whispered in the sounds of silence."
(Simon and Garfunkel, "The Sounds of Silence")

It was a little over five years ago when I first heard the preacher on Market Street. After 17 years of working in the Philadelphia suburbs, I was starting a new job and returning to the familiar confines of Center City, where I had previously worked for 15 years, as well as attended high school and college.

As I emerged from the subway station that late summer morning, the preacher stood at 16th and Market streets loudly barking like a Wildwood boardwalk pitchman seeking players for his rigged game. I'm paraphrasing, but he was shouting, "Jesus welcomes all to his kingdom, saints and sinners alike". His powerful voice could easily be heard over the considerable traffic and construction noise of the city. "Christ is the way and the truth", he continued. "It is only with Him and through Him that you can attain true happiness". I smiled as I heard it and thought to myself, "Wow, I forgot about all of the kooks down here. Welcome back!"

My fellow subway denizens and I shuffled past him like a herd of sheep as he continued to loudly ramble on – some nonsense about the Bible, wickedness, the light, and judgment day. He appeared too well dressed to be homeless, so I simply assumed that he was just crazy. I continued to walk towards my office building and the preacher's voice began to fade. As I looked back at him with mild amusement, several people bumped into me, and gave me angry looks. Unfortunately, my navigation skills within a rushing Center City crowd had diminished, and it was one of the many things that I'd have to learn again. As it turned out, I'd eventually learn much more.

The preacher was still there when I headed home from work that night, as well as the next day, and the day after that. As a matter of fact, he's been preaching there just about every day since I've been back downtown, and probably a lot longer. He's become somewhat of a permanent fixture of the Center City landscape.

Over the years, I've heard him preaching on that street corner on blistering hot days, bitterly cold nights, in the rain, the wind, and the snow. I'd developed a certain admiration of his perseverance, even though I thought his preaching was a waste of time as nobody ever seemed to listen to what he was saying. Every time I saw him, or heard him, I would think of the old phrase: 'heart of gold, head of wood'.

All of that has changed now. Just a few days before the recent "Blizzard of 2016", a close friend and mentor unexpectedly died. His death was the latest of many among my family and friends that have darkened my world over the last 18 months. I read of his passing while at work, and I accomplished very little that day. That evening, in the bitter cold, I walked in a semi-daze towards the subway entrance. Suddenly I heard the voice of the preacher. I don't know what prompted me to do it, but I walked up to him. He stopped preaching and looked at me. "My friend just died" I said to him in a quivering voice. "Everyone seems to be dying."

He clutched my hand, closed his eyes, and said, "Pray with me, brother. Jesus, comfort this man as he has lost another dear friend. He needs your strength, comfort, and blessings during this time of great sorrow. Let him know that he is never alone, and that you will always be there for him. Let him see your light in this temporary darkness. Amen." He opened his eyes and said, "Bless you brother."

My personal views on God, religion, life after death, and the universe are heavily influenced by science, and very much different than the preacher's views. But, I have to admit that I was surprised at how much comfort his words had given me. I've come to learn that the preacher's basic messages embrace values that we should all live by, regardless of our religious views: respect one another, be kind, and help those in need.

I now have a greater admiration for the preacher, and as I headed home recently, I waved to him. He waved back and said, "Have a blessed evening." I slowly descended down the subway steps, and the preacher's voice from above gradually diminished with each step down. This time, however, I actually listened to what he said, for I've come to the realization that the words of the prophets aren't always written on the subways walls, but often resonate within them. And the echo of these words, like the voices of lost loved ones, should be remembered for they will inevitably fade to a faint whisper, until they're lost forever in the wells of silence.

AFTERWORD

My friend who had died, and prompted me to write this essay, was Joe Flaherty. Although he was 20 years older than me, we had become friends over the last several years as a result of our involvement in Roman Catholic High School's Alumni Association. Prior to his passing, Joe had just completed a 2-year term as Alumni Association President, and I would often see him at the school as he continued to tirelessly work on numerous alumni activities. Joe was truly one of the most dedicated alums in school history, and, not surprisingly, in 2015 he was selected as one of Roman's "125 Men of Distinction" in conjunction with the school's 125 year anniversary. His death was sudden, unexpected, and really shook me. At the end of Joe's funeral mass, a group of Roman students led the attendees in singing the school song, The Purple and Gold. *There wasn't dry eye to be found in the church.*

As for the preacher, he and I have spoken to each other a bit more since this essay was published. He told me that his name is Gregory, and he appreciated my kind words about him in the essay. When he sees me now, he always asks how I am doing and to "have a blessed day." An e-mail that I received from an Inquirer *reader informed me that Gregory's words are a source of comfort for him as well: "Nice words about Brother Greg. I walk by his corner in the morning. I have been doing so for years. Some time ago, we made eye contact and acknowledged each other. Then he would simply say "Have a blessed day" whenever I passed and our eyes met. Like you, I am more influenced by science than religion, but I have to say that I always felt good (and still do) about receiving Brother Greg's blessing as I start my day. It is a genuine wish from a good man. Thanks for sharing how he helped you. Although I'm sure he's helped many more people than just us, he'd be happy to know that his words resonated with at least two people."*

THE BRIDGE

Searching for span's hidden message

(Edited version published in the November 27, 2016
Philadelphia Inquirer)

The bridge at Henry and Valley Aves. (Chris Gibbons photo)

"The darkest night is often the bridge to the brightest tomorrow."
(Jonathan Lockwood Huie)

I was barely awake on that recent mid-summer morning as I started to read the text from Ed, one of my closest childhood friends. It had been sent hours before, while I slept. My heart raced faster as I read each word.

"Oh my God!", I uttered. My wife sat up in bed, alarmed by the pained expression on my face. "What?! What is it?!", she asked. I was still trying to comprehend what I was reading and didn't respond. "Tell me!", my wife yelled. "It's….it's Ed's little daughter, Julia. She was rushed to the hospital. She's really sick. Something in her brain." I immediately called Ed, completely forgetting that it was 5am in Los Angeles. As we spoke, for the first time in the 48 years that I've known him, I sensed fear in his voice.

In the days and weeks following that call, I couldn't stop thinking about the terrible anxiety and heartache that Ed and his family were enduring, and how life, at times for all of us, can seem so difficult and unfair. I was occasionally overwhelmed with feelings of helplessness in knowing that my friend and his family were struggling and there was nothing that I could do.

It was also during this time that "The Bridge" seemed to be reaching out to me. Although I've driven over the bridge at Henry and Valley Avenues in Roxborough hundreds of times in the last 40 years, I hadn't really given much thought to the teenage years that I'd spent there with Ed and the other guys from our "crew". But now it seemed that each time I drove over it, something seemed to seep within my sub-conscience, a faint message tantalizingly close to clarity, yet elusive as the wind. Maybe it was just simple nostalgia, or perhaps little Julia's struggle triggered in me that innate desire, shared by many of us, to return to a simpler time when there was no fear, a time when the pressures wrought by the complexities of life didn't seem to exist, a time when Ed and I had yet to cross over the threshold from adolescence into adulthood. I cannot say. But something linked to the bridge seemed to be calling out to me with an indistinct message that lay just beyond the periphery of my understanding. I decided to go back to the bridge to see if I could find what that message may be.

As I walked towards the bridge on that hot summer day I wasn't really sure of what I was looking for or what I'd find, but the memories of my days there suddenly flooded back. I remembered that people in the surrounding neighborhood thought that it was strange that my buddies and I "hung out" under a bridge, and called us "trolls". We weren't offended by the name, and actually reveled in the unique identity it created for us. The bridge had a 50 foot x 15 foot leveled, compacted-dirt ledge directly underneath its northern side with a 9 foot floor to ceiling headroom. It became our sanctuary that not only shielded us from the wind, rain, and snow, but also temporarily safeguarded our carefree teen spirit from the ever encroaching world of adulthood and responsibility.

I bounded down the old path that led underneath the bridge and my nostalgic visit to the past quickly became a sobering meeting with the present. It seemed darker and colder than I remembered. Spray-painted, bubble-letter graffiti, commonly found on old Philadelphia warehouse buildings, now adorned the walls. It also appeared that someone was living there as a chair was positioned in front of a still-smoldering fire-pit. There was an old coat, fast-food trash, jugs of water, and a large plastic container strewn around the dirt ledge. All remnants of our days there were gone, and my positive memories of the place where lifelong friendships had been forged were now tarnished by what it had become. It felt strange, yet oddly familiar, and as I looked at the empty chair, I couldn't help but view it as an ominous warning of a life that may have been.

I walked up the path from underneath the bridge that day, convinced that there was no hidden message to be found there, but as I looked out onto Henry Avenue, I immediately noticed something very odd – there were no cars on the usually bustling roadway. In that silent, surreal moment, I looked across the empty bridge towards the other side, and realized for the first time just how sharply it curved around the bend. You couldn't see what was on the other side of the bend, or where the road led – just like life.

It was then that I finally understood the elusive message: rather than being a sanctuary, the bridge was akin to a damp cellar in which we hid. It was only when we emerged from underneath it, and traveled on the road above it, did all of us finally reach the unique destinations that awaited us. Many of us were fortunate enough to bring new lives into this world, which brought great joy and meaning to our journeys. But Julia's plight embodied the fear and heartache that can sometimes accompany us as we travel on the road of life. The key is to confront and overcome these obstacles, rather than try to escape from them.

Thankfully, the news from Julia's doctors gradually improved with each passing day. It turns out that she has an AVM, a tangle of abnormal blood vessels connecting arteries and veins in her brain, but Julia's case is highly treatable and she's expected to make a full recovery. The last time that I spoke to Ed, the fear in his voice was gone and I was proud of the way he and his wife, Adrianna, bravely confronted what has to be every parent's nightmare.

I drove over the bridge recently, and noticed thin wisps of smoke drifting up from below. It curled up and over the bridge, momentarily morphing into the ghostly apparitions of young boys and drifting far up into the sunlit sky until gradually fading away. I watched it disappear as I crossed the bridge, and rounded the bend, towards whatever destination awaited me on the other side.

Under the bridge - 2016 (Chris Gibbons photo)

AFTERWORD

As I write this in January, 2020, I'm happy to report that Julia has recovered quite well over these last 3 ½ years, and, now a vibrant, young teenager, is doing just fine. In regards to the Bridge, some of my friends thought that I was a bit too harsh in my assessment of it (ie:"… rather than being a sanctuary, the bridge was akin to a damp cellar in which we hid."), as they have many fond recollections of our days and nights spent there. I have great memories of it as well, but metaphorically speaking, I still believe that the Bridge represented the path that we had to take in order to cross that sometimes scary gulf separating adolescence and adulthood - my friends and I temporarily stopped our journey, and went under the Bridge until we were ready to cross it. Looking back, perhaps I was a bit harsh - because we sure did have a lot of fun under it before the time had come to finally cross it!

SAVING A SEAT AT THE BAR

(Published on my website June 2016)

My Dad and my brother, Jack - 1954

It was the winter of 1982, and proud of my very recent attainment of 'legal drinking age' status, I decided to stop in the old Domino Lounge in my Roxborough neighborhood in the hopes that I might run into my brothers and finally have a beer with them at a bar. The smoky, dimly-lit bar was nearly empty, and after a quick glance around I didn't recognize any of the few patrons and started to leave. "Chris!", a familiar voice called out from the far-end of the bar.

I squinted through the smoky haze and saw that it was my Dad. I walked down to the end of the bar, and he patted the bar stool next to him and said, "Here…I saved you a seat." I looked around at the numerous empty bar-stools and smiled as I said "Thanks." Over the years, whenever I ran into my Dad at the Domino, he would always welcome me the same way. Even in his later years at Sea Isle City's VFW Post, although the once booming voice had been reduced to a faint, raspy whisper, I was still greeted with: "Here…I saved you a seat."

Today marks two years since my Dad passed away and I've often found myself thinking of these seemingly mundane moments while reflecting upon his life

My Dad was born in 1930, and raised in the ethnic-Irish North Philadelphia enclave known as "Swampoodle." When he was just a toddler, my grandmother returned to her native Ireland with my Dad in tow. Remarkably, although he was very young and was there less than a year, he once told me that he could still envision the lush green fields of Ireland, the only memory he had of the trip.

A Depression-era child, Dad would often tell my brothers and sisters that his family was so poor that one particular Christmas his only gift was "a can of peaches." But, he didn't tell that tale to garner sympathy. He usually used that story out of his extensive repertoire of life experiences when one of us was complaining about what we didn't have. My parents raised 11 children, and complaints of what we didn't have were common, so all of us heard that story so many times that we would imitate my Dad, right down to his "Archie Bunker" style of delivery. When he was older, we once gave him a can of peaches for Christmas, and I detected just a hint of a smile as he unwrapped it.

Dad was proud of his Catholic roots and often talked fondly of his school days at St. Columba's and Roman Catholic High School. In the late 1940's he enlisted in the Army and eventually fought in the Korean War. He didn't like to talk about what he experienced there, but readily shared the more lighthearted stories of military life. A favorite of mine was the time that he was traveling at night across the desolate U.S. mid-west on a bus that was loaded with soldiers. It was a long trip through mostly barren desert, and when the bus temporarily stopped on the roadside so the men could relieve themselves, they noticed a flashing neon sign way off in the distance. Initially, they couldn't make out what the distant sign was flashing until one of the sharper eyed soldiers said, "I think it says car....wait a second.....no....it's bar!" The soldiers began to run towards the sign, stripping off their back-packs while ignoring their sergeant's orders to stop. My Dad would always laugh as he said, "But there was no stopping us! Even the sergeant wound up running with us."

The fashion and hair-style changes that accompanied the social upheaval of the 1960's were not enthusiastically welcomed by my Dad, but did provide ample material for his sardonic wit. I once proudly entered the kitchen with collar length hair and wearing my new multi-color, striped, bell-bottom pants before leaving for a grade school dance. He just shook his head and said, "You look like a carnival clown!"

Unfortunately the early 1970's were difficult years for my family. My oldest brother, Jack Jr., tragically drowned, and my Mom and Dad were never really the same after that. But, I was very proud of the example that the two of them set for us. In the face of great personal tragedy, they showed that you must go on and rise above adversity - qualities that I've tried to emulate as an adult.

There's an old saying regarding the passing of a loved one: All that's left are the memories. But, when I think of my Dad, that's not exactly true for me. I do have the memories, but I also often play a hopeful scenario in my mind that helps to ease the pain of his loss

I like to imagine that shortly after he passed, Dad found himself in his version of heaven, where he was walking in a lush green field, like the one in Ireland he remembered as a toddler. He wasn't old and frail like he was when he died, but young and strong, with the jet-black hair that I remember from the 1960's. And as he walked across the field, he spotted two figures off in the distance - an older man with his arm around a teenager. My Dad then ran towards them as he realized that it was his father and my brother, Jack. As the three of them embraced, I can just imagine my grandfather speaking with his thick Irish brogue: 'Don't worry, Jack...I took good care of eem 'til ya got here. Welcome home." And the three of them then walked together towards a flashing neon sign off in the distance.

I sincerely hope that my Dad found his heaven after he passed, and if he did, I know that he's saving a seat for me at the bar.

AFTERWORD

Shortly after my Dad passed away, my brother Pat asked me to do his eulogy. I hadn't even thought about it, as I assumed one of my older brothers was going to give it. But when I thought about some of the things that I would say, I feared that I wouldn't be able to get through it without breaking down in front of all in attendance. I told Pat that I couldn't do it, as it would be too difficult for me. As the months passed, it slowly weighed on my conscience. I began to write down the things that I would have said had I given his eulogy, and this essay was the result. Since my Dad's passing, whenever I attend a funeral mass and a eulogy is given, I take particular notice of those that are extremely difficult for the speaker to get through, but, I've always found that they do eventually get through it. Telling my brother Pat that I couldn't do my Dad's eulogy because "I wouldn't be able to get though it" was wrong. I should have tried, and will always regret that I didn't.

ABOUT THE AUTHOR

Chris Gibbons is a freelance writer from the Philadelphia area whose stories and essays have been primarily published in the Op-Ed pages of the Philadelphia Daily News and Philadelphia Inquirer, but have also been published in other outlets as well, such as the Washington Times, Houston Chronicle, Arizona Desert Sun, Savannah Morning News, Orlando Sentinel, the History Channel Magazine, America in WW 2 magazine, and PhillyMan magazine. Because of his life-long interest in military history and NASA, Chris's stories often focus on veterans and space exploration, but he also often writes about his experiences while growing up in a large family in Philadelphia during the 1960's and 1970's. A graduate of Drexel University, as well as Roman Catholic High School in Philadelphia, Chris serves on the Executive Committee of Roman's Board of Trustees. He is currently the 1st Vice President of Roman's Alumni Association and is also Chairman of the Association's Veterans Committee and leading the effort to find the names of the Roman alumni who gave their lives in World War I.

Chris also serves as an Officer with the American Catholic Historical Society, and he's a 40-year member of the Planetary Society. Chris can be reached at: gibbonscg@aol.com.